Art in the Cinema

Art in the Cinema

The Mid-century Art Documentary

Edited by Steven Jacobs,
Birgit Cleppe and
Dimitrios Latsis

BLOOMSBURY ACADEMIC

LONDON • NEW YORK • OXFORD • NEW DELHI • SYDNEY

BLOOMSBURY ACADEMIC
Bloomsbury Publishing Plc
50 Bedford Square, London, WC1B 3DP, UK
1385 Broadway, New York, NY 10018, USA

BLOOMSBURY, BLOOMSBURY ACADEMIC and the Diana logo are trademarks of
Bloomsbury Publishing Plc

First published in Great Britain 2021

Cover design by Charlotte Daniels
Cover image: The Open Window directed by Henri Storck, 1952
(© The Henri Storck Foundation)

A catalogue record for this book is available from the British Library.

A Library of Congress Cataloging-in-Publication Data
Names: Jacobs, Steven, 1967- editor. | Latsis, Dimitrios, editor. | Cleppe, Birgit, editor.
Title: Art in the cinema : the mid-century art documentary / edited by Steven Jacobs,
Dimitrios Latsis, and Birgit Cleppe.
Description: London ; New York : Bloomsbury Academic, [2020] |
Includes bibliographical references and index. |
Identifiers: LCCN 2020009084 (print) | LCCN 2020009085 (ebook) |
ISBN 9781788313674 (hardback) | ISBN 9781350160316 (epub) |
ISBN 9781350160309 (pdf)
Subjects: LCSH: Art, Modern. | Documentary films–History and criticism. |
Experimental films–History and criticism.
Classification: LCC N6350 .A635 2020 (print) | LCC N6350 (ebook) | DDC 791.43/657—dc23
LC record available at https://lccn.loc.gov/2020009084
LC ebook record available at https://lccn.loc.gov/2020009085

ISBN: HB: 978-1-7883-1367-4
         ePDF: 978-1-350-16030-9
         eBook: 978-1-350-16031-6

Typeset by RefineCatch Limited, Bungay, Suffolk
Printed and bound in Great Britain

To find out more about our authors and books visit www.bloomsbury.com
and sign up for our newsletters.

Contents

List of Figures

Notes on Contributors

Birgit Cleppe is currently preparing a PhD on European art documentaries of the 1940s and 1950s at the Department of Art History at Ghent University. She studied Architecture at Ghent University, Belgium, and the Politecnico di Milano, Italy. She also works as an art and architecture critic and as a guest professor, she teaches architecture history and urbanism at KASK School of Arts in Ghent.

Angela Dalle Vacche is Professor of Cinema Studies at the Georgia Institute of Technology. She is originally from Venice, Italy, and before coming to Atlanta, she taught at Vassar College and at Yale University. She is the author of *The Body in The Mirror: Shapes of History in Italian Cinema* (1992), *Cinema and Painting: How Art is Used in Film* (1996) and *Diva: Defiance and Passion in Early Italian Cinema* (2008). She has edited *The Visual Turn: Classical Film Theory and Art History* (2008), *The Color Reader* (2006) and *Film, Art, New Media: Museum without Walls* (2012). Dalle Vacche is currently working on her fourth book *Andre Bazin's Cinema: Art, Religion, Science*.

Henning Engelke teaches art history and film at Goethe-University, Frankfurt. He has published in journals and anthologies on experimental film, documentary, production design and film theory. He is the author of *Dokumentarfilm und Fotografie. Bildstrategien in der englischsprachigen Ethnologie 1936–1986* (2007) and *The Art That Never Was: US-amerikanischer Experimentalfilm, 1940–1960* (2016).

Steven Jacobs is an art historian who has published in *Art Journal, History of Photography, Millennium Film Journal, October, Oxford Art Journal* and in numerous edited volumes. He also wrote or co-authored *The Wrong House: The*

Architecture of Alfred Hitchcock (2007), *Framing Pictures: Film and the Visual Arts* (2011), *The Dark Galleries: A Museum Guide to Painted Portraits in Film Noir* (2013), *Screening Statues: Cinema and Sculpture* (2017) and *The City Symphony Phenomenon: Cinema, Art, and Urban Modernity Between the Wars* (2018). He teaches at Ghent University and University of Antwerp, Belgium.

Dimitrios Latsis is Assistant Professor of Film Studies at the School of Image Arts, Ryerson University in Toronto where he teaches in the Film Studies and Film and Photography Preservation and Collection Management programs. He received his PhD in Film Studies from the University of Iowa and completed a post-doctoral fellowship in Visual Data Curation at the Internet Archive where he served as film archivist. He recently edited a special issue of the journal of the Association of Moving Image Archivists on Digital Humanities and/in Film Archives. He is currently writing a monograph on the historiography of American cinema during the early and silent years.

Emanuele Pellegrini is Associate Professor of Art History and director of the PhD track in Analysis and Development of Cultural Heritage at IMT School for Advanced Studies, Lucca (Italy). He has been a researcher at Ca' Foscari University of Venice, Scuola Normale Superiore in Pisa and University of Udine. He has been a Chercheur Invité at INHA Paris, and visiting professor at Renmin University, Beijing. Pellegrini is a member of the scientific committee of the Fondazione Ragghianti in Lucca and director of the international magazine *Predella: Journal of Visual Arts*. His research interests are mainly centred on art criticism between the eighteenth and twentieth centuries. He has published books and articles on Carlo Ludovico Ragghianti, Roberto Longhi, the protection of cultural heritage in Italy during the nineteenth and twentieth centuries.

Lucy Reynolds has lectured and published extensively, most particularly on questions of the moving image, feminism, political space and collective practice. She is Senior Lecturer in the Department of Media, Arts and Design at Westminster University. Her articles have appeared in a range of journals such as *Afterall, Moving Image Review and Art Journal, Screen* and *Screendance*.

She writes for *Art Agenda* and *Millennium Film Journal,* and has curated exhibitions and film programmes for a range of institutions from Tate and MUHKA, Antwerp to the ICA and the South London Gallery.

Natacha C. Ritsma has obtained her PhD at the Department of Communication and Culture and American Studies at Indiana University and is currently a curator at the Loyola University Museum of Art in Chicago. Her research interests include experimental and documentary film; educational and non-theatrical film production, distribution and exhibition; and films about art and artists.

Joséphine Vandekerckhove studied Art History at Ghent University and at Sapienza Università di Roma and did a postgraduate in Curatorial Studies at Ghent University/Hogeschool Ghent (KASK). She is currently enrolled as a PhD student (Fellow of the Research Foundation – Flanders) at the Department of Art, Theatre and Music Sciences of Ghent University and Università di Verona. Her PhD research focuses on a comparative study of mid-twentieth-century art documentaries of the art historians and filmmakers Paul Haesaerts and Carlo Ludovico Ragghianti in Belgium and Italy, under supervision of Steven Jacobs.

John Wyver is Senior Research Fellow at the University of Westminster. He is Principal Investigator on the research project *Screen Plays: Theatre Plays on British Television* (2011–15), funded by the Arts and Humanities Research Council. He is the author of *Vision On: Film Television and Arts in Britain* (2007). In 1982 he co-founded the independent production company Illuminations, and for BBC, Channel 4, Sky Arts and other broadcasters he has produced numerous arts documentaries and performance films, including *Hamlet* (2009), *Macbeth* (2010) and *Julius Caesar* (2012). His work as a producer has been honoured with a BAFTA Award, an International Emmy and a Peabody Award. He is Media Associate for the Royal Shakespeare Company and he produces the Live from Stratford-upon-Avon cinema broadcasts.

Preface and Acknowledgements

Art documentaries, which most of us know through television, usually evoke tiresome didacticism and droll ponderousness. This has not always been the case, however. Before the breakthrough of television in most European countries, the art film was applauded as an avant-garde film genre. In the years immediately following the Second World War, art documentaries played an important part in an emerging cinephile culture favouring experimental shorts. The 1940s and 1950s can be considered as the Golden Age of the art documentary – not only because literally hundreds of art documentaries were produced but also because of the high quality and highly innovative or experimental nature of many of these films. With the exception of Alain Resnais's *Van Gogh* (1948), Henri-Georges Clouzot's *Le Mystère Picasso* (1956) and a few others, most of the art films of the 1940s and 1950s fell into oblivion and they have received only meagre scholarly attention. This book aims to remedy this situation by discussing the most innovative, experimental and influential post-war art documentaries while also drawing attention to lesser-known productions.

In an extensive introduction to this volume, the art documentaries of the 1940s and 1950s are situated in the context of the post-war reconstruction and international cultural exchange, epitomized by international organizations such as FIFA – the International Federation of Films on Art. Discussing films by major figures such as Alain Resnais, Luciano Emmer, Henri Storck, Paul Haesaerts and Carlo Ludovico Ragghianti, the introduction also chronicles the debates surrounding the status of films on art as 'art films' in their own right. In addition, the introduction draws attention to the particular formal and thematic concerns of documentaries on painting and sculpture while also focusing on the highly important subgenre of films showing artists at work.

Finally, the phenomenon of the art documentary is placed in a broader context of the dissemination and popularization of art enabled by the museum, the art book and the emerging medium of television.

Following this introductory chapter, nine chapters, each written by specialists in the field, deal with a specific theme or a key film. The first two chapters focus on the social, political and institutional context of mid-twentieth-century art documentaries. Birgit Cleppe demonstrates how the rise of the post-war art documentary is closely connected to new museological developments, while Dimitrios Latsis discusses two key American art documentaries in the light of Euro-American cultural and political relationships at the start of the Cold War. Subsequently, both Chapter 3 and Chapter 4 deal with the ways art historians have used the medium of film as instruments of art historiography enabling new visual research methods. In their chapters on the films by Paul Haesaerts and Carlo Ragghianti, Steven Jacobs and Joséphine Vandekerckhove, and Emanuele Pellegrini respectively, show how these art historians went beyond the traditional role of advisory experts or authors of a voice-over text, taking full responsibility for the film's form and content. The following chapters focus on specific films: Angela Dalle Vacche discusses André Bazin's unrealized film project on the Romanesque churches of the Saintonge region in France, while Natasha Ritsma, John Wyver and Lucy Reynolds focus on Willard Van Dyke's *The Photographer* (1948), John Read's *A Sculptor's Landscape* (1957) and Dudley Shaw Ashton's *Figures in a Landscape* (1953) respectively. In the final chapter, Henning Engelke discusses the art documentaries made by visual artists, focusing on Ilya Bolotowsky's film experiments.

To a large extent, this book is the result of a research project (2014–18) sponsored by the FWO Research Fund Flanders that enabled Birgit Cleppe to complete her PhD thesis on post-war art documentaries under the supervision of Steven Jacobs at Ghent University. However, the foundations of this book go back to earlier initiatives such as the symposium and film programme *Art & Cinema: On the Aesthetics, History and Theory of the Art Documentary*, which took place at KASK Cinema in Ghent in December 2013 and included screenings of films by Charles Dekeukeleire, Paul Haesaerts, Glauco Pellegrini, Luciano Emmer, Umberto Barbaro and Roberto Longhi, Pierre Alechinsky,

Luc de Heusch, John Read, Bruce Conner and Hans Cürlis, introduced by Susan Felleman, Steven Jacobs, Brigitte Peucker, Paola Scremin, Angela Dalle Vacche and John Wyver, among others. This symposium and film programme was part of a research project on the interactions between film and the visual arts at the School of Arts (KASK), University College Ghent, which also resulted in the release of the DVD box and booklet on *Art & Cinema: Belgian Art Documentaries* by Cinematek in Brussels in 2013.

A similar film programme and symposium entitled *The Cinematic Museum: The Post-war Art Documentary* took place at the same venue in December 2017, including films by Henri Alekan, Dudley Shaw Ashton, René Huyghe, Mark Lewis, Carlo Ludovico Ragghianti, Alain Resnais and Robert Hessens, and lectures by Birgit Cleppe, Steven Jacobs, Dimitrios Latsis, Mark Lewis, Emanuele Pellegrini and Lucy Reynolds, among others. We would like to thank all universities, museums, archives and individuals who made possible these events and offered us the opportunity to watch some amazing films and discuss these with several experts of the field: KASK Cinema, Cinea Brussels, the Brussels Cinematek, the BOF Research Fund of Ghent University, Laura Bonne, Lisa Colpaert, Bert Lesaffer, Elisa De Schepper, Bart Versteirt, Joséphine Vandekerckhove and Leen Vanderschueren.

Both film programmes brought several contributors to this volume together and this was also the case with a panel on the post-war art documentary at the 2015 SCMS conference in Atlanta, where Birgit Cleppe, Henning Engelke, Steven Jacobs and Natasha Ritsma gave papers that were the basis for their chapters in this volume. We would like to thank all participants, chairs and audience members for their contributions and valuable comments. We would additionally like to acknowledge Hilde D'haeyere, Leon Duyck, Joni Kinsey, Patricia Oman, Sara Kosiba, Roger Hallas, Jennifer Wild and the staffs of the Archives of American Art, Berkeley Art Museum and Pacific Film Archive, and San Francisco Museum of Modern Art for their advice, research help and invitations to share this work. Last but not least, we also owe thanks to Madeleine Hamey-Thomas at I.B. Tauris and Claire Constable, Anna Coatman and Rebecca Richards at Bloomsbury.

Introduction: the mid-century celluloid museum

STEVEN JACOBS AND DIMITRIOS LATSIS

In a 1991 survey of art documentaries, its authors state that many of the art films of the 1940s and 1950s 'seem dated and too "arty" today'.[1] The aim of this book is to contradict this statement, advocating that mid-twentieth-century art documentaries are often highly personal, poetic, reflexive and experimental films that, still today, offer a thrilling cinematic experience in contrast with many of the didactic art documentaries produced during the following decades. Furthermore, the 1940s and 1950s can be considered 'the Golden Age' of the art documentary as illustrated by the sheer quantity of such films produced in that era. Several surveys commissioned and published by international organizations such as UNESCO include listings of literally hundreds of art documentaries made in many countries.[2] This vast quantity went hand in hand with the exceptional quality of many innovative landmark documentaries such as *Le Monde de Paul Delvaux* (Henri Storck, 1946), *La Leggenda di S. Orsola* (Luciano Emmer, 1948), *Van Gogh* (Alain Resnais and Robert Hessens, 1948), *Rubens* (Henri Storck and Paul Haesaerts, 1948), *Thorvaldsen* (Carl Theodor Dreyer, 1949), *Jackson Pollock 51* (Paul Falkenberg and Hans Namuth, 1951), *Les Statues meurent aussi* (Alain Resnais and Chris Marker, 1953), *Le Mystère Picasso* (Henri-Georges Clouzot, 1956), *A Sculptor's Landscape* (John Read,

1957) and *L'Enfer de Rodin* (Henri Alekan, 1959). An impressive list of leading and famous filmmakers contributed to these films, some of which won Academy Awards and other important film prizes in those years.[3] In addition, art documentaries were discussed extensively at international conferences, in publications of professional associations, in leading film and art journals and by prominent critics and film theorists such as André Bazin, Pierre Francastel, Henri Lemaître, Siegfried Kracauer and Rudolf Arnheim, among others.[4] Leading universities started collecting, studying and disseminating these films, albeit in the context of the overall genre of educational films.[5]

Pre-war developments

The flourishing of highly innovative art documentaries in the wake of the Second World War would not have been possible without pre-war experiments. Films on art go back to the 1910s when scenics and travelogues documented sights and monuments of historical cities. Architecture and monumental sculpture were the pre-eminent subjects of early films on art, owing to the fact that they could be filmed in natural light.[6] Moreover, these public sculptures could be viewed from different or even shifting viewpoints, mobilizing the static artwork – a goal that many later art documentaries also attempted to reach.

Another way to mobilize or 'animate' immobile works of art was to show the process of their creation. Already in 1915, Sacha Guitry made *Ceux de chez nous* (*Those of Our Land*) on leading French writers and artists including Degas, Monet, Renoir and Rodin.[7] The film basically consists of a series of vignettes showing celebrities posing for the camera but some footage focuses on artists working in their studio – in many cases the sole cinematic record of the artists. Showing an artist at work would become one of the most successful formulas throughout the history of the art documentary. In the late 1930s, Elias Katz made the *Artists at Work* series, consisting of simple 10-minute glimpses of artists such as Lynd Ward, William Groper and George Grosz at work.[8] Similarly, many American educational films on decorative art of the 1920s and 1930s show us, for instance, how to weave baskets, how to make pottery, how native Americans made their blankets and so forth.[9]

The most impressive early film project dealing with artists at work, however, originated in the Berlin *Institut für Kulturforschung*, which was founded in 1919. Under the direction of art historian Hans Cürlis, this 'Institute for Cultural Education' was one of the first organizations that favoured film as a mediator for art appreciation and instruction.[10] Together with cinematographer Walter C. Türck, Cürlis started the landmark film cycle *Schaffende Hände* (*Creating Hands*) in 1922 using 'over the shoulder' shots showing prominent artists such as Max Liebermann, Lovis Corinth, Käthe Kollwitz, Max Pechstein, Wassilly Kandinsky, Otto Dix and George Grosz at work.[11] Several of these films document the creation of a work of art in the length of a single take, dwelling on the artist's gestures, movements and hesitations. As we will demonstrate in one of the following paragraphs, the theme of the artist at work proved highly important for mid-twentieth-century art documentaries, particularly those on artists using styles marked by gestural brushwork and physical movements such as Abstract Expressionism and lyrical abstraction.

Apart from Cürlis's institute, several small studios as well as UFA, Germany's major studio, produced films on visual arts during the interwar period. UFA even included a unit that produced popular educational shorts for both theatrical and non-theatrical release and listed art subjects in its catalogues as early as 1922. An often noted UFA Kulturfilm was *Die steinernen Wunder von Naumburg* (*Stone Wonders of Naumburg*, 1935) by Rudolph Bamberger and Curt Oertel, in which the camera explores the architecture and the sculpted Gothic figures of Naumburg cathedral. Described by Arthur Knight as the first film 'that suggested the possibility of granting an art experience through the medium of motion picture', the film has its verbal information restricted to a minimum and it first and foremost delivers its message visually.[12] Oertel went on to make art documentaries, including the landmark *Michelangelo: Das Leben eines Titanen* (1940), a feature-length film telling the story of Michelangelo's dramatic life, which is evoked not with reliance on re-enactments, but by the spectacular visualization of his art.

By means of location shots, vivid montages, light- and sound effects, (subjective) camera movements and point-of-view shots, Oertel carries us along through intrigues, conspiracies and civil wars in Renaissance Florence and Rome. Gliding over Michelangelo's paintings and sculptures, Oertel's

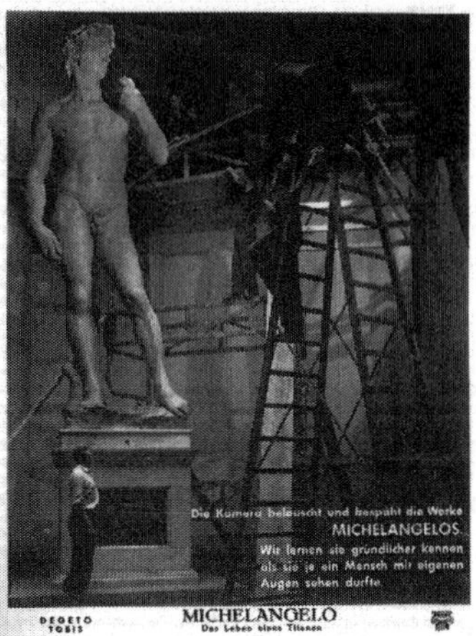

Figure 0.1 Michelangelo: Das Leben eines Titanen *(Curt Oertel, 1938). Lobby card.*

camera evokes the dramatic tension of Michelangelo's works, which are beautifully captured through chiaroscuro lighting. The creation and history of the statue of David (1501–4), for instance, is evoked through a succession of striking images. First, we see the statue's face luring from behind bars, as if it is still in Michelangelo's studio, but further shots suggest that the statue is travelling through Florence. Later, an attack on Florence is evoked as we see a missile falling and shattering the arm of the statue, followed by dramatic close-ups of David's face and shattered marble pieces. Turning the contemplation of art into a thrilling cinematic experience, Oertel's film was re-edited in 1950 by Richard Lyford under the supervision of Robert Flaherty and Robert Snyder. Distributed as *The Titan: The Story of Michelangelo*, the film won an Academy Award for Best Documentary Feature.

Other internationally acclaimed art documentaries released shortly before the Second World War were produced in Belgium – the magazine *Design Review* later noted that 'Belgium's contribution to the art film was out of all proportion to its limited geographical surface area.'[13] *Thèmes d'inspiration* (*Themes of Inspiration*, 1938) by Charles Dekeukeleire 'animates' static artworks by showing painted images that are interwoven with footage of the world that inspired Flemish painters. A highly lyrical film, *Thèmes d'inspiration* juxtaposes details of paintings of Old and Modern Masters with footage of real landscapes, faces and objects, evoking the world that inspired the artists. Marked both by the impressionist avant-garde (to which Dekeukeleire had contributed earlier) and by the new documentary trends of the 1930s, *Thèmes d'inspiration* focuses on the telluric alignment of characters in paintings by Pieter Bruegel, Joachim Patinir, Jacob Jordaens and Constant Permeke. Dekeukeleire's film focused not only on artworks but additionally explored the phenomena that inspired them, pioneering a format appropriated by many films to come.

The most influential pre-war Belgian art film was André Cauvin's *L'Agneau mystique* (*The Mystic Lamb*, 1939), which deals with the famous fifteenth-century altarpiece by Jan and Hubert Van Eyck.[14] In an 8-minute film, the voice-over is confined to a minimum in favour of a visual exploration of the painting. Scanning the altar's panels, the camera moves slowly so there is time to contemplate the many details rendered in close-up. For the first time, an art film drew attention to the aesthetic coherence of a single (though multi-panelled) piece of art enabling the viewer to make a formal analysis. Together with Cauvin's similar film, *Memling* (1939), *The Mystic Lamb* was commissioned by the Belgian government for its pavilion at the 1939 New York World's Fair where it made a lasting impression. Arthur Knight described *The Mystic Lamb* as 'probably the first of the new art films on an adult level to be seen by any considerable audience in America'.[15] Writing in 1952, Iris Barry stated that *The Mystic Lamb* 'has not even now, after so many other cinematic studies of paintings, been surpassed'.[16]

Post-war reconstruction and cultural organizations

Films released in the late 1930s such as Dekeuleire's *Themes of Inspiration*, Cauvin's *The Mystic Lamb* and Oertel's *The Titan* marked the start of a boom for art films that was only slowed down by the advent of the Second World War. In the decade following the War, literally hundreds of art documentaries were released in several countries. This post-war 'renaissance' of art documentaries can, no doubt, be linked to the conditions of a society recovering from the traumas of the War. After the barbarism of Nazism and the devastation of war, film, in its capacity as a mass medium, was called upon for the accomplishment of a humanist ideal of cultural emancipation through education. Art came to be seen as a necessary and even a fundamental part of education for all. These changing attitudes about the place of the visual arts in education, culture and society were unmistakably beneficial to the production and exhibition of films on art.[17] Considered to be an efficient device for the proliferation, democratization and popularization of high culture, the art documentary developed in tandem with an expanding participation of the middle and lower classes to the sphere of art and culture, as evidenced by growing museum attendance and cultural tourism. This ideal of social and cultural emancipation also inspired the foundation of UNESCO, the United Nations' scientific and cultural agency, in 1945. International cultural organizations such as UNESCO and the Fédération internationale des Archives du Film (FIAF) played an important role in the support of the production, distribution and critical contextualization of art documentaries, which were presented as devices for cultural and educational progress. This was also the aim of more specialized organizations such as IAFF (International Art Film Federation), CIDALC (Comité Internationale pour la Diffusion des Arts et des Lettres par le Cinéma) and IIFA (International Institute of Films on Art).

Last but not least, leading artists such as Fernand Légér, filmmakers such as Luciano Emmer, Henri Storck and Alain Resnais, museum officials such as René Huyghe (Louvre), James Johnson Sweeney (Guggenheim Museum, New York) and Paul Fierens (Royal Museums of Fine Arts, Brussels), and film archivists such as Henri Langlois (Cinémathèque française) and Iris Barry (MoMA Film Library, New York) were involved in the development of FIFA (Fédération Internationale du Film sur l'Art).[18] Founded in 1948, FIFA organized three International Art Film Congresses, which took place at the Louvre in Paris in 1949, at the Palais des Beaux-Arts in Brussels in 1950 and at the Stedelijk Museum in Amsterdam in 1951. Throughout the 1950s, FIFA would become an important platform for the debates on art films, facilitating their international distribution.[19]

Although, in many cases, nationalist agendas, economical protectionism or just a pride of a local cultural heritage made the production of such films possible, most if not all of the mid-twentieth-century art documentaries were

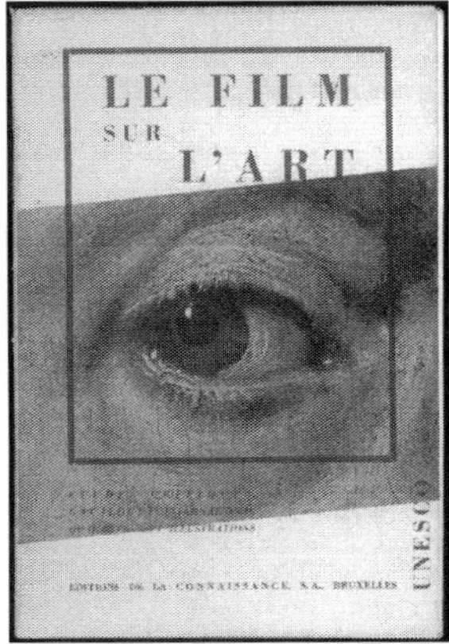
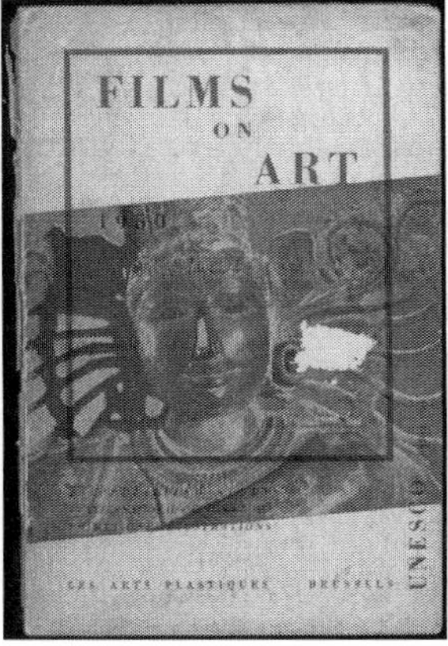
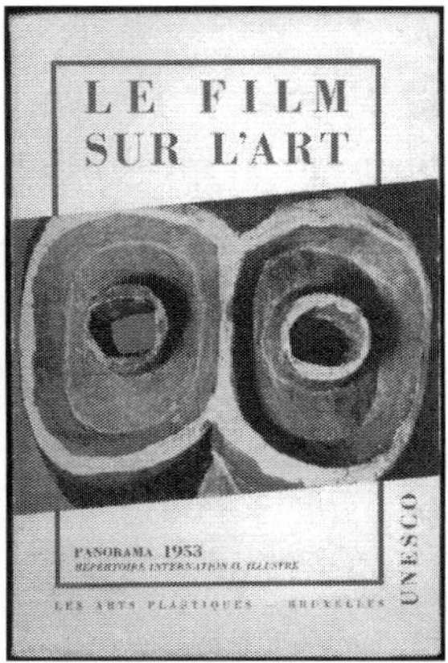

Figure 0.2 Films on Art *books published by UNESCO in 1949, 1951 and 1953.*

first and foremost inspired by this belief in the possibilities of cultural exchange and international understanding through culture and education.

This dialectic between internationalism and nationalism also marks the production and distribution of American art documentaries of the Cold-War era, such as the landmark film *The Photographer* (Willard Van Dyke, 1948), discussed extensively by Natasha Ritsma in Chapter 6. While rivalries between the US and the Soviet Union in science, including the 'Space Race', are widely known to historians of the period as well as the general public, scholars like Lisa Davenport and Michael Krenn have shown that dispute in the cultural and intellectual sphere was at least as intense.[20] With abstract expressionism, jazz and creative writing at the forefront, the United States actively sought to demonstrate its artistic supremacy over the socialist realism of the Soviet Union by promoting individualism and the market as the avatars of a 'national aesthetic'. The USIA (United States Information Agency) and private production companies made and distributed films on Jackson Pollock, Alexander Calder and Isamu Noguchi, which actively departed from the regionalist-representational bent of the New Deal sponsored art of the 1930s. In addition to exhibitions, publishing and the explosion of the art market, it was films like these that can be credited with the ascendance in public perception of New York as the new art capital of the world.[21]

Writing in 1949, critic and curator Arthur Knight found films on art produced in the United States quite wanting in matters of aesthetics, labelling them 'invariably pedestrian', 'often crude' and 'oversimplified classroom demonstrations' when compared to the more famous examples of the genre made in France, Belgium and Italy.[22] Despite this qualitative deficit, the American Federation of Arts' Guide to Art Films published in 1950 listed no fewer than 353 such titles, more than a hundred of which had been produced in the preceding year alone. By 1960, films on art were being nominated for Academy Awards on a regular basis (e.g. *Rembrandt: A Self-Portrait*, 1954 and *The Living Stone*, 1959), artists like Marie Menken and James and John Whitney made audacious experimental films still being taught today and specialized companies (like Pictura Films Corporation) and divisions of educational film producers (e.g. Encyclopaedia Britannica and Films Inc) had emerged to serve a wide market that included museums, schools and art appreciation programmes. As we will see in Chapter 2, this (brief) renaissance of the documentary on art in North America was part and parcel of the rise of the United States as a leading cultural power in the 'free' world of liberal democracies and was thus imbricated in the cultural rhetoric of the Cold War, with lines drawn on aesthetic as much as geopolitical grounds.

Major figures in Europe: Emmer, Storck, Resnais

The major figures of the European films on art in the 1940s and 1950s were Luciano Emmer, Henri Storck, Paul Haesaerts and Alain Resnais, working in Italy, Belgium and France – countries with a rich artistic (particularly pictorial) past.[23] In Italy, the production of innovative art documentaries started in the late 1930s and early 1940s when painter Luciano Emmer joined forces with Enrico Gras to produce a series of innovative and commercially successful short art documentaries such as *Racconto da un affresco* (1938), *Cantico delle creature* (1943), *Fratelli miracolosi* (1946), *Il Dramma di Cristo* (1948), *L'Invenzione della croce* (1948) and *La Leggenda di S. Orsola* (1948).[24] Emmer and Gras attempted to transpose the narrative aspects of paintings into film. Emmer was convinced that cinema had inherited the narrative functions that painting once exercised. Not coincidentally, most of Emmer's films deal with the rich tradition of *trecento* and *quattrocento* painting by artists such as Giotto,

Piero della Francesca, Vittore Carpaccio and Fra Angelico among others, who replaced the iconic stasis of the medieval and Byzantine tradition with a more dynamic and an openly narrative character.

Rather than documentaries on art, Emmer created narrative films that use painted images instead of actors, sets, props and locations. *Il Dramma di Cristo* (1948) is therefore not so much about Giotto but rather about the life of Christ, told with the help of Giotto's frescoes of the story. In so doing, Emmer isolated details of the paintings in succession, almost evoking classical continuity. After a shot of a landscape, for instance, Emmer cuts into the picture with a medium shot on an isolated fragment of the picture, followed by a close-up reaction shot of a character, in its turn succeeded by close-ups of bystanders or significant objects. Using camera movements to point out details, creating rhythm through editing to impart action to the static actors, and working very closely with the musical score (often composed by Roman Vlad) and a minimal voice-over commentary, Emmer transformed static paintings into stories. Most of the shots of an Emmer film focus on narrative elements in the paintings – elements that painters had themselves used in order to create a narrative such as gestures or facial expressions of the characters. As in a feature film, however, Emmer uses inserts of details from the painting that have no specific narrative function – a bird on a tree, a vase on a window sill – but that help to create an atmosphere and a setting for the story. Frequently, Emmer introduces a kind of cinematic suspense, as when he first shows the feet of a person before showing their character in its entirety, contradicting the logic of the painting displaying all its details simultaneously. Although unmistakably based on the narrative organization of the paintings, Emmer's films present themselves as creative translations or transpositions rather than reproductions.

Another major mid-twentieth-century contribution to the development of the art film was made by Henri Storck, who had already directed *Regards sur la Belgique ancienne* in 1936. In the late 1940s he made landmark films on artists such as Delvaux and Rubens – the latter made in collaboration with Paul Haesaerts. In contrast with Cauvin's film on Van Eyck's Mystic Lamb and most of Emmer's films, Storck did not base his films on individual paintings but rather on a collage of details from various works. While Emmer wanted to tell stories that were also the subject of his filmed paintings, Storck developed essay films with a thematic and formal analysis of the artworks. As its title suggests, *Le Monde de Paul Delvaux* (*The World of Paul Delvaux*, 1946), which Storck made in collaboration with poet and essayist René Micha, deals with surrealist painter Delvaux's entire *oeuvre* rather than with his biography or a specific painting. Delvaux's famous nudes and uncanny cityscapes merge with objects and fragments from different paintings crystallizing into an oneiric and melancholy universe. To achieve this effect, Storck and Delvaux did away with the frames of the pictures and in some cases lined them up one next to the other so that Storck's camera could pass without interruption between them.[25] Accompanied by a poem by Paul Eluard and music by André Souris, *Le Monde de Paul Delvaux* animates static images: cinema itself almost magically contributes to the 'Pygmalionesque' dimension of Delvaux's petrified nudes in nocturnal cityscapes.

Besides Italy and Belgium, the art documentary in the late 1940s flourished in France, where its production was encouraged by a decree obliging cinema owners to include short features in their programmes. Moreover, producers such as Anatole Dauman (Argos Films) and Pierre Braunberger (Les films de la Pleiade) financed and promoted documentaries by experimental filmmakers.[26] A key figure in the development of the post-war French art documentary was Alain Resnais, who would become one of the major *auteurs* of French post-war cinema. After having made a series of small film portraits of painters such as Hans Hartung, César Doméla and Max Ernst in 1946–7, Resnais created *Van Gogh* (1948, in collaboration with Robert Hessens), which was commissioned by the Amis de l'Art, a circle founded with the purpose of stimulating the proliferation of art by means of lectures and films. This society was presided over by art historian Gaston Diehl, who asked Resnais to make a film 'in the style of Luciano Emmer' who would write the film's commentary.[27] The film tells the tragic story of the life of Vincent Van Gogh, who had already become the perfect embodiment of the romantic myth of the artist as an unrecognized, tormented, self-destructive and tragic individual.[28] Strikingly, Resnais tells this myth by means of a cinematic manipulation of Van Gogh's paintings. On the whole, the film consists of a masterful succession of 207 shots of details of paintings, evoking the continuity of a feature film. In the first place, Resnais constructs a drama with the help of montage effects, a wide variety of transitions (from straight cuts to slow lap dissolves), and all kinds of camera movements. Given this perspective, the film is more in line with Van Gogh biopics (such as Vincente Minelli's 1954 *Lust for Life*) than with most of the many art documentaries that have since been dedicated to the painter. In doing so, Resnais masterfully combined the innovations introduced earlier by Curt Oertel (telling the biography of an artist through the illustration of his works), Luciano Emmer (creating narrative and drama by means of a continuity of shots showing details of paintings) and Henri Storck (mixing parts of different paintings, presenting the artist's entire oeuvre as a single vast image). As in Storck's film on Delvaux, a mobile camera and an eye-catching montage reveal the essence of the formal language of the artist. The story is told from within the painter's mind and the world is seen through the eyes of Van Gogh. After the success of *Van Gogh*, Resnais made similar films on *Gauguin* (1950) and Picasso's *Guernica* (1950).

Education and research

The mid-twentieth-century art documentaries by Emmer, Storck, Resnais, Haesaerts and many others had unmistakably educational ambitions. They attempted to take the visual arts outside the museum, bringing them to wider audiences. Producers of mid-twentieth-century art documentaries often made these ambitions more explicit. As scholars like Natasha Ritsma and Suzanne Regan have shown, films on art were among the earliest subgenres of 'educational films' and formed an integral part of the non-theatrical programmes from the early days of cinema.[29] Films like *The Art of Timothy Cole; the Last of the Wood Engravers* (made for the Boston's Museum of Fine Arts in 1930) and *The Art City of Munich* (1912) were among many listed in early catalogues published by pioneers of educational cinema George Kleine and Charles Urban. Indeed, before its emergence as a separate niche in the 1930s, short (single reel or split-reel) films on art were often subsumed under the category of travelogues or 'scenics', films that aimed to replicate something of the experience of the Grand Tourists of the Age of the Enlightenment by combining travel, sightseeing and art appreciation in an easily digestible package. Such films were screened in cinemas as part of what came to be known as 'the complete program' (combining a feature with non-fiction, comedic and animation shorts) during the 1920s, but they were also disseminated by a robust distribution network that catered to church groups, primary and secondary schools, art academies and even prisons and the military.[30]

Furthermore, art documentaries were frequently presented as instruments of learning and even as new models of art historical scholarship in their own right. Strikingly, leading art historians such as Gaston Diehl in France, Roberto Longhi and Carlo Ludovico Ragghianti in Italy, or Paul Haesaerts in Belgium, participated in the production and, occasionally, direction of these films. Their involvement thus surpassed their traditional role of adviser or author of the commentary. As demonstrated in Chapter 3, Belgian art historian and critic Paul Haesaerts collaborated with Henri Storck on the landmark film *Rubens* (1948), which provided a formal analysis of the works of the baroque painter. To do so, Haesaerts and Storck employed the entire repertory of the film medium: irises, close-ups, camera movements, and even rapidly rotating images reveal Pieter Paul Rubens' predilection for spiral-shaped structures; animated lines point out the characteristics of Rubens' compositions, while dissolves to footage of water, clouds and flames evoke Rubens' idea of a fertile universe in motion. By means of split screens, Haesaerts and Storck compare Rubens with other artists. Two years later, Haesaerts used similar diagrams, split screens and animations in *De Renoir à Picasso* (1950) as a commentary about modern art in general, tracing three inspirational sources: the so-called sensual or carnal (Renoir), the cerebral (Seurat) and the instinctual or passionate (Picasso).

For Haesaerts, conventional art criticism and art history were outdated and unadjusted to their objects. 'Let the image now replace the word, let discourse become an eloquent succession of images.'[31] Calling cinema a 'new instrument of investigation and thinking' that enables us to comprehend the artworks, Haesaerts developed a concept of '*cinéma-critique*'.[32]

Likewise, in Italy, art historian Carlo Ludovico Ragghianti developed the concept of the *critofilm*, which he saw as a form of art criticism 'made through cinematographic means instead of words'.[33] As demonstrated in Chapter 4, his

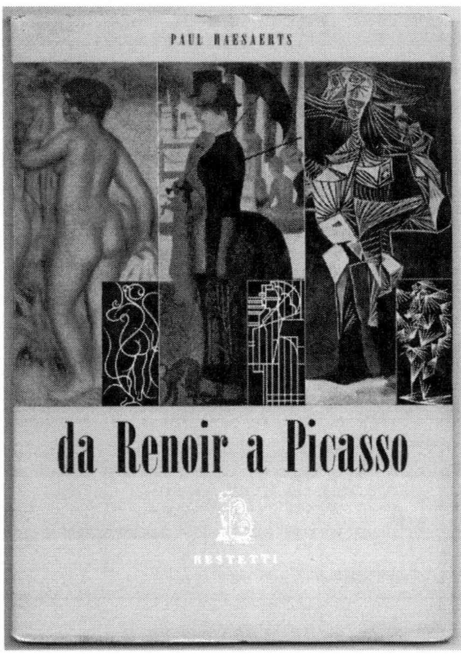

Figure 0.3 *Book with texts by Paul Haesaerts and Umbro Apollonio published on the occasion of the Italian release of* De Renoir à Picasso *(Paul Haesaerts, 1950).*

series of about twenty critofilms started in 1948 with a now lost film, *Lorenzo Il Magnifico* and concluded in 1964 with a film essay, *Michelangelo*, the longest of the series. As an author of writings on cinema as a visual art form since the 1930s, Ragghianti believed strongly that our understanding of visual language could be improved if we use images instead of words in order to 'decode' artworks. Unlike many of their colleagues, Haesaerts and Ragghianti went beyond the traditional role of expert or author of the text, taking full responsibility of a film's construction.

The art documentary as art

Despite these educational purposes, many art documentaries of the era also displayed self-consciously artistic and cinematic ambitions. According to Siegfried Kracauer, *Rubens* by Haesaerts and Storck 'is neither pure cinema nor merely a teaching instrument. It is a glamorous hybrid'.[34] Although some stated that the medium of film remained 'predominantly a machine for seeing better, a remote cousin of the magnifying lens, a periscope, a pair of opera glasses,'[35] filmmakers such as Alain Resnais, Henri Storck and Luciano Emmer presented their 'documentaries' not as mere registrations or reproductions of artworks. A film on art had to be an interesting *art film*, exploring the essential characteristics of the film medium and investigating the tensions between movement and stasis, the two- and three-dimensional, narrative and iconic images, and the real and the artificial. This autonomization of the film *vis-à-vis* the original artwork was an important subject for debate in those years. FIFA itself embodied this ambiguity as the two last letters of the abbreviation were defined as *films sur l'art* on some occasions and *films d'art* on others. Many of these films were screened as part of film programmes combining art documentaries with experimental films by artists such as Norman McLaren, Hans Richter or Fernand Léger.

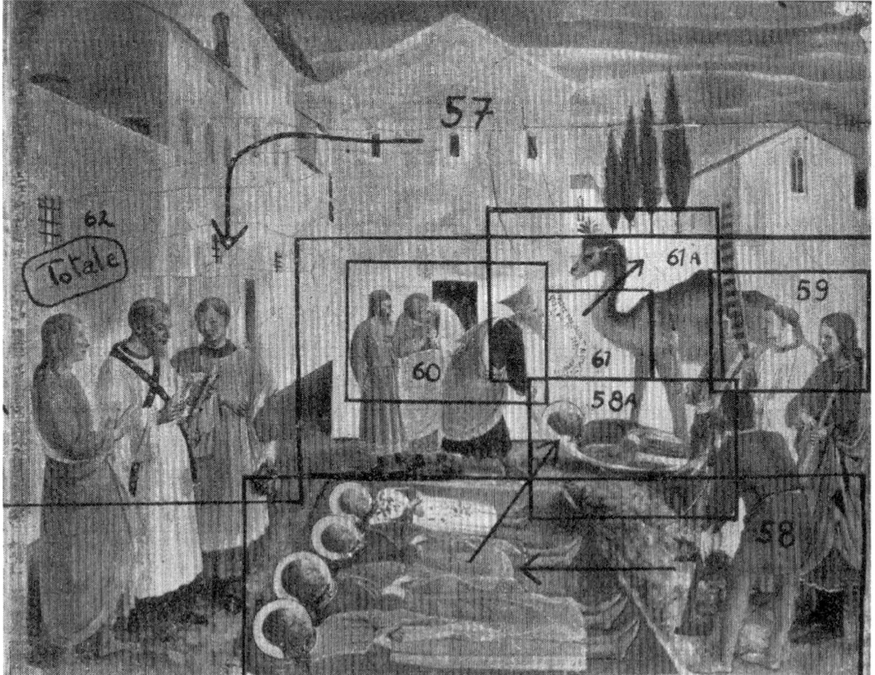

Figure 0.4 *Luciano Emmer, technical indications for the filming of a painting by Fra Angelico (c. 1948).*

This 'arty' and experimental dimension of mid-twentieth-century art documentaries contributes to their poetic dimension, intellectual depth, astounding visuals and their exceptional quality, which surpasses those of most later art documentaries complying with the standardized 'illustrated lecture' format. Not coincidentally, the experimental art documentaries of the 1940s and early 1950s developed in tandem with the so-called essay film, which combined the look of a documentary with a personal perspective and a highly reflexive dimension.

The essay film at least partly derived from the art documentary and its productive tension inherent in the translation of painting, sculpture or architecture into film. Resnais' early art documentaries on *Van Gogh* (1948) and *Guernica* (1950) paved the way for his essay films of the 1950s. His *Les Statues meurent aussi* (with Chris Marker and Ghislain Cloquet, 1953) about African art and the effect of colonialism on its reception is a perfect example of an essay film characterized by a self-reflexivity that can be found in the works by Dziga Vertov and Jean Rouch. *Les Statues meurent aussi* prefigures several later art documentaries such as *Ways of Seeing* (John Berger, 1972) or *Cézanne: Dialogue avec Joachim Gasquet* (Jean-Marie Straub and Danièle Huillet, 1989), which, akin to the new deconstructivist methods of art history, subverted voices of authority and, inspired by a Brechtian aesthetics, questioned the illusionistic possibilities of film.[36]

This autonomization of the art documentary *vis-à-vis* the original artwork was an important subject for debate among the critical reflections on the genre by Resnais, Emmer, Storck and Haesaerts. These debates also reveal that these filmmakers refused to make a clear-cut distinction between the film on art on the one hand and the art film on the other. Writing in a 1950 issue of *Sight & Sound*, Jean Queval explicitly denied the need for rigid delineations of type, arguing that at 'present, there is little to be gained from introducing rigid categories into a genre that is still searching for principles.'[37] Paradoxically, Siegfried Kracauer situated the autonomy of the new experimental art documentaries in an art historical tradition. Referring to the use of pieces of antique architecture in Piranesi's engravings, or the presence of French and Italian fountain sculptures in Watteau's *fêtes champêtres*, Kracauer stated that objections against these art films usually fail 'to take into account the fact that within the traditional arts themselves, transfers of works of art from their own medium to another are fairly frequent and are considered quite legitimate'.[38]

According to Beatrice Farwell, however, art documentaries are confronted by a dilemma by definition. 'The more a film on art succeeds as a film, the less likely it is to increase one's understanding of painting.'[39] Alluding to the film by Storck and Haesaerts, Farwell deals with the example of the art of Rubens, which, at first sight, seems like a natural for film treatment because his art is full of movement. The point, however, is that Rubens was capable of creating this movement in a static medium. When a painting is set into motion by means of cinematic devices, the illusion Rubens skilfully created is lost. A new filmic illusion is constructed, which, according to Farwell, falsifies Rubens' art and which can even lead to a misinterpretation of the art of painting in general. Furthermore, the medium of film was often denounced by art historians because films did not show the entire work in a single shot or at a single glance. At the third FIFA conference in Amsterdam in 1950, an art critic even argued for the obligation of filmmakers to show the artwork entirely and in colour at the beginning of their films.[40] Such considerations ignore the basic qualities and possibilities of art documentaries, which not only 'represent' artworks but also reproduce, duplicate, reconfigure, re-imagine or remediate them with the help of the cinematic or audio-visual devices such as close-ups, montage, camera movements, etc. In the process, art documentaries transform or translate the original artworks from one medium to another, creating a new hybrid.

Camera and canvas: documentaries on painting

The demand to 'show the artwork entirely and in colour at the beginning of a film' and the rather naïve assumptions on the transparency of film also ignore the essence of the film medium, which exceeds or at least questions the dichotomy based on Lessing's division between spatial and temporal arts. Art documentaries can even be said to exemplify the complexity of film as both a spatial and temporal discipline. This is already clear from Emmer's films where various stages of a narrative painting (such as *The Legend of Saint Ursula* by Carpaccio) are seen simultaneously by the beholder of the original artwork as forming part of a single pictorial composition unfolding in time by means of camera movements and editing techniques.

However, on a more fundamental level, the maker of an art film faces additional problems. Even when a shot attempts to record a painting entirely, the artwork as a *Gestalt* is lost by definition because, almost always, the proportion of the painting does not completely coincide with the aspect ratio of the film camera and film screen. The filmmaker, consequently, has to crop the image or the frame will also include a part of the world that falls outside the painting. Strikingly, in the most interesting art films, filmmakers deal with their framings in a highly conscious way and create new visual balances and tensions within them. In the films by Emmer, Storck and Resnais, this even becomes a *conditio sine qua non*.

Given this perspective, one should also point out that not only the vast majority of art documentaries and the most interesting and innovating ones among them have painting as their subject, whereas the film medium seems more appropriate for the registration of sculpture and architecture, both of which imply a mobilized beholder. This pronounced focus on painting cannot entirely be explained by referring to the prominent position the medium of painting has occupied since the Renaissance. The preference for painting as a subject might be related to the visual primacy of film whereas architecture and sculpture have traditionally been thought of as more tactile – an aspect that will be dealt with in the following paragraph. First and foremost, however, it is precisely the confrontation between the frame of the painting and that of the camera as well as the interference of two kinds of two-dimensionality that turn the film of a painting into an interesting artistic challenge. At the precise moment when the avant-garde emphasizes the integrity of the pictorial surface (for example, the insistence on flatness throughout Clement Greenberg's writings of the 1940s and 1950s), filmmakers played on the ambivalence of the film image which, according to Arnheim, presents each object 'in two entirely different frames of reference, namely the two-dimensional and three-dimensional'.[41] By focusing on painting, Emmer, Storck and Resnais presented the genre of the art documentary as a means to investigate the limits of film as a medium by juxtaposing movement versus stasis, narrative versus iconic images, and cinematic space versus pictorial surface.

The juxtaposition between two frames was also the subject of one of the major essays André Bazin dedicated to the relation between painting and cinema.[42] According to Bazin, the fixed frame of painting enclosed a world that exists entirely by and for itself; it draws the attention of the spectator in a centripetal way to a static composition. The frame of the film camera, by contrast, is mobile and implies a centrifugal space extending beyond the frame into the smallest and most remote corners of everyday life. When we show a part of a painting on a film screen, the space of the painting loses its orientation and it is presented as something borderless and hence as something that extends beyond the frame. Apart from the (educational or democratizing) fact that cinema is capable of bringing a painting closer to a wider audience, film presents a painting as part of the world. According to Bazin, Resnais precisely succeeded in introducing this centrifugal space of film into the centripetal space of painting. By switching between paintings and by letting the camera glide over surfaces the limits of which remain invisible, Resnais breaks through the spatial restraints of painting. According to Bazin, Resnais' art documentaries are therefore hybrid or symbiotic works. On the one hand, they cannot simply be considered as documentary recordings of another art form because the material provided by the other medium is transformed. On the other hand, they are not autonomous films since they remain dependent on other arts.

Key documentaries on sculpture

'An object in space is a better proposition for a film on art than a two-dimensional work like a painting, an illuminated manuscript, or a goblin,'[43] wrote Josef Paul Hodin in his review of *Looking at Sculpture* (Alexander Shaw, 1949), a film focusing on statues in the Victoria and Albert Museum. Indeed, cinema has consistently been presented as the perfect instrument to document sculpture. 'Short of a field trip, the best way to teach sculpture is with cinematic visual aids,' Sally Chappell wrote in 1973. 'The flow of images and the inherent motion of changing camera distance and angle simulate the live three-dimensional experience of sculpture better than a series of front, side, and back view slide reproductions. The cinema can also reproduce the movement of light, so important in rendering the material of sculpture – the shifting reflections in Brancusi's metals, for example, or the glowing transparencies in Pevsner's plastics.'[44]

Apart from the aforementioned *The Titan*, the most interesting examples of documentaries on sculpture include *Aristide Maillol, sculpteur* (Jean Lods, 1943), *Alexander Calder: Sculpture and Constructions* (Hartley Productions for MoMA, 1944), *Visual Variations on Noguchi* (Marie Menken, 1945), *Looking at Sculpture* (Alexander Shaw, 1949), *Forms in Space: The Art of Sculpture* (Sidney Lubow and Arthur Swerdloff, 1949), *Thorvaldsen* (Carl Theodor Dreyer, 1949), *Henry Moore* (John Read, 1951), *Les Pierres vives* (Fernand Marzelle, 1951), *Jacques Lipchitz* (Frank Stauffacher, 1951), *Works of Calder* (Herbert Matter, 1951), *Les Statues meurent aussi* (Alain Resnais and Chris Marker, 1953), *Figures in a Landscape* (Dudley Shaw Ashton, 1953), *The Gates of Hell* (Albert Elsen, 1954), *L'Enfer de Rodin* (Henri Alekan, 1957), *Gyromorphosis* (Hy Hirsch, 1958) and *A Sculptor's Landscape* (John Read, 1958).[45] None of these films, with the exception of *Les Statues meurent aussi*, have received major critical or scholarly attention. This list comprises a wide variety of titles, ranging from didactic documentaries (Shaw, Lubow and Swerdloff) that attempt to explain the quintessence of sculpture, to artists' films (Menken, Hirsch) that use sculptures to create abstract visual studies, to poetic film essays by major filmmakers (Dreyer, Alekan, Resnais and Marker). Arguably coming closest to the format of the essay film is *Les Statues meurent aussi* (*Statues also Die*) by Resnais and Marker. Dealing with African art and voicing a vehement criticism of colonial politics, this famous film is marked by the self-reflexivity characteristic of essay films. As Resnais and Marker focus on the sculptures' eyes, on beholders looking, and on practices of museum display, the film is a meditation on the cinematic gaze and how it visualizes or represents sculptures. In so doing, the film definitely reflects on the encounter between film and sculpture.

This dimension also marks other key documentaries on sculpture of the 1940s and 1950s, which additionally juxtapose an optic visuality to a haptic one. On the one hand, films such as *Thorvaldsen* and *L'Enfer de Rodin* enable us

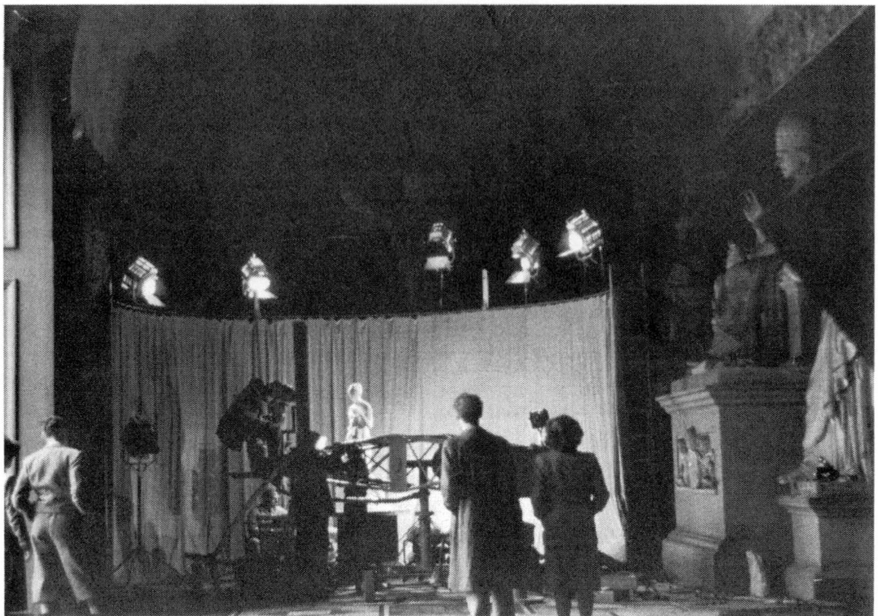

Figure 0.5 *Carl Theodor Dreyer filming in the Thorvaldsen Museum, Copenhagen, 1949. Production still. Courtesy of the Danish Film Institute.*

to 'feel' the three-dimensionality, weight, and even texture of sculptural volumes through the use of light, a scanning camera or revealing close-ups.

Here, film also makes manifest the fact that sculptures are situated in the same physical space as their beholders, emphasizing the bodily interactions between statue and onlooker. This 'reality effect' of sculpture is emphasized by the filming of sculptures against natural backgrounds such as shifting clouds or moving foliage in documentaries such as *Figures in a Landscape* and *A Sculptor's Landscape*. On the other hand, the moving image inevitably transforms sculptures into pure optical phenomena. In films like *L'Enfer de Rodin* and *Visual Variations on Noguchi*, even the most heavy and solid volumes are turned into floating, airy shapes on the screen. Movement within the shots, shifting viewpoints, camera movements, light and fragmenting and alienating close-ups transpose the sculpture from its real and physical space to an imaginative realm. These films demonstrate that the medium of film is able to transform sculptures into a pure optical experience reminiscent of *Ein Lichtspiel: Schwarz Weiss Grau* (1930), László Moholy-Nagy's landmark film that is more of an extension of his kinetic light sculpture rather than a mere document of it.

Contemporary artists and acts of creation

Showing a static artwork in the dynamic medium of film has often been considered an uninteresting or unchallenging task by filmmakers. That's why so many art documentaries have shifted their focus from the finished artwork to its process of creation, i.e. the development of the artwork through time. Long after Cürlis' 1920s series of *Schaffende Hände* (creating hands), the motif of the artist at work remained important throughout the art documentary's entire history. In the 1940s and 1950s, the act of creation became the subject of key films such as *Visite à Picasso* (Paul Haesaerts, 1950), *Jackson Pollock 51* (Paul Falkenberg and Hans Namuth, 1951) and *Le Mystère Picasso* (Henri-Georges Clouzot, 1956). The first of these films, Haesaerts' *Visite à Picasso*, contains a remarkable sequence

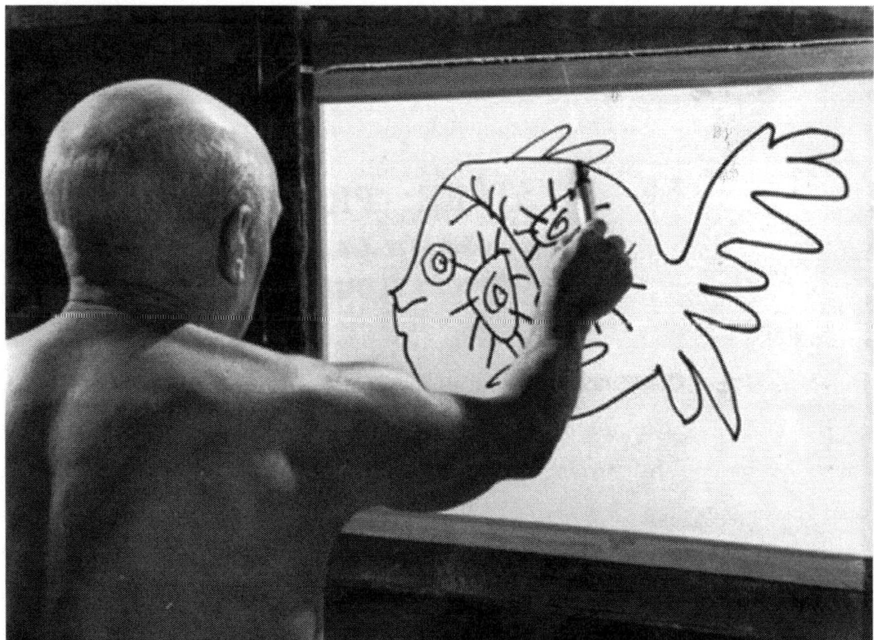

Figure 0.6 Le Mystère Picasso *(Henri-Georges Clouzot, 1956). Digital still.*

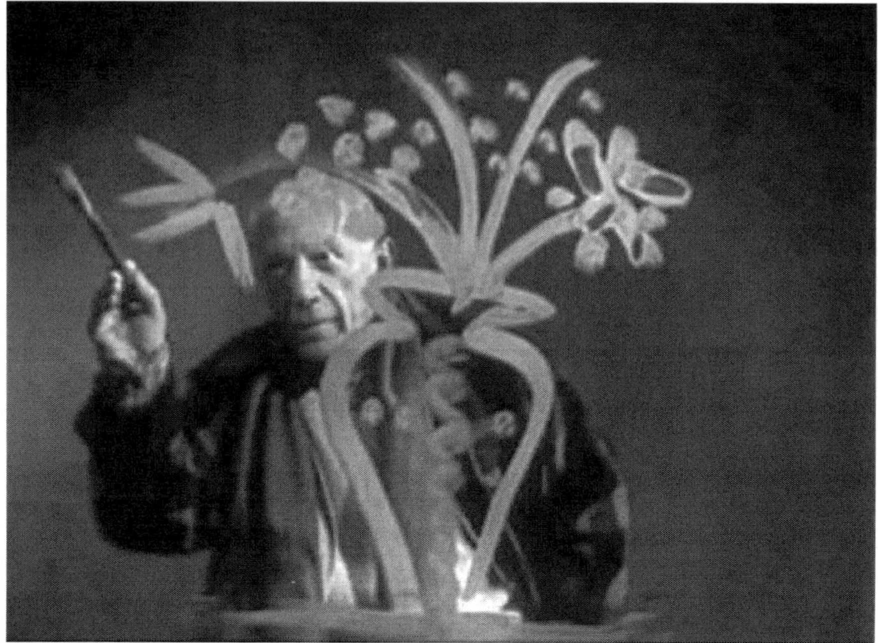

Figure 0.7 Visite à Picasso *(Paul Haesaerts, 1950). Digital still.*

showing Picasso painting various forms (a bird, a vase with flowers, various zoomorphic figures) on a sheet of Plexiglass mounted between himself and the camera. The effect is striking – shown against a dark background, it looks as if Picasso draws white lines into the space in front of him. The use of a glass pane in order to show the creation process itself was adopted by Falkenberg and Namuth's highly influential *Jackson Pollock 51*. Pollock's large-format drippings can be understood as an almost seismographic registration of his bodily movements and their effect on film is very powerful. Similarly, *The Reality of Karel Appel* (Jan Vrijman, 1962) features artist Karel Appel, who was a member of the CoBrA movement (1948–51), flicking paint at the camera, peeping through a hole in the canvas.[46] The most famous variation of the artist painting on a glass pane can be found in Clouzot's feature-length *Le Mystère Picasso*.[47]

Noirish black-and-white shots of Picasso at work alternate with long takes in colour of a porous white screen on which Picasso paints or draws. Clouzot's long takes reproduce the duration of the painting process. The screen is filmed frontally from behind so that the artist remains invisible. As a result, the screen becomes a kind of 'automatic painting' transforming or morphing, for instance, the initial image of a flower into a fish, then a hen, a human face, and finally the head of a faun.

In these landmark films by Haesaerts, Namuth and Falkenberg, and Clouzot, we are witnessing the creation and development of a painting through its succeeding stages. According to André Bazin, who famously labelled the Clouzot documentary a 'Bergsonian film', time and duration have become the instruments and even the subject of the film, which consists for the most part of uninterrupted long takes that reproduce the duration of the painting process.[48] For Bazin, Clouzot's film on Picasso shifts the emphasis from the simultaneous presence of all the elements of a finished work to the progressive duration of the creative act. Both the Picasso films by Haesaerts and Clouzot and *Jackson Pollock 51* by Namuth and Falkenberg largely consist of scenes in which we see the artist at work filmed through a plate of glass or translucent material. In the films by Haesaerts and Namuth and Falkenberg, the artists themselves seem to be immersed in their paintings, emphasizing the physical dimension of the pictorial act.

The fascination for the artist at work tallies perfectly with the stylistic preoccupations of the artists being filmed. After all, artistic currents such as Action Painting, Tachisme and CoBrA (often grouped under labels such as abstract expressionism, lyrical abstraction or gestural abstraction), favoured experiment, irrational spontaneity, improvisation and a highly physical way of painting. Referring to Action Painting, Harold Rosenberg famously noted in 1952 that 'the canvas began to appear [...] as an arena in which to act – rather than as a space in which to reproduce, redesign, analyze, or "express" an object, actual or imagined. What was to go on the canvas was not a picture but an event'.[49] In addition, emphasizing on process over product, Rosenberg concluded that 'a painting that is an act is inseparable from the biography of the artist. The painting itself is a "moment" in the adulterated mixture of his life. [...] The act-painting is of the same metaphysical substance as the artist's existence. The new painting has broken down every distinction between art and life'.[50] Likewise, CoBrA artist Jorn noted that the psychic automatism favoured by the pre-war Surrealists, had been exchanged for a more physical activity.[51]

This entanglement of physical and biographical aspects made gestural abstraction highly attractive for filmmakers as the artworks themselves enticed the spectator to see them in an organic relationship with the artists who made them. Post-war lyrical abstraction provided filmmakers with images that are static (and hence un-cinematic) but the paintings evoke the painter's movements and his physical actions – hence notions such as 'Action Painting', 'Gesture Painting' or 'Gestural Abstraction'. In the context of these artistic currents, a painting can be read as an almost seismographic registration of the movement of the artist's hand or entire body. As a result, movements of the hand or bodily manipulations of canvasses, stretchers, pencils, and paint are emphasized in the films by Haesaerts, Clouzot, and Falkenberg and Namuth as well in other films such as *Calligraphie japonaise* (1955) by CoBrA member Pierre Alechinsky. In the context of Gestural Abstraction, painting becomes a performance. In so doing, the films on Picasso and Pollock at work paved the way for the increasing importance of the bodily presence and the performative self of the artist. These films construct a narrative around the body of the artist and track his fluid and gestural creative process in a way at once more sophisticated and critical than portrayals of artists in older films like *Works of Calder* of *Art Discovers America*. These films resonate, for instance, with the work of Georges Mathieu, who occasionally introduced a performative dimension to his painting in the 1950s, executing large canvases before audiences.[52] Likewise, several artists of a later generation experimenting with performance and happenings (Allan Kaprow, Yves Klein, Fluxus artists) have mentioned the importance of the ubiquitous photographic and cinematic representations of Jackson Pollock at work.[53]

Gestural Abstraction not only appeals to cinematic representation because of the importance of physical actions and gestures, but also because of the temporality that is inscribed in the paintings. Gottfried Boehm not only sees 'movement, physically manifested in and through the artist's body' as a common denominator in most of these artworks but also notices 'a heightened temporality that communicates itself to the works'.[54] This notion of painting as a process of constant metamorphosis is also a crucial issue in Picasso's work of that era as demonstrated in the films by Haesaerts and Clouzot. Moreover, changing, transforming, metamorphosing an image also implies destruction – 'to paint is to destroy what preceded', Karel Appel stated.[55] As the act of creation, destruction implies the subjection of the artwork to a physical act, which makes it attractive for filmmakers – it is not a coincidence that the filmed biographies or so-called biopics of famous or fictitious artists often contain scenes in which the artist destroys his creations.[56]

Films showing or evoking the acts of creation are ambivalent. On the one hand, they contribute to a demystification of romantic notions about the artist genius, inspiration, and creation. They unveil the act of creation, showing that the production of artworks involves lots of preparations, numerous mistakes and recapitulations, mundane labour and even boredom. On the other hand, however, such films seem to be unable to deconstruct the mythic image of the artist as demiurge. On the contrary, they almost inevitably present the artist as a 'heroic individual' tallying with the post-war cult of major artists as celebrities. According to Lotte Eisner, in showing the immediacy of the act of creation, 'an astounding presence is revealed, stripped naked in all its complexity'.[57] Thanks to the film medium, the artists acquire an almost shamanistic power. Focusing on the act of creation, these films, in the words of Philip Hayward, contribute to an 'extreme fetishization of the actual moment of creation'.[58] In films showing artists at work, Patrick Hayman notes, the magic of painting 'comes across in a splendidly satisfying way, as the painting itself grows and changes under the joyful brush of the artist'.[59] Many of these films are so powerful because they hint at an essential feature of many art currents of the beginning and middle of the twentieth century. As indicated by authors such as Konrad Fiedler and Paul Valéry, the act of creation acquired a new meaning in the development of modern art since the late nineteenth century.[60] Instead of presenting the hand as a mere servant of the artist genius, merely giving form to an idea or *disegno*, modern art saw the struggle against the materials or against earlier stages of the artwork as an essential element of its aesthetic power. Combining seeing and doing in all kinds of bodily relations, the act of creation became a staple image of the art documentary.

Finally, the motif of the artist at work was also used in contexts in which the process of artistic creation does not involve the physical action or virtuoso drawings emphasized in the films on Picasso or Pollock. In *Magritte, ou la leçon de choses* (Luc de Heusch, 1960), the stereotypical image of the artist struggling with paint and brushes in an untidy studio is replaced by footage of the famous Surrealist dressed in suit and tie, who works in the homely living room of his house – his 'work' seems only to consist of moving and manipulating frames and canvasses as well as giving (sometimes ironic) titles to already finished paintings.[61]

Art book and museum

In their attempts to convey works of art, art documentaries should be situated in a long tradition reaching back to ekphrastic writing in Antiquity and the development of all kind of practices and devices of display and means of mediating art works, such as prints, photography, illustrated books and museums. Moreover, the Golden Age of the art documentary coincides with a period of major changes in the fields of publishing and museums, following on the heels of the popularization of the fine arts in the decades following the Second World War. The cultural participation of the middle and lower classes was expanding – a phenomenon resulting in increasing number of visitors to museums as well as in the breakthrough of the illustrated art book, epitomized by the success of publishers specializing in high-quality art books such as Skira and Phaidon.

The art book had already undergone some major changes shortly before the war. Kenneth Clark, for instance, who would much later write and present the milestone BBC television art documentary *Civilisation* (1969), published *One Hundred Details from Pictures in the National Gallery* in 1938. The book became an instant success and was followed by the publication of *More Details from Pictures in the National Gallery* in 1941. Inspired by the improvement of photographic reproduction techniques, both books were made for the pleasure of the eye. Although a few details had been selected 'for historical or iconographical reasons', most details 'have been chosen chiefly for their beauty', Clark emphasized in the introduction. Clark further remarked that the book contained many details that viewers had never noticed. This means that 'we do not look at pictures carefully' and that 'the great value of these photographic details is that they encourage us to look at pictures more attentively, and show us some of the rewards of patient scrutiny'.[62]

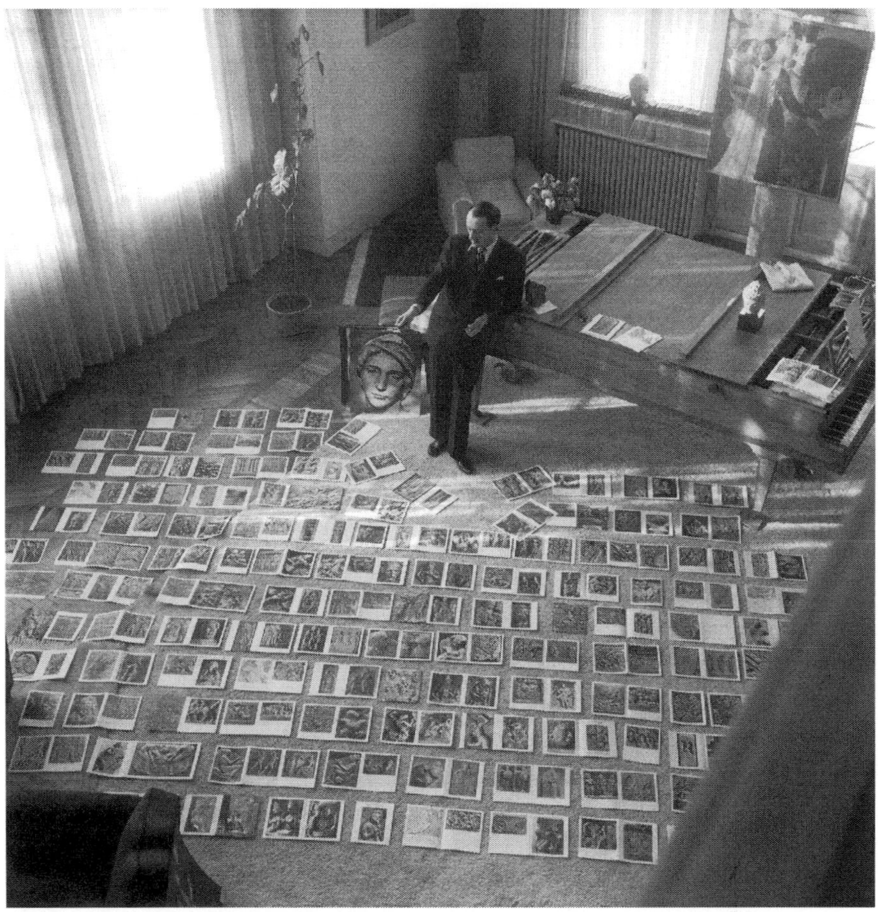

Figure 0.8 *André Malraux (photograph by Maurice Jarnoux, 1954).*

First and foremost, the late 1940s and early 1950s was also the era in which André Malraux developed his *Musée imaginaire*.[63] According to Malraux, the traditional physical museum could be exchanged for a kind of virtual all-encompassing photographic archive, embodied in the phenomenon of the illustrated art book. In contrast to the traditional museum, which stimulated the contemplation of unique and isolated masterpieces, the *Musée imaginaire* was rather based on the juxtaposition of artworks of divergent styles, periods and cultures. Whereas, according to Walter Benjamin, photography and film had destroyed the *aura* of the traditional work of art, for Malraux, modern techniques of mechanical reproduction had a rather ambivalent role.[64] Photography was unmistakably capable of disconnecting the work of art from its original context but could also reinforce its aura by emphasizing its affinity with other artworks or with human creativity as such. Strikingly, for Malraux, the medium of photography supplies the materials for the art book but it is cinema that provides its organizational model.

According to Malraux, the art book was, just like a film, a succession of images arranged on the basis of a technique of montage.[65] Like many art books, many art documentaries can be considered as virtual museums; they are cinematic equivalents of a curatorial endeavour: creating successions of artworks and isolating masterpieces through montage, camera movements, light, etc.

What is more, the production of numerous high-quality art documentaries and Malraux's project of the *Musée imaginaire* also coincided with important museological innovations. The late 1940s saw the establishment of the International Council of Museums (ICOM), which had ambitions to pioneer new curatorial practices. As Birgit Cleppe has demonstrated in her chapter in this volume, right from its inception, ICOM showed great interest in the art documentaries and museums were often involved in their production.

Museum collections and major exhibitions have also been the subject of early newsreels and seminal art documentaries. The Metropolitan Museum of Art in New York, for instance, figured prominently in the self-produced films having already adopted film by 1925 and showing its own movies at the museum.[66] The Metropolitan also produced *Behind the Scenes: The Working Side of the Museum* (1928), an early example of the popular subgenre of behind-the-scenes tours of museums. With *Kurgäste hinter Museumsmauern* (1934) and *Heilbehandlung von Kunstwerken* (1939), which deal with the conservation laboratories of Berlin museums, Hans Cürlis contributed to this subgenre as well. In the 1930s, Cürlis also made films focusing on collection highlights of a single museum or several museums in films such as *Aus Berliner Museen* (1937) and *Schatzkammer Deutschland* (1939).[67] After the war, leading museums continued to produce films or were the subject of art documentaries. The Louvre, for instance, features in numerous documentary films with various approaches and perspectives. Some of these films, such as *Images de l'ancienne Egypte* (Maurice Cloche, 1951), show artworks isolated from their context without the disturbing details that might thwart an intimate encounter with the artworks during a real museum visit. Others, such as *Les Pierres vives* (Fernand Marzelle, 1951), bring together works from different galleries to evoke an actual museum visit as the camera goes from one room into the other, approaching the exhibits from an oblique angle. In so doing, rather than merely documenting the museum, the film aims to extend the museum experience, translating it into a thrilling cinematic adventure while constructing a new virtual collection.[68]

Television: standardization and deconstruction

The landmark art documentaries by Oertel, Emmer, Storck, Haesaerts and Resnais of the late 1930s and 1940s preceded the spread of the medium of television in their countries of origin. In the decade following the Second World War, the mid-twentieth-century documentary on the visual arts found its most fertile non-theatrical base in the culture of ciné clubs, art societies, museums and schools. From the 1950s onwards, however, television became the most important medium for the production and distribution for art documentaries. It should be noted that television's relationship with the visual arts goes well beyond the format of the feature-length art documentary as the arts also became occasionally the topic of newsreels, talk shows, TV revues and other types of programmes. Moreover, this relationship has been largely determined by the process of transmission as many programmes were live or recorded broadcasts of events from a television studio or an outside location. In the United States, the rapid rise of network television and its incessant demand for programming played a major role in the coverage of art for a mass audience. Lynn Spiegel has amply demonstrated that such programmes were used by broadcasters to bolster 'their reputations as public servants' and 'to convince sponsors, audiences and government regulators at the Federal Communications Commission (FCC) that their companies were not just economically sound, but also socially valuable'.[69]

Apart from featuring artworks and artists in all kinds of programmes, television became a major (co-)producer of art documentaries, which could now reach a far greater audience than ever before. The first major advances in the 1950s were made in Great-Britain where John Read (see Chapter 7) made seminal films on such contemporaneous British artists as Henry Moore, Graham Sutherland and Stanley Spencer. Impressed by Emmer's films and convinced that 'the educational is implicit in the artistic', Read focused on direct encounters with the artists. His films, in the words of John Wyver, 'can feel strikingly "open" for the viewer to bring his or her own responses'.[70] Some interesting films on art were also produced within the context of *Monitor* (1958–65), arguably television's first arts magazine. Noteworthy among them are Ken Russell's portraits of composers such as Elgar and Debussy and *Pop Goes the Easel* (1962), his account of the development of Pop Art in Britain using a kind of collage-aesthetic echoing the works of the artists being discussed in the film.

Directed at a mass audience without a specialist knowledge, for better or worse television contributed to the standardization of the art documentary taking the format of a didactic historical tour with an on-camera host whose words are often juxtaposed with footage of artworks. This format was pioneered by Kenneth Clark, who created art programmes from the late 1950s onwards and who became famous with the highly successful thirteen-part series *Civilisation: A Personal View* (1969).[71] In *Civilisation*, Clark delivers his lectures in magnificent settings all over western Europe thanks to a budget that enabled extensive location shooting. Combining the art history lecture with a Grand-Tour-travelogue format, *Civilisation* harmoniously pairs spectacular images with music and a narration marked by 'the effortless confidence' and patrician erudition of Clark's judgements.[72] This on-camera presence of an expert would subsequently mark many similar series for decades, from John Berger's riposte to Clark's *Civilisation* in *Ways of Seeing* (1972), and Robert Hughes' *Shock of the New* (1979) to Simon Schama's *Power of Art* (2006), and the recently broadcast 'sequel' to *Civilisation*, entitled *Civilisations* (BBC/PBS, 2018) which Schama co-hosted with Mary Beard and David Olusoga.

Despite the didacticism of this dominant format, television has occasionally also offered possibilities to question or deconstruct the voice of authority speaking on- or off-camera and giving an art history lecture supported by the camera's exploration of artworks or buildings. Berger's *Ways of Seeing* (1972) not only dealt with art but also addressed the very process of its dissemination and commercialization by the mass media. Inspired by Marxist art theorists such as Frederick Antal and Walter Benjamin (to whom Berger explicitly refers in the first programme) as well as by the 'new art history', Berger demystified traditional notions of art, revealing its hidden ideologies. Dealing with themes likes reproduction, the female nude, the role of the art market, and the seduction of advertising, *Ways of Seeing* relates both art and popular visual culture to social and economic reality.

The diversity in approaches, formats and content suggested by these few examples of the art documentary's afterlife on the small screen could well be thought of as a second Golden Age of the genre, one that brought it to a much larger public while retaining stylistic traits pioneered by earlier filmmakers (camera movement over artworks, chronological or geographic succession in editing, etc). Furthermore, from the late 1960s to the early 1990s, state television in many European countries facilitated the production of experimental and highly self-reflexive art documentaries such as productions by Jean-Christophe Averty in France, Gerry Schum in Germany, Mike Dibb and John Wyver in the United Kingdom, and Jean-Paul Tréfois, Jef Cornelis and Stefaan Decostere in Belgium.[73] Their new televisual formats were closely connected to changes in the arts themselves. Unmistakably, the medium of television was at its best when dealing with contemporary practices and issues. Rather than visualizing or reproducing artworks that already existed, new artworks were created *through* the interaction with television, in line with new artistic currents such as happening, performance, process art, land art, conceptual art and video art. Coinciding with the development of these new ideas and practices, television became an important channel of production for many vanguard artists. Gerry Schum's *Fernsehgallery* or 'TV Gallery' contains an episode entitled *Identifications* (1970) showing performances or interventions by Joseph Beuys, Gilbert & George, and Richard Serra among others. Likewise, artists such as Peter Weibel, Valie Export, Maria Lassnig and Arnulf Rainer were able to create works for/on Austrian art programmes such as *Kontakt* or *Impulse* in the early 1970s. Although they 'documented' artworks in a certain sense, these programmes presented themselves as artworks in line with new conceptions and definitions of 'art objects' among the vanguard art currents of the late 1960s and 1970s.

In a world in which television programming has increasingly migrated to streaming and online platforms and the self-contained, feature-length documentary is increasingly superseded by seriality, interactivity, virtual and augmented reality, we would do well to remember that despite its nearly century-long evolution, the art documentary is deeply rooted in the cinematic tradition of non-fiction, the populism of the Visual Instruction movement and the vision of filmmakers like Emmer, Storck and Resnais that sought to bring their passions for visual art and the motion picture together. It is to their work that the contributors to this volume pay tribute.

Notes

1   Henriette Montgomery and Nadine Covert, 'Art on Screen: Films and Television on Art – An Overview', in Nadine Covert (ed.), *Art on Screen: A Directory on Film and Videos about the Visual Arts* (New York/Los Angeles: Metropolitan Museum of Art/J. Paul Getty Trust, 1991), 1.

2   See, for instance, William Mck. Chapman, *Films on Art* (New York: American Federation of the Arts, 1952), *Le film sur l'art* (Paris: UNESCO, 1953) and Carlo Ludovico Raghianti, *Répertoire général international des films sur l'art* (Roma: Edizone dell' Ateneo, 1951), containing 453, 729 and 1,109 titles respectively.

3   In 1950, Alain Resnais received an Oscar in the Best Short Subject category for *Van Gogh*, whereas Robert Flaherty and Robert Snyder won the Academy Award for Best Documentary Feature with *The Titan*. *1848* (Marguerite de la Mure and Victoria Mercanton) and *Rembrandt: A Self-Portrait* (Morrie Roizman) were nominated in 1949 and 1954, respectively, for best documentary shorts. For the importance of art documentaries at the Venice Film Festival, see Luisella D'Alessandro, *La Mostra del cinema di Venezia e la fortuna del documentario d'arte in Italia* (Università di Teramo, MA diss., 2007).

4   The two most important texts by Bazin on this topic are 'Peinture et cinéma' (written between 1943 and 1951) and 'Un film Bergsonien: Le Mystère Picasso' (1956), which are both included in *Qu'est-ce que le cinéma?* (Paris: Éditions du Cerf, 2007), 187–92, 193–202. See also Rudolf Arnheim, 'Painting and Film', in *Film Essays and Criticism* (Madison, WI: University of Wisconsin Press, 1997), 86–92; Siegried Kracauer, *Theory of Film: The Redemption of Physical Reality* (Princeton, NJ: Princeton University Press, 1960), 195–201; Pierre Francastel, 'A Teacher's Point of View', in *Films on Art* (Paris

and Brussels: UNESCO and Les Arts plastiques, 1951); and Henri Lemaître, *Beaux-arts et cinéma* (Paris: Les Éditions du Cerf, 1956).

5   For a prominent case study see Natasha Ritsma, *The Postwar 'Arts Explosion' in an Age of Mechanical Reproduction: the Production, Distribution and Exhibition of Non-Theatrical Films on Art* (PhD diss: Indiana University, 2014).

6   See Jens Thiele, *Das Kunstwerk im Film: Zur Problematik filmisher Präsentationsformen von Malerei und Grafik* (Bern: Herbert Lang/Frankfurt: Peter Lang, 1976), 14.

7   See Alain Carou, 'Ceux de chez nous: galerie de portraits, théâtre de la mémoire', in Noëlle Giret and Noël Herpe (eds), *Sacha Guitry, Une vie d'artiste* (Paris: Gallimard, 2007), 55–61.

8   Katz was a student at the American Artists School. See 'PM Shorts', *PM Magazine* (1 December 1937): 84.

9   See Arthur Knight, 'A Short History of Art Films', in Chapman (ed.), *Films on Art 1952*, 8–9.

10   See Thiele, *Das Kunstwerk im Film*, 15–18; Reiner Ziegler, *Kunst und Architektur im Kulturfilm 1919–1945* (Konstanz: UVK Verlaggesellschaft, 2003), 35–40, 45–54 and 302–9; Ulrich Döge, *Kulturfilm als Aufgabe: Hans Cürlis (1889–1992)* (Berlin: CineGraph Babelsberg, 2005); and Rainer Ziegler: 'Schaffende Hände: Die Kulturfilme von Hans Cürlis über bildende Kunst und Künstler', in Klaus Kreimeier, Antje Ehmann, Jeanpaul Goergen (eds), *Geschichte des dokumentarischen Films in Deutschland. Band 2: Weimarer Republik 1918–1933* (Stuttgart: Reclam, 2005), 219–27.

11   Cürlis was not known for his use of animation and other special effects – his films were billed as 'Trick- und Animationsfilme'. See Peer Moritz, 'Berthold Bartosch', in *CineGraph Lexikon zum deutschsprachigen Film* (Munich: edition text + kritik, 1984).

12   Knight, 'A Short History of Art Films', 10. See also Ziegler, *Kunst und Architektur im Kulturfilm*, 290–1 and 315–17.

13   Gordon Mirams, 'Art and the Cinema', *Design Review* 3, 2 (September–October 1950): 39–41. See also Steven Jacobs, *Art & Cinema: Belgian Art Documentaries* (Brussels: Cinematek, 2013).

14   See Steven Jacobs, 'The Silence of the Mystic Lambs: Jan van Eyck and André Cauvin's film about The Mystic Lamb (1939)', *Simiolus: Netherlands Quarterly for the History of Art* 39, 1–2 (2017): 102–10.

15   Knight, 'A Short History of Art Films', 11.

16   Iris Barry, 'Pioneering in Films on Art', in Chapman (ed.), *Films on Art 1952*, 2.

17   Katerina Loukopoulou, 'Museum at Large: Aesthetic Education through Film', in Devin Orgeron, Marsha Orgeron and Dan Streible (eds), *Learning with the Lights Off: Educational film in the United States* (New York: Oxford University Press, 2012), 357.

18 See Leon Duyck, *FIFA: Fédération Internationale du Film d'Art Onderzoek naar de samenstelling, doelstellingen, werking en activiteiten van de FIFA en de ondersteuning van de kunstdocumentaire na WOII tot en met de jaren '60* (Ghent University, MA diss., 2014).

19 See the volumes published by UNESCO such as *Films on Art* (Paris: Unesco, 1949); *Films on Art* (Paris: UNESCO/Brussels: Les Arts plastiques, 1951); and Francis Bolen (ed.), *Films on Art: Panorama 1953* (Paris: UNESCO, 1953).

20 Lisa E. Davenport, *Jazz Diplomacy: Promoting America in the Cold War Era* (Jackson: University Press of Mississippi, 2009) and Michael L. Krenn, 'The Golden Age of Cultural Diplomacy', in *The History of United States Cultural Diplomacy: 1770 to the Present Day* (London: Bloomsbury, 2017), 95–126.

21 Serge Guibault, *How New York Stole the Idea of Modern Art* (Chicago, IL: University of Chicago Press, 1983).

22 Arthur Knight, 'Art Films in America', in *Films on Art: A Specialized Study and International Catalogue* (Brussels: Editions de la Connaissance, 1949), 44.

23 Steven Jacobs, 'Camera and Canvas: Emmer, Storck, Resnais and the Post-war *Art Film*', in *Framing Pictures: Film and the Visual Arts* (Edinburgh: Edinburgh University Press, 2011), 1–37.

24 On Emmer, see Lorenzo Codelli, 'Un Sandwich par jour: Entretien avec Luciano Emmer', *Positif* 543 (May 2006): 100–5; Luciano Emmer and Enrico Gras, 'The Film Renaissance in Italy', *Hollywood Quarterly* 2, 4 (July 1947): 353–8; Francis Koval, 'Interview with Emmer', *Sight & Sound* 19, 9 (January 1951): 354–6; Herbert F. Margolis, 'Luciano Emmer and the Art Film', *Sight & Sound* 16, 61 (Spring 1947): 1–3; Paola Scremin, 'Luciano Emmer: Récits sur l'art', *Zeuxis* (Autumn 2005): 55–62; Lauro Venturi, 'Italian Films on Art', in *Films on Art* (Paris: UNESCO/Brussels: Editions de la connaissance, 1949), 32–41.

25 Paul Davay, 'Compelled to See', in *Films on Art* (Paris: UNESCO/Brussels: Editions de la connaissance, 1949), 16–17. See also Steven Jacobs, 'Henri Storck's *Le Monde de Paul Delvaux* (1946) and Pygmalionist Cinema', in Roger Hallas (ed.), *Documenting the Visual Arts* (London: Routledge, 2019), 23–33.

26 See Roger Odin, *L'Age d'or du documentaire*, Vol. II (Europe, années cinquante), (Paris: L'Harmattan, 1998), 9–15; and Dominique Bluher and François Thomas (eds), *Le Court métrage français de 1948 à 1968* (Rennes: Presses Universitaires de Rennes, 2005).

27 See Suzanne Liandrat-Guigues and Jean-Louis Leutrat, *Alain Resnais: Liaisons secrètes, accords vagabonds* (Paris: Cahiers du cinéma, 2006), 212. In the interview included in this volume, Resnais mentions that he started *Van Gogh* before having seen a film by Emmer. He nevertheless recognizes the latter's influence on *Guernica*.

28 See Griselda Pollock, 'Artists Mythologies and Media Genius: Madness and Art History', *Screen* XXI, 3 (1980): 57–96; and Griselda Pollock, 'Crows, Blossoms, and Lust for Death: Cinema and the Myth of Van Gogh the Modern Artist', in *Looking Back to the Future: Essays on Art, Life and Death* (London: Routledge, 2000), 277–310.

29 Natasha Ritsma, *The Postwar 'Arts Explosion' in an Age of Mechanical Reproduction: The Production, Circulation, and Exhibition of Nontheatrical Films on Art* (PhD diss., Indiana University, 2015) and Suzanne Regan, *The Utilization of the Film Medium by American Art Museums* (PhD diss., University of Massachusetts, Amherst, 1981).

30 For more on the distribution practices of educational cinema see Katerina Loukopoulou, 'Museum at Large: Aesthetic Education Through Film', in Dan Streible, Devin Orgeron and Marsha Orgeron (eds), *Learning with the Lights Off: Educational Film in the United States* (New York: Oxford University Press, 2012), 356–76 and Zöe Druick, 'UNESCO, Film and Education', in Charles Acland and Haidee Wasson (eds), *Useful Cinema* (Durham, NC: Duke University Press, 2011), 81–102. University extensions catering to adult (further) education became increasingly important distributors of educational films (including art documentaries) as evidenced by the prominent example of Indiana University's Audio-Visual Center discussed by Natasha Ritsma in *The Postwar 'Arts Explosion' in an Age of Mechanical Reproduction* and in her chapter in this volume.

31 Paul Haesaerts, 'Sur la critique par le cinéma', in *Le Film sur l'art 1950* (Paris: UNESCO, 1950), 26. See also Céline Maes, 'Paul Haesaerts et le film sur l'art: pour un cinéma-critique', in Valentine Robert, Laurent Le Forestier and François Albera (eds), *Le film sur l'art: Entre histoire de l'art et documentaire de création* (Rennes: Presses universitaires de Rennes, 2015), 153–64.

32 Paul Haesaerts, 'Arts plastiques et caméra', *Festival (Cahier 4)* (Brussels, 21 June 1947). Also published in *Arts de France* 23–4 (1948): 25–31.

33 On Ragghianti, see Marco Scotini (ed.), *Carlo Ludovico Ragghianti and the Cinematic Nature of Vision* (Milan: Charta, 2000).

34 Siegfried Kracauer, *Theory of Film: The Redemption of Physical Reality* (Princeton, NJ: Princeton University Press, 1960), 198.

35 Barry, 'Pioneering in Films on Art', 1.

36 Judith Wechsler, 'Art History and Films on Art', in Nadine Covert (ed.), *Art on Screen: A Directory of Films and Videos About the Visual Arts* (New York: The Metropolitan Museum, 1991), 10–11.

37 Jean Queval, 'Film and Fine Arts', *Sight & Sound* (February 1950): 35.

38 Kracauer, *Theory of Film*, 197

39 Beatrice Farwell, 'Films on Art in Education', *Art Journal* 23, 1 (Fall): 39–40.

40 Bolen, 'Le Film à la rencontre des arts plastiques', 7.

41 Rudolf Arnheim, *Film As Art* (Berkeley, CA: University of California Press, 1957), 59.

42 Bazin, 'Peinture et cinéma', 187–92.

43 J.P. Hodin, 'Two English Films', *Films on Art* (Brussels/Paris: Les Arts Plastiques/ UNESCO, 1951), 22.

44 Sally A. Chappell, 'Films on Sculpture', *Art Journal* 33, 2 (Winter 1973–4): 127–8.

45 See Steven Jacobs, 'Carving Cameras on Thorvaldsen and Rodin: Mid-Twentieth-Century Documentaries on Sculpture', in Steven Jacobs, Susan Felleman, Vito Adriaensens and Lisa Colpaert, *Screening Statues: Sculpture and Cinema* (Edinburgh: Edinburgh University Press, 2017), 65–84.

46 The Danish-Belgian-Dutch CoBrA movement (an acronym for the capitals of these countries) produced several interesting art documentaries showing artists at work although all of these films were made after the dissolution of the movement in 1951. Apart from *De werkelijkheid van Karel Appel* (Jan Vrijman, 1962), documentaries on CoBrA artists include three versions of a film on painter and poet Lucebert by Johan Van der Keuken: *Een film voor Lucebert/Lucebert, tijd en afscheid* (*A Film for Lucebert/ Lucebert, Time and Farewell*, 1962/1967/1994); and two films by Luc de Heusch on two of CoBrA's founding members: *Alechinsky d'apres nature* (*Alechinsky from Life*, 1970) and *Dotremont: Les logogrammes* (*Dotremont: The Logograms*, 1972). In 1955, painter Pierre Alechinsky made an interesting film on *Japanese Calligraphy*. See Steven Jacobs, 'CoBrA, Canvas, and Camera: Luc de Heusch Filming Alechinsky and Dotremont at Work', in Rachel Esner and Sandra Kisters (eds), *The Mediatization of the Artist* (London: Palgrave Macmillan, 2018), 115–29.

47 See Bazin, 'Un Film Bergsonien'; Smith, 'Moving Pictures', 163–73; and Philippe Fauvel, '*Le Mystère Picasso*: De la Tyrannie de la réalité, en peinture, à la litanie de la peinture, en réalité', *Positif* (May 2009): 96–9.

48 Bazin, 'Un Film Bergsonien', 193–202.

49 Harold Rosenberg, 'The American Action Painters' (1952), included in Charles Harrison and Paul Wood (eds), *Art in Theory 1900–1990: An Anthology of Changing Ideas* (Oxford: Blackwell, 1993), 581.

50 Harrison and Wood, *Art in Theory 1900–1990*, 582.

51 Richard Miller, 'De CoBrA-geste', in Anne Adriaens-Pannier and Michel Draguet (eds), *COBRA* (Tielt: Lannoo, 2008), 241.

52 See Georges Mathieu, *Georges Mathieu: 50 ans de création* (Paris: Hervas, 2003); Lydia Harambourg, *Georges Mathieu* (Lausannes: Ides et Calendes, 2013); and Georges Mathieu, *L'Abstraction prophétique* (Paris: Gallimard, 1984).

53 See, for instance, Allan Kaprow, 'The Legacy of Jackson Pollock' (1958), in Allan Kaprow, *Essays on the Blurring of Art and Life* (Berkeley, CA: University of California Press, 1993), 1–9.

54 Gottfried Boehm, 'The Form of the Formless: Abstract Expressionism and Art Informel', quoted in *Action Painting: Jackson Pollock and Gesture in Painting* (Ostfeldern: Hatje Cantz, 2008), 39.

55 Karel Appel, quoted in Hugo Claus, *Karel Appel Painter* (New York: Abrams, 1962), 152.

56 On artists biopics, see Steven Jacobs, 'Vasari in Hollywood: Artists and Biopics', in Jacobs, *Framing Pictures: Film and the Visual Arts* (Edinburgh: Edinburgh University Press, 2011), 38–64. It should be remembered that the ephemeral aspect of art in these films is reinforced by the fact that works produced during their making was always meant to be destroyed afterwards.

57 Lotte Eisner, quoted in Philip Hayward, 'Introduction', in Philip Hayward (ed.), *Picture This: Media Representations of Visual Art and Artists* (London: John Libbey, 1988), 7.

58 Philip Hayward, 'Introduction', in Hayward (ed.), *Picture This*, 7.

59 Patrick Hayman, quoted in Philip Hayward, 'Introduction', in Hayward (ed.), *Picture This*, 7.

60 Dominique Chateau, 'L'acte de création comme problème esthétique', in Pierre-Henry Frangne, Gilles Mouëllic and Christophe Viart (eds), *Filmer l'acte de création* (Rennes: Presses universitaires de Rennes, 2009), 81–7.

61 Steven Jacobs, 'Cinema, Surrealism, and Object Lessons: On Luc De Heusch's 1960 *Magritte ou la leçon de choses*', *Art Journal* 77, 1 (2018): 54–70.

62 Kenneth Clark, 'Introduction', in *One Hundred Details from Pictures in the National Gallery* (London: Printed for the Trustees of the National Gallery, 1938), v–vi.

63 *Le Musée imaginaire* was originally published in 1947 as the first volume of *Psychologie de l'art* (Genève: Skira) and was later adapted to become a part of *Les Voix du silence* (Paris: Gallimard, 1951). In 1965, the text was republished as *Le Musée imaginaire* (Paris: Gallimard). The three volumes of *Le Musée imaginaire de la sculpture mondiale* (Paris: Gallimard) were published in 1952–4.

64 For a fresh look at Malraux's project and a comparison with the work of Benjamin and Aby Warburg, see Walter Grasskamp, *The Book on the Floor: André Malraux and the Imaginary Museum* (Los Angeles, CA: Getty Research Institute, 2016).

65 See Douglas Smith, 'Moving Pictures: The Art Documentaries of Alain Resnais and Henri-Georges Clouzot in Theoretical Context (Benjamin, Malraux and Bazin)', *Studies in European Cinema* 1, 3 (2004), 163–73. See also Grasskamp, *The Book on the Floor*.

66 Haidee Wasson, 'Big, Fast Museums/Small, Slow Movies', in Charles R. Acland and Haidee Wasson (eds), *Useful Cinema* (Durham, NC: Duke University Press, 2011), 178–204. Another example from this period is *Franklin Watkins* (1950) produced by the Philadelphia Museum of Art for their exhibition of the artist's work that year.

67 See Bénédicte Savoy, *Vom Faustkeil zur Handgranate: Filmpropaganda für die Berliner Museen 1934–1939* (Köln: Böhlau Verlag, 2014).

68 See Steven Jacobs and Birgit Cleppe, 'A Museum of Moving Images: Mid-Twentieth-Century Art Documentaries on the Louvre,' *Oxford Art Journal* 42, 3 (2019): 373–93.

69 Lynn Spiegel, *TV by Design: Modern Art and the Rise of Network Television* (Chicago, IL: University of Chicago Press, 2008), 4. See also Maurice Berger, *Revolution of the Eye: Modern Art and the Birth of American Television* (New York: The Jewish Museum, 2015).

70 John Wyver, *Vision On: Film, Television and the Arts in Britain* (London: Wallflower Press, 2007), 22.

71 Clark had made some experimental forays into art programmes for BBC Television even before the Second World War, with his *Artists at Work* series (1937–8). See Wyver, *Vision On*, 16. His *Civilisations* (1969) would even get a limited release in cinemas, including at the National Gallery of Art in Washington DC, testifying to the fact that distinctions between television and cinema were often blurred in the production and circulation of art documentaries.

72 John Wyver, 'Television', in Chris Stephens and John-Paul Stonard (eds), *Kenneth Clark: Looking for Civilisation* (London: Tate Britain, 2014), 124.

73 See Dorine Mignot (ed.), *Revision: Art Programmes of European Television Stations* (Amsterdam: Stedelijk Museum, 1987).

1

The institutional breeding grounds of the post-war film on art: key figures and networks behind the first International Conference on Art Films

BIRGIT CLEPPE

From 26 June to 2 July 1948, the French art circle Les Amis de l'Art (Friends of the Arts) organized the first International Conference on Art Films.[1] For the organization of the conference, Les Amis de l'Art managed to gather an impressive list of co-organizing partners: UNESCO, the International Council of Museums (ICOM), the Cinémathèque française and the French Ministries of Education and Foreign Affairs. Held at the Louvre and the Musée de l'Homme, the conference was also supported by two leading French museums. Moreover, the conference coincided with two other major events within the art world. From 21 to 27 June, the first International Conference of Art Critics was held in Maison de l'UNESCO in Paris, while from 28 June to 3 July, ICOM organized its first general conference in the Louvre.[2] The conference on art films was attended by a variety of filmmakers, artists, museum officials, film archivists and art historians, who had already shown interest in the genre of the film on art. The event, with film screenings and lectures, was presented to all the attendants of the other two conferences. At the end of the conference, the organizers provided a long-term institutional endorsement of the film on art by establishing the Fédération International du Film sur l'Art (FIFA, or the International Federation of the Film on Art).

This chapter aims to uncover the roots of this outspoken interest by prominent cultural and political authorities in the fairly new film genre of the art documentary. By mapping who was involved in the organization of this first conference, it unravels a heavily intertwined network of institutions and individuals that supported the foundation of FIFA. By tracking down how the film on art fits alongside their other activities, it will not only bring to light the divergent ambitions behind the institutional infrastructure of the film on art, but also investigates whether there are common interests and concerns to be found within this chaotic amalgam of personal opinions and ambitions, and institutional agendas. More particularly, this chapter will demonstrate the dominance of the museum world in the development of the post-war art documentary and FIFA. In addition, the ambitions of the attendants of FIFA's first conference in 1948 will be discussed in the light of FIFA's 1966 report entitled 'Problems of the Film on Art', included in FIFA's final publication, the film catalogue *Dix ans du film sur l'art* (Ten Years of the Film on Art).[3] In so doing, I will question if and how the origins of this institutionalization enhanced, delimited or to some extent even predetermined the future production, diffusion and promotion of films on art. After all, the interest in film was far from an unconditional love for a new art form, as most museums reduced art documentaries to functional tools, serving their own agendas.

Joining forces: who founded FIFA?

In a brief report on the conference, Henry de Morant, director of the Fine Arts Museum in Angers, stated that 'until now, the film on art was the result of isolated directors working with limited resources and without any link between them'.[4] These isolated initiatives, Morant added, 'were highly unfavorable for the proliferation and even the creation of films on art'. According to Morant, the principal result of the conference was 'to make those interested aware of their common strength and group them into a Fédération internationale du film d'art et du film expérimental.'[5]

'The organizers of the first FIFA conference, and first and foremost Mr Diehl', Morant added, had modelled themselves on 'the scientific film, that started to become well-known and appreciated thanks to the initiatives of Jean Painlevé, D. Commandon and others'.[6] In 1947, Painlevé had established the International Scientific Film Association (ISFA) under UNESCO's patronage and as part of the Fondation de l'Union Mondiale du Documentaire with, among others, Joris Ivens, Henri Langlois, Iris Barry and Henri Storck. Its goal was 'to join scientific, technical and film circles'.[7] Painlevé had attributed a central role to UNESCO, because 'this organization could allow to regulate efficiently the participation of all member states and particularly facilitate the circulation of educational films'.[8] The association strengthened its ability to distribute films worldwide by also inviting organizations such as the Fédération Internationale des Archives du Film (FIAF) and the Fédération Internationale des Ciné Clubs (the latter directed by Painlevé since its creation in 1947) to participate at its first conference in October 1947.[9] Similarly, with the foundation of FIFA, 'the objective of the federation is to group the persons and institutions interested in art and cinema. It tries to encourage the realization and diffusion of the film on art [...] through the rapprochement among its members'.[10] It will, therefore, consciously use their institutional structures and networks. As a result, Morant concludes, 'it is not said that the films will always remain unknown to the big masses', while admitting in a footnote of his report that 'currently they are definitely! And if I say that I have never seen a single one of them, it is not to distinguish myself of my brother historians.' For the international dissemination of art documentaries, the patrongage of UNESCO was fundamental.

Les Amis de l'Art

One of the speakers at the conference was French art historian and critic Gaston Diehl, who explicitly referred to 'the systematic experiments which had been carried out in the past four years by Les Amis de l'Art (Friends of Art) in various circles of Paris and the Provinces'.[11] Founded immediately after the liberation in October 1944 by Diehl, the Parisian Mouvement des Amis de l'Art, often shortened to Les Amis de l'Art, aimed to spread knowledge of contemporary art all over France. It did so by setting up local branches, organizing conferences, film screenings, and establishing the *Prix de la jeune peinture*.[12] The organization also published a journal whose subtitle reveals its true ambition: *Mouvement de propagande et de culture artistiques*.[13] The film on art fitted perfectly within this mission. In his book *La peinture en France dans les années noires (1935–1945)*, which can be regarded as his memoirs, Diehl summarizes the humanist emancipatory mission of the organization in a chapter entitled 'Le regard devant l'oeuvre' as 'apprendre à voir' or 'learn to look'.[14] Apart from being 'an end in itself for artists (painters, sculptors, architects and engravers) who might use it as a new visual medium', Diehl pointed at the possibilities of the art film 'for the artistic education of the public'.

As part of the activities of Les Amis de l'Art, Diehl frequently screened films.[15] It was at one of Les Amis' events that young filmmaker Alain Resnais would meet painter Robert Hessens as well as Gaston Diehl, who invited Resnais to direct a 16mm film on the the Van Gogh exhibition held at the Musée de l'Orangerie, from January to March 1947, 'in the style of Luciano Emmer'.[16] By the time of the 1948 conference, Les Amis de l'Art had already produced several influential art documentaries. *Van Gogh* (Alain Resnais and Robert Hessens, 1948) would eventually win the Academy Award for Best Short Subject in 1950.[17] In the same period, Diehl, Hessens and Resnais collaborated on *Malfray* (1948).[18] In 1949–50, Hessens and Resnais produced *Guernica*, and in 1950, Diehl would write the scenario for *Gauguin*, directed by Resnais.[19]

Having founded the Salon de Mai during the Occupation, where artists who had been disregarded as degenerate by Nazi ideology were invited to exhibit their works, and having written *Les problèmes de la peinture* (The Problems of Painting) in 1945, Diehl's interest primarily focused on contemporary, often abstract, art and painting. Les Amis de l'Art would also publish the booklet *Pour et contre l'art abstrait* (In Favour and Against Abstract Art), as an issue of *Les Carnets*, written by Diehl and Denys Chevalier.[20]

As Marianne Le Galliard has observed – partly quoting the voice-over commentary of Alain Resnais' film on Henri Goetz (1947) – this fitted well in the post-war Parisian context. In a world turned upside down by the Second World War, there was a predominant spirit of humanism based on subjectivity and the defence of individuality. Abstract art, at the time of the Liberation, responded for some to this dynamism, to this

> new world that arises. Thus, in Paris, new galleries are opened (Conti Gallery, Allendy or Denise René) and new associations are formed, such as Les Amis de l'Art, founded by Gaston Diehl in 1944 whose goal is to disseminate this new art through projections, publications, 'educational' conferences.[21]

Another reason that may explain Diehl's interest in all varieties of artistic education was his dissatisfaction with conventional museum displays. Diehl had graduated from the École du Louvre in 1936, where he may well have been in touch with Louvre curators René Huyghe and Jacques Jaujard who were then in the midst of realizing their art documentary *Rubens et son temps* on the eponymous exhibition at the Musée de l'Orangerie.[22] In 1943, René Huyghe would become one of the members of the honorary committee of Diehl's Salon de Mai, together with his colleague at the Louvre's painting department, Germain Bazin, who would later collaborate on the Louvre documentary *A Golden Prison: The Louvre* (John Sughrue, 1964). In his book on French painting between 1935 and 1945, Diehl dismisses his classical education at the École as it 'had not prepared him at all to sift the wheat from the chaff and rather tended to mislead him in the name of the so-called tradition'.[23] Instead of an academic or art historical understanding of the artwork, Diehl propagated a more direct and visual approach to the canvas, in which 'its sensitive strength to communicate' could be revealed.[24] At the 1948 conference, he took this stance when he stated that the film on art's 'purpose was not so much to describe a work of art accurately and in detail but rather to evoke its inward essence'.[25] Instead of giving solid art historical background, the films should stimulate 'the curiosity and appetite of the observer, finally encouraging him to visit the museum in order to see and study the original work, with the spirit and detail of which he would be already familiar'.

The conference's honorary committee

A quick glance at the honorary committee of the conference reveals the interest in the art documentary among national and international institutions, government officials and leading figures in the fields of cinema and the visual arts. All of them shared the interest of Les Amis de l'Art in the film on art as a new medium for artists, but also as a tool for artistic education as well as a revolutionary reproduction method that enhanced national and international distribution of artworks. Strikingly, most of the organizations involved were fairly young. The French Cinémathèque, which had been founded in 1936, was represented by its founding director Henri Langlois. Langlois was bewildered by Luciano Emmer's *Racconto da un affresco* (1938), and appreciated his films on Italian Renaissance painting first and foremost as independent works of art. Emmer himself would state that 'shooting a short film was no longer about rigging up a series of photographed paintings'.[26] Langlois would be the first to screen Emmer's work in France.[27] Subsequently, Emmer's films were applauded by prominent film critics such as André Bazin, Jean George Auriol and Jean Cocteau.

Likewise, the French Centre National de la Cinématographie (CNC), which had just been established in 1946, was represented by its director Michel Fourré-Cormeray as well as Claude Jaeger and Jacques Chausserie-Laprée, who were responsible for the production of films and documentary shorts respectively. As a non-commercial documentary film genre, the film on art was well within the scope of the CNC that had the task of 'ensuring the dissemination of documentary films and the development of a non-commercial cinema sector'.[28]

Whereas CNC and the French Cinémathèque could furnish the necessary contacts and technical knowledge from a cinematic point of view, the French Ministry of Foreign Affairs could provide the necessary support on the political level. Its Cultural Relations Department and its Cultural Interchange Department were represented by Louis Joxe and Roger Seydoux respectively. Philippe Erlanger attended the conference as director of the Association française d'Action Artistique, its core business also being the development of international cultural exchanges.[29] Jacques Jaujard, former Director of National

Museums, represented the French Ministry of Education. The composition of the honorary committee of the conference thus mainly revealed the interest in the art documentary on an institutional, often political level, centred around France's national interests and the international ambitions of its ministries and some of its organizations.

UNESCO: a fresh impulse to the dissemination of culture

Non-French members of the honorary committee of the 1948 Conference on Art Film included Grace McCann Morley and Ernest Borneman who represented UNESCO's Museum Division and Film Unit. UNESCO's interest in the art documentary comes as no surprise. UNESCO was founded during the last months of the Second World War with a strong belief in the value of cultural interchange between people for the establishment of world peace. Its mission was

> to contribute to peace and security by promoting collaboration among the nations through education, science, and culture in order to further universal respect for justice, for the rule of law, and for human rights and fundamental freedoms, which are affirmed for the peoples of the world without distinction of race, sex, language, or religion, by the charter of the United Nations.[30]

In his appraisal of UNESCO's activities in the early years of its existence, Walter Sharp, distinguishes three ways it had to achieve its main purpose.

> First among the means proposed for realizing this noble goal is the advancement of mutual knowledge and understanding through all means of mass communication; that is to say, 'the free flow of ideas by word and image.' [...] The second suggested method is to 'give fresh impulse to popular education and to the spread of culture,' by promoting equality of educational opportunity. [...] The third is to 'maintain, increase and diffuse knowledge,' for its own sake, by conserving the world's cultural inheritance,

by encouraging international exchange of persons and publications, and by assuring world-wide access to the products of the world's scholars, scientists and creative artists.[31]

It is clear that the art documentary could play an important role in all three. As filmic reproductions of art, art documentaries exhibit artworks in a cinematic way, bringing the museum to the cinema theatre. By adding movement, comparing details, or showing artists at work, art documentaries could show even more than the real museum, and it could reach wider audiences. The very first issue of the *UNESCO Courier* stated that the visual reproduction of art was 'to be encouraged [...] as a means of assisting art education and stimulating cultural exchange'.[32] As part of UNESCO's Arts and Letters programme, a detailed catalogue of paintings reproduced in colour

> will be discussed with experts in colour reproduction, art education and the history of art who are to meet in Paris this summer at the same time as the Conference of the International Council of Museums. To complement these lists, to bring them alive as it were, an exhibition will be held consisting of the best colour prints available to illustrate the techniques of colour printing and their role in art appreciation and education.[33]

In many of its early issues, the *UNESCO Courier* expressed its interest in reproductions of artworks and, consequently, also in the medium of film as a means of popular communication about the arts. The fourth issue announced the production of a 'Film Catalogue on International Understanding', referring to a 'draft catalogue of filmstrips and films on the crafts and arts'.[34] Another article in the same issue emphasized the importance of improving colour reproductions of paintings, adding that 'attention is also urged towards improving the colour fidelity in films of works of art'.[35]

Though both are part of UNESCO, an interesting antagonism can be found between the progressive approach of UNESCO's film unit and a more conservative stance towards the film on art by its Museum division. In his talk at the International Art Film Festival at the Metropolitan Museum in New York, held on 26 April 1957, Belgian film archivist Francis Bolen, who represented UNESCO's Film Unit, described the organization's supportive role.[36] While never directly financing the production of films on art, with the exception of Paul Haesaert's *L'Humanisme: Victoire de l'esprit* (1955), it tended to support existing initiatives.[37] From 1953 onwards, FIFA was granted a yearly sum of $2,000 and it published several catalogues listing the existing films on art (one of them edited by Bolen himself). The film on art also benefitted from several more general UNESCO policies, such as its Film Coupons, which had been introduced in order to overcome the different currencies of its member states.

UNESCO's film unit regarded the film on art as a means of mass communication, being able to distribute art on a massive scale, maybe even with a possibility of realizing André Malraux's contemporaneous ideas on the imaginary museum. UNESCO's museum division, on the other hand, saw things from a different angle, as we can conclude from both Grace McCann Morley's writings in the *Burlington Magazine* in 1947 and the Museum guide it published in 1960.[38] The Museum Division regarded the film on art merely as an educational tool, as a technical aid that should never distract the visitor from 'the real contact with the objects' because 'real objects seen in their best setting can accomplish this far more effectively than can a second-hand experience.'[39] By no means, could film be a replacement of the actual museum.

ICOM: a new method for revealing art

The *UNESCO Courier* published a short report on the 1948 ICOM conference that expressed the shared views of UNESCO and ICOM on the importance of museums: 'With UNESCO, ICOM believes that museums can have great value in furthering understanding among peoples and can have strong influence in the educational training of both youth and adults.'[40] Founded with the support of UNESCO in 1946, ICOM intended to introduce new museological practices. In his introduction to the very first issue of ICOM's periodical *Museum*, Georges Salles, Directeur des Musées Nationaux in charge of the Louvre, succinctly summarized the then prevailing ideas on museum innovation, aimed at transforming the museum from an elitist storehouse of art treasures into a medium of mass communication.

> Like books and the radio, the museum is on the way to becoming one of the principle media of knowledge: it must therefore adapt itself to all subjects and all public to be at the same time a means of study and stimulating entertainment, a storehouse and an organ of widespread diffusion.[41]

Right from its inception, ICOM showed great interest in the art documentary. In the second (double) issue of *Museum* dedicated to 'Museums and Education', the fourth and final chapter dealt with films on art, with articles such as 'The Film and the Art Museum', 'The Function of the Art Film', 'Art and the Camera Eye in Italy' and 'The Use of Motion Pictures in Museums of the Present Day'.[42] The editorial stated that 'art museums should take note of the outstanding developments in this new method of revealing art'.[43]

The honorary committee of the first Conference on Art Films may not have included any ICOM members, but the organizing committee contained several museum officials, often very active within ICOM and within FIFA. As 'representatives of national commissions', René Huyghe and Charles Sterling represented France. Both were working at the painting department of the Louvre. Having produced an art documentary himself, Huyghe lectured at the conference on his colour film *Rubens et son temps* (René Huyghe and Jacques Jaujard, 1938) emphasizing 'the extraordinary mobility and supersensitivity of the camera's eye and its ability to magnify an isolated detail'. Huyghe furthermore emphasized the added value of film over the museum because the observer's eye could

> be guided on a real tour of the picture, so that, by revealing the balance of the composition, the secrets of technique and the intrinsic vigour of the forms, the camera can impart a more profound understanding of the intentions of the artist.[44]

Huyghe was very interested in developing new museological paradigms. In the first issue of *Museum,* he wrote about the rearrangement of the Louvre's painting collection that 'a museum is not a fixed frame into which exhibits can be fitted like soldiers enrolled in a unit; the setting must be an expression and a natural extension of the work of art'.[45] For ICOM's second biennial conference in London in 1950, Huyghe wrote an influential report on 'the Coordination of international art exhibitions', tackling the conflicting ambitions of a museum that wants to attract as much people as possible on the one hand, and aims to conserve its artworks in the best conditions on the other.[46] With the possibilities of art documentaries in mind, Huyghe's central question in this report almost sounds rhetorical: 'How can we satisfy the growing appetite of the public and avoid disappointing the highly desirable curiosity they are showing in works of art, while at the same time reducing the movement of works to the minimum?'[47] Together with Italian art historian Lionello Venturi, Huyghe would act as a vice president of FIFA from its establishment. Working for the Louvre where FIFA had its headquarters, and being an active member of ICOM, Huyghe would be one of the strongest links between the art documentary phenomenon and the museum world in the early days of FIFA.

Coinciding with both the first FIFA Congress and the first 'Congress of Art Critics', UNESCO's report on ICOM's first 'Biennial International Museum Conference' also mentions 'a special evening of the members of ICOM held on the evening of 29 June'.[48] This event was clearly aimed at convincing leading museum officials and art critics of the importance of the art documentary, as indicated by this quote from Louvre curator René Huyghe's speech:

> At the present time, the film is one of the most valuable instruments we have for the proliferation and appreciation of art. With the help of the camera, the material structure and the essential content or character of works of art can now be analysed in detail. People do not generally know how to look at pictures. The film enables us to hold the spectator's eye and guide it step by step through the descriptive and visual detail of a work of art.[49]

In general, approbation for the film on art often went hand in hand with a dismissal of traditional 'dull' museum displays. For instance, UNESCO's report on the first conference is introduced with the essay 'The Art Film in the Museum' by Gordon Mirams that would later appear in ICOM's periodical *Museum*. Associating museums with 'dreadful paintings' in 'dim corridors',

Mirams evokes a 'nightmare' in which he would be 'locked up in the local museum at closing time and forced to spend the night among the mummies, the skeletons, the devil-masks, and the stuffed lions and tigers'. But 'if I had access to the museum's movie projector and a supply of its art films', Mirams writes, 'I would even welcome the opportunity'.[50]

Another leading museum official involved in the institutional network of art documentaries was Willem Sandberg. Serving as director of the Stedelijk Museum in Amsterdam since 1945, Sandberg attended the conference as a representative of the Dutch National Commission. Under the direction of D.C. Roëll, he had been responsible for the contested reorganization of the Stedelijk in May 1938, executed within the context of the exhibition *A Hundred Years of French Painting*. The entrance hall and staircase, the walls of which had previously been of red and yellow brick and had been decorated with green tiles, was painted white. In addition, the lilac wainscoting was removed, the yellow glass was replaced by plain glass and light was tempered by awnings. Organizing over 300 exhibitions in a period of seventeen years, Sandberg was more interested in the museum as an active player within the field of visual arts than in a treasury for a precious collection. In 'An Old Museum Adapted for Modern Art Exhibitions' published in *Museum* in 1951, he asks the question boldly in the first paragraph of his article: 'Why was our modern art museum built? [...] As a place in which to collect exhibits, or to demonstrate to the general public a line of evolution, a given development, a progression of ideas?'[51] As an advocate of the second conception, Sandberg defended the decision to turn the Stedelijk as much as possible into a *white cube*. 'Emphasis has been placed on general simplification of rooms to make them adaptable for different types of exhibitions.' For Sandberg, a museum's exhibition space had to be as neutral as possible, in order to receive the most divergent types of exhibitions, just like the white screen in the movie theatre is apt to host any kind of film.

Next to his quest for innovation within the field of museum display, Sandberg's interest in the film on art can also be related to the great importance he attached to art reproductions and their ability to disseminate art around the globe. He was part of the scientific committee that prepared UNESCO's aforementioned *Catalogue of Colour Reproductions of Paintings*.[52] Apart from the catalogue, the committee was also asked to consider themes for future

UNESCO Travelling Exhibitions of Reproductions.[53] For the second and third publication of the catalogue, Sandberg was joined by two other individuals that can be linked to the film on art: his FIFA fellow, Italian art historian Lionello Venturi, and the French director of the Musée de l'Art Moderne Jean Cassou, who wrote the scenario and narrated the French voice-over commentary in *La Fenêtre ouverte* (Henri Storck, 1952).[54]

AICA: art criticism on screen

The most direct liaisons with FIFA are perhaps to be found within the circles of the International Association of Art Critics (AICA)., with several individuals holding AICA's highest positions remaining loyal towards FIFA from its very beginning up to its slow decay at the end of the 1950s. Both Cassou and Venturi were mentioned as vice-presidents of the first International Congress of Art Critics. Together with René Huyghe, Lionello Venturi would become vice president of FIFA and would remain so until 1958.[55] The president of the AICA Congress was Paul Fierens, the director of the Belgian Royal Museums of Fine Arts, who would become FIFA's president in 1951.[56] Two vice-presidents of that congress, Herbert Read and James Johnson Sweeney, can also be linked to FIFA. Renowned art historian Herbert Read was the father of film director John Read who would join FIFA in 1959, during the final years of its existence.[57] Director of the Solomon R. Guggenheim Museum and AICA director from 1957, James Johnson Sweeney is mentioned as a member of FIFA's administrative board in 1953.[58] Sweeney would collaborate with animation artist John Hubley for the scenario of the film *Adventures of an Asterisk* (John and Faith Hubley, 1957), 'which brilliantly visualized in terms of design and characterization the clash between representational and non-representational art'.[59] In 1952, Jean Cassou and James Johnson Sweeney commissioned the production of the film *L'Oeuvre du vingtième siècle: Musée national d'arts modernes: Peintures et sculptures*, about the exhibition of the same name curated by Sweeney for the Musée de l'Art Moderne in Paris.[60] In *Les Arts Plastiques,* Jean Cassou compared the different presentations when the exhibition travelled to the Stedelijk Museum in Amsterdam and the Palais des Beaux-Arts in Brussels subsequently. Cassou was especially struck by Sandberg's asymmetric display of the artworks without any consideration of school or chronology. 'This dissymmetry is concerted and studied, and there's an idea behind it,' Cassou writes:

> It arouses the attention and directs it. When entering, a certain capital piece may seem to be relegated in the corner of the room. The room's door is not situated on the room's central axis though, but opens up exactly towards this corner, so that, if you pass by in the neighbouring room, you continue to perceive the work of art, standing out and framed, and persistent in its manifestation. And you finally understand the wish of the curator is to call your attention and not let it rest.[61]

The presentation thus evoked an almost cinematic experience, where suspense is constructed from one work of art to another.

Next to Sweeney and Venturi, among the twenty-four members of the general assembly, Simone Gille-Delafon is also mentioned as a delegate for France. Starting in 1949, she became AICA's secretary-general. Francis Bolen mentioned her as executive secretary of FIFA from 1954 onwards.[62] Gille-Delafon was very active in the final years of AICA, establishing a bigger network of sixteen independent national departments and moving FIFA's seat from the Louvre to FIAF.[63] She also tried, though not always successfully, to establish connections with other organizations with parallel ambitions such as the Institut International du Film sur l'Art (IIFA) and the Conseil International du Cinéma et de la Télévision (CICT).[64] In 1965, she became part of FIFA's expert committee that edited the last catalogue on art film: *Dix ans du film sur l'art*.[65]

For the final session of the AICA Congress, the official agenda referred to the 'Opening of the Congress of films on Fine Arts', held in the Salle de l'École du Louvre, with an 'address by Messrs. René Huyghe and Fernand Léger'.[66] Part of the FIFA conference was thus embedded in the AICA Congress. In his talk, Léger described the art of cinema as 'a new means of self-expression' and emphasized the similarities with painting, because both are trying 'to find a means of correspondence with the visual feeling of their time'.[67] In the entire FIFA conference this is the only intervention that does not somehow instrumentalize the film on art but frames it as an independent art form.

The other interventions merely approach the film on art as a tool for art criticism.

For the third AICA conference, held in the Netherlands in 1951, René Huyghe was invited to be one of the speakers. Though his speech 'Psychology of Art' does not touch on the film on art, it does express a similar aversion towards a documentary, factual approach of art criticism similar to that expressed by Diehl. Because, according to Huyghe, 'the critic would not be worthy of his task if he did not understand at first that any form of expression [...] responds to [...] internal necessities raising from temperament.'[68]

Belgian art critic and filmmaker Paul Haesaerts also lectured at the 1951 conference, speaking on 'Art criticism through the cinema'. Haesaerts explicitly distanced himself from films on art with a pure 'art historical' bias and pleaded for films with a critical stance.

> Let's forget about fiction films inspired by the painter's style, or by a civilization. Let's forget about the cinematic representation of the flask of which an artist made a legendary episode. Let's forget about the documentaries on the context, work and studio of an artist, and let's pass on to the craft of cinema used as a means to realize that what we might call 'animated painting'. Let's focus only on this part of the 'Cinema on Art' that has brought us new possibilities of critical expressions, of new tools.

Furthermore, Haesaerts pointed out the difference, the added value of a visual critique over a written text:

> Because this time the artwork, intransigent testimony, is constantly present. The thousand images of it in the film, replace the letters, the words of our sentences, so far removed of that of what they are speaking. Writing only allows us to circulate in memories, while film offers us the present – a fictional present, most certainly, but in a way more complete, more diverse than the real present. Currently, if that what the critic says is true, this truth is directly verifiable, immediately within reach of the eye and the judgment, almost of the hand.[69]

Being more easily transportable than real paintings and sculptures, the visual language of art criticism through the cinema also enhanced an international distribution of ideas. This dovetailed well with AICA's statutes, aiming at 'bring[ing] together art critics, wishing to improve international cooperation in the realm of the plastic, graphic and applied arts, and of architecture' and 'to facilitate information and international artistic exchanges'.[70]

Film: seminars of the arts

Whereas the honorary committee of the conference did not include a filmmaker, the organizing committee, as well as the board of directors of FIFA, included several. In comparison to the honorary committee, the organizing committee more closely reflected the international cinephile circles in which the art documentary came about. The conference was chaired by French artist Fernand Léger, who had already animated his own art on screen in 1924 with his landmark experimental film *Ballet mécanique*. One of the vice chairmen of the organizing committee was Belgian filmmaker Henri Storck, who had gained fame with his *Regards sur la Belgique ancienne* (*Views of Ancient Belgium*, 1936), a colour film on the art treasures of Belgium in which he experimented for the first time with the cinematic exploration of artworks through montage and animation. The other vice president, American journalist Willam Mck. Chapman, would soon start filming prehistoric cave paintings for *Lascaux, Cradle of Man's Art* (1949–50). The report furthermore mentions Luciano Emmer, who had made *Racconto di un affresco* (1938) and *Il paradiso terrestre* (1946), as 'general representative'.[71] Other members of the organizing committee included filmmaker and Emmer's creative partner Enrico Gras, photographer Thomas Bourchard who had made *Fernand Léger in America, his New Realism* (1943), Belgian filmmakers André Cauvin and Jean Cleinge, French filmmaker Maurice Cloche who had made several films on the Louvre collection including *Images de l'ancienne Egypte* (1951), Robert Hessens who collaborated with Alain Resnais and Gaston Diehl on the production of *Van Gogh* (1948) and *Malfray* (1948), German filmmaker Curt Oertel who had made the landmark *Michelangelo: Das Leben eines Titanen* (1940) and French filmmaker Roger Leenhardt, who would direct a fair number of biopics on French artists like *Daumier* (with Henri Sarrade, 1958), *Le maître de Montpellier: Frédéric Bazille* (1960), and *Pissarro* (1976) as well as the television series *La vie des Estampes* (1976) on the engravings and prints of Abraham Bosse, Claude Lorrain, Cochin le père, Moreau le jeune, François Daumier, Henri de Toulouse-Lautrec, Jean-Emile Laboureur and Victor Vasarely.[72]

Belgium was represented by the brothers Luc and Paul Haesaerts neither of whom was a museum official but who both had strong connections with Belgian museum institutions. In 1938, they established Les Compagnons de l'Art, assembling influential contemporary Belgian artists such as René Magritte, Léon Spilliaert, Edgar Tytgat and Constant Permeke. Renowned as an art critic, Paul Haesaerts published widely on twentieth-century painting in Belgium as well as producing numerous art documentaries. He became a member of the Commission de Peinture Moderne of the Museés Royaux des Beaux-Arts de Belgique. In 1945, Luc Haesaerts founded the Séminaire des Arts (Arts Seminar), together with a periodical of the same name (*Les Carnets du Séminaire des Arts*) publishing six issues between March and August 1945.

To revive their Club de l'Écran after the Second World War, Henri Storck, André Thirifays and Piet Vermeylen, who had also founded the Belgian Cinémathèque in 1938, decided to integrate it into Haesaert's Séminaire des Arts. This resulted in a new ciné club, named Écran du Séminaire des Arts (Screen of the Arts Seminar) that soon had up to 3,000 members. Both Écran and the Cinémathèque owed their survival mainly to the Palais des Beaux Arts in Brussels, where most of the film screenings took place. The Écran film programme leaflets were written and presented by Belgian journalist Paul Davay, while the programming of the screenings was the work of Jacques Ledoux, who also made the selection for the first Festival mondial du Film et des Beaux-Arts (World Festival of Film and the Fine Arts) in 1947.[73]

In the first issue of the *Carnets,* in March 1945, Paul Haesaerts announced the initiative of the founding of les Archives cinématographiques des Arts within the context of the Séminaire. 'From now on,' Haesaerts wrote, 'methodical and concerted efforts will be undertaken within a domain where, up to this moment, only fantasy and coincidence ruled.' Haesaerts was referring to Sacha Guitry's *Ceux de chez nous* (1915), 'a piece of film dedicated to Auguste Renoir, a moving document where one sees the old painter in his wheelchair, his brushes tight to his fingers with bandages, at work with a surprising energy'. Regretting that 'no similar documents exist on Douanier, Modigliani or

Vuillard', Haesaerts mentioned the efforts of Robert Cocriamont who dedicated 'some excellent meters of film to Gustave De Smet' and 'also shot René Magritte'. The establishment of the Archives cinématographiques des Arts was an attempt to change this with additional initiatives for the production of films. 'For the *Séminaire*, Henri Storck went to film James Ensor in Ostend', Haesaerts wrote, while also mentioning Storck's *Le Monde de Paul Delvaux* (The World of Paul Delvaux, 1946) that had been released to coincide with an exhibition at the Palais des Beaux Arts in Brussels. While hinting at the Séminaire's next ambitions, similar films on Permeke, Tytgat, Daeye, Brusselmans or Spilliaert, Haesaerts explicitly announced the emergence of a new film genre: 'We are practicing. It's a totally new craft to learn. It is, in cinema, the inauguration of a new genre, the cinematic art critique.'[74] Already in the third issue of *Carnets,* the sponsorship of such filmic projects was announced. The association Les Amis de l'Art Populaire was prepared to finance the Séminaire and its Archives filmées des Arts with an amount of 25,000 BFr.[75] After this, no more references were made to the archives or the film productions, although these initiatives may be understood as embryonic predecessors of FIFA's ambitions, such as the establishment in 1951 of an art film library and distribution centre based in the Stedelijk Museum in Amsterdam. The discussions at the Séminaire about portraying leading artists at work in line with Guitry's landmark 1917 film, may also lay at the basis of Paul Haesaerts own films dealing with artists at work such as *Visite à Picasso* (1950) and *Quatre peintres belges au travail* (Four Belgian Painters at Work, 1952).

As a successor of *Les Carnets du Séminaire des Arts*, Luc Haesaerts founded the monthly periodical *Les Arts Plastiques: carnets du séminaire des Arts* together with Ernst Goldschmidt.[76] Whereas within the Séminaire's activities the interest in the film on art is developed, within that of Les Arts Plastiques the network of protagonists of the first Conference on Art Films, and as a result, of FIFA, becomes apparent. Already in the first issues, a considerable number of authors appear who would develop strong connections with both the museum world and FIFA: Jean Cassou, Gaston Diehl, Paul Fierens, Paul Haesaerts, René Huyghe, Herbert Read, and Lionello Venturi wrote contributions. Painter Albert Dasnoy, who would later figure in Paul Haesaerts' *Quatre peintres belges au travail* (1952) and René Micha, who would collaborate

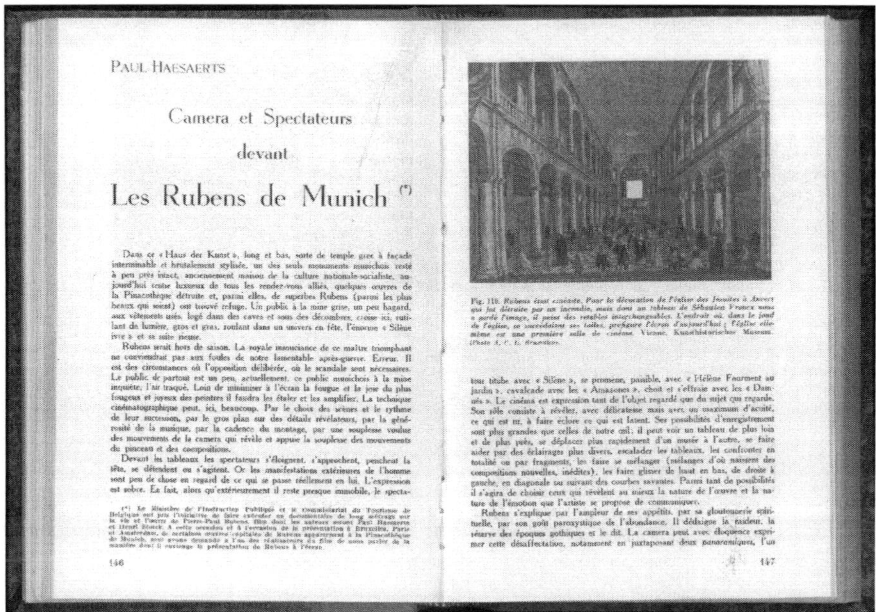

Figure 1.1 *Paul Haesaerts, 'Caméra et spectateurs devant les Rubens de Munich',*
Les Arts Plastiques 2, 3–4 (1948): 146–4

on several art documentaries such as *Le Monde de Paul Delvaux* (Henri Storck, 1946), *Noblesse du bois* (Charles Dekeukeleire, 1955) and *Paul Klee ou la genèse* (René Micha, 1958) contributed to the journal as well.[77]

Starting in 1948, *Les Arts Plastiques* often focused explicitly on the art documentary. In his 1948 article 'Caméra et spectateurs devant les Rubens de Munich', Paul Haesaerts included a frame enlargement of his *Rubens* film: a manipulated reproduction of Sebastian Vrancx' painting of the Jesuits' church in Antwerp, in which the location for Rubens' interchangeable paintings above the altar is coloured white as if it were a cinema screen.

'Rubens was a film director', Haesaerts writes, 'the location where, at the very end of the church, his canvases alternated each other, prefigures the screen of today; the church itself is a first cinema theatre.'[78] In January 1949, *Les Arts Plastiques* even dedicated an entire issue to the art documentary, containing an extensive list of films on art together with articles on the art documentary in several countries.[79] An offprint of this issue was later republished by UNESCO and counts as its first Catalogue on Films on Art.[80] The second and third UNESCO catalogue would also be offprints of *Les Arts Plastiques*.[81]

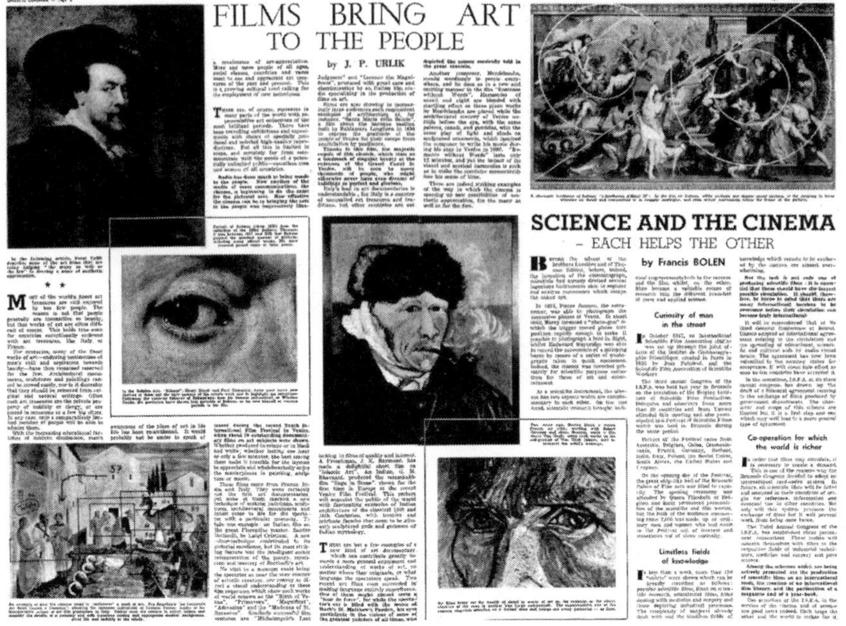

Figure 1.2 *Articles on art documentaries in* UNESCO Courier 11 12, January 1950, 6–7.

Breeding ground or burial ground?

The number of intertwined voices that gathered during this single week in the summer of 1948 in Paris is astounding. The paragraph of the conference report entitled 'Result of the Conference' testifies to this flurry of activity, stating that 'an International Federation for Art Films was established, with M. Fernand Léger as President; the vice-presidents were chosen from Italy (Lionello Venturi), France (René Huyghe) and the United States of America (William Chapman). Delegates will be appointed in all countries. The Headquarter of the Federation is: Palais du Louvre, Direction des Musées nationaux, Paris.'[82]

FIFA had been born. The majority of films produced after 1948 that were included in the 1953 catalogue are proof of the enthusiasm within the film-on-art community. But this initiative never really gained momentum. At the third conference, which took place in July 1951 in Amsterdam, only twenty-three films from eight countries were shown, whereas the 1948 one had featured sixty-four films from eleven countries. The enthusiasm already seemed to have dissipated right after the first conferences in Paris in 1948 and in Brussels in 1949.

Undoubtedly, the disparity of interests put everything on hold. In all these conferences, numerous hours were spent discussing whether FIFA should be focusing on art films, films on art or artists' films. In Amsterdam, FIFA members would agree on the following description of its aims: 'to promote, through an as broad as possible international cooperation, the making, the knowledge, the study, the conservation, the circulation, and the dissemination of works related to the Arts'.[83] The organization's acronym (FIFA) would henceforth tellingly stand for Fédération Internationale du Film d'Art, and no longer for Film *sur* l'Art – an International Federation of Art Films rather than Films *on* Art. A working document entitled 'Projet de Statuts' found among the FIFA files in the EYE Film Museum in Amsterdam uses 'Fédération Internationale du Film Artistique', indicating that a third option was suggested.[84]

Within the next few years, the constitution of FIFA's general assembly changed numerous times. Between 1948 and 1958, the presidency of the organization shifted from Fernand Léger to Paul Fierens, Pierre Francastel, Iris Barry, Denis Forman and René Huyghe. In the same period, the seat of the organization moved from the Louvre in Paris to the Stedelijk in Amsterdam in 1954, only to return to the Louvre, then to the FIAF headquarters in 1956, and finally back to the Louvre in 1958. The number of filmmakers who sat on FIFA's board diminished. In 1958, the board consisted of René Huyghe, Simone Gille-Delafon, Lionello Venturi, James Johnson Sweeney, Umbro Apollonio, Willem Sandberg, James Quinn, Mary Meerson and Henri Storck. The latter was the only filmmaker, who eventually had to leave as well, passing on his responsibilities as secretary-general to Simone Gille-Delafon.[85]

In his 1966 report, Henri Lemaître divided films on art into four categories: (a) entertaining films for everyone, without the necessity of prior knowledge of art history; (b) cultural films for a wide public, with the ambition to initiate the viewers into an art historical theme; (c) cinematic museums, functioning as a filmic accompaniment to museum exhibitions, libraries and universities; and (d) films with a scientific ambition, produced within the context of specific academic activities, by cinematic 'laboratories' studying the artworks in depth.[86] It is telling that all categories referred to the film on art in an instrumentalizing way. It would seem that from early on, FIFA lost track of its most inspiring advocates: the filmmakers – especially those who advocated and made lyrical, highly personal films on art. As we have seen, this narrowing down of the film from an artistic product to a functional tool already existed within the mission statements of the different institutions involved. For UNESCO, the art documentary was at best a tool for international communications, for ICOM an entertaining extra to the museum or an educational instrument, and for AICA a visual device for art criticism. For neither of them, films on art were first and foremost self-standing works of art, they were 'second-hand experiences' of art. The institutional breeding grounds of the art documentary were from the very beginning destined to also be its burial grounds.

Notes

1   The organization is mainly mentioned in articles concerning its founder, Gaston Diehl. See for instance, Pierre Restany (ed.), *Gaston Diehl (1912–1999). Un homme, une Empreinte* (Paris: Fondation National des Arts Graphiques et Plastiques, 2000); and Gaston Diehl, *La Peinture en France dans les années noires, 1935–1945* (Nice: Z'éditions, 1999).

2   In the course of this chapter, these events will be referred to as 'AICA Congress' and 'ICOM Conference'. For more information on AICA's and ICOM's history, see Hélène Lassalle, *Histoire de l'AICA France 1949–1990* (Paris: AICA, 1990), 6. http://aicafrance. org/wp-content/uploads/2014/04/AICA-France-1949-1990.pdf; and Sid Ahmed Baghli, Patrick Boylan and Yani Herreman (eds.), *Histoire de l'ICOM (1946–1996)* (Paris: ICOM, 1998), 15–17.

3   Henri Lemaître, 'La culture artistique et les moyens audiovisuels. Problèmes du film sur l'art au cinéma et à la télévision', in *Dix ans de films sur l'art (1952–1962): Peinture et sculpture* (Paris: UNESCO, 1966), 11–100.

4   Henry de Morant, 'Enfin les films sur l'art', in Pierre Francastel, 'Art et histoire de l'art', *Annales. Economies, sociétés, civilisations* 5, 3 (1950): 366.

5   De Morant, 'Enfin les films sur l'art', 366.

6   De Morant, 'Enfin les films sur l'art', 366.

7   Marie Berne, 'Autoportrait du scientifique en artiste: Jean Painlevé', *Mnemosyne o la costruzione del senso* 6 (2013): 150.

8   Roxane Haméry, *Jean Painlevé, le cinéma au cœur de la vie* (Rennes: Presses universitaires, 2013), 153.

9   Roxane Haméry, 'Au cœur des institutions cinématographiques', in Haméry (ed.), *Jean Painlevé*, 153–4.

10   Lemaître, 'La culture artistique et les moyens audiovisuels', 92.

11   Film Unit Projects Division, Department of Mass Communications, UNESCO, *Report of the First Conference on Art Film* (Paris: UNESCO, 1948), 9. (UNESCO/MCF/Conf. 1/1, Paris, 15 September 1948).

12   Natalie Adamson, *Painting, Politics and Struggle for the École de Paris (1944–1964)* (London: Routledge, 2017).

13   Within its short period of existence, it changed name three times. In 1945–6, the first four issues were called *Les Cahiers des Amis de l'art*; in 1946–7 *Cahiers des Amis de l'Art: mouvement de propagande et de culture artistiques*; in 1948–52: *Les Amis de l'Art*.

14   Diehl, *La Peinture en France dans les années noires*, 15–17.

15   Marianne le Galliard, 'Alain Resnais: initiation à l'art abstrait (1946–1948)', *Culture visuelle* 10 (March 2014), http://attractions.hypotheses.org/55

16   Film producer Pierre Braunberger had it realized in 35mm. See Suzanne Liandrat-Guigues and Jean-Louis Leutrat, *Alain Resnais: Liaisons secrètes, accords vagabonds* (Paris: Cahiers du cinéma, 2006), 212.

17   Liandrat-Guigues and Leutrat, *Alain Resnais*, 212.

18   Francis Bolen mentions all three of them as directors of the film. See Francis Bolen, *Le Film sur l'art. Panorama 1953. Répertoire international illustré* (Bruxelles/Paris: Les Arts Plastiques/UNESCO, 1953), 46. Other sources only mention Resnais and Hessens as directors, and Diehl as commentator, for instance Gisèle Breteau, *Abdécadaire des films sur l'art moderne et contemporain 1905–1984* (Paris: Centre Georges Pompidou/Centre national des arts plastiques, 1985), 150.

19   Francis Bolen mentions all three of them as directors of the film in Bolen, *Le Film sur l'art*, 45.

20   Denys Chevalier and Gaston Diehl, 'Pour et contre l'art abstrait', *Cahier Des Amis de l'Art* 11 (1947): 58.

21   Le Galliard, 'Alain Resnais'.

22   https://www.archivesdelacritiquedart.org/auteur/diehl-gaston

23   Diehl, *La Peinture en France dans les années noires*, 15.

24   Diehl, *La Peinture en France dans les années noires*, 17.

25   Film Unit Projects Division, *Report of the First Conference on Art Film*, 8. (UNESCO/MCF/Conf. 1/1, Paris,15 September 1948), 9.

26 Luciano Emmer, 'Pour un nouvelle avant-garde', *Cinéma d'aujourd'hui. Cahiers de Traits* 10 (1945): n.p.

27 Francis Guermann, 'La Féderation International du Film sur l'Art (FIFA)', *Zeuxis, films sur l'art/film on art* 1 (2000): 14–19.

28 Jean-Pierre Jeancolas, 'Structures du court métrage français, 1945–1958: De l'âge d'or aux contrebandiers', in Dominique Bluher and François Thomas (eds), *Le Court Métrage français de 1945 à 1968* (Rennes: Presses universitaires de Rennes, 2005), 29–46.

29 For a precise definition, see http://www.associations-midipy.org/aide.php?n=218

30 Walter Sharp, 'The Role of UNESCO. A Critical Evaluation', *Proceedings of the Academy of Political Science* 24, 2 (1951): 101–14.

31 Sharp, 'The Role of UNESCO', 101–14.

32 N.N., 'Fine art reproductions to be encouraged', *The UNESCO Courier* I, 1 (February 1948): 8.

33 N.N., 'Fine art reproductions to be encouraged', 8.

34 N.N., 'Film Catalogue on International Understanding', *The UNESCO Courier* I, 4 (May 1948): 5.

35 N.N., 'UNESCO Research Needs in Communication Techniques', *The UNESCO Courier* I, 4 (May 1948): 8.

36 An Italian translation of Bolen's speech was published in the review *SeleArte*. Francis Bolen, 'Per il film sull'arte', *SeleArte* VI, 31 (July–August 1957): 27–34.

37 Bolen, 'Per il film sull' arte', 31.

38 N.N., 'UNESCO and the Future of Museums', *The Burlington Magazine for Connoisseurs* 89, 527 (February 1947): 29–30; Grace L. McCann Morley, 'UNESCO and the Future of Museums', *The Burlington Magazine for Connoisseurs* 89, 530 (May, 1947): 136–7; N.N., *The Organization of the Museum: Practical Advice* (Paris: UNESCO, 1960).

39 N.N., 'The Organization of the Museum', 49.

40 N.N., 'Museum Directors Gather at First World Conference', *UNESCO Courier* I, 6 (July 1948): 3.

41 In 1945, Georges Salles had succeeded Jacques Jaujard as director of Les Musées de France. See Georges Salles, 'The Museums of France', *Museum* 1, 1–2 (1948): 10.

42 Gordon Mirams, Francesco Monotti, et al., 'The Film and the Art Museum', *Museum* 2, 3–4 (1948): 196–7; Gordon Mirams, 'The Function of the Art Film', *Museum* 2, 3–4 (1948): 198–203; Francesco Monotti, 'Art and the Camera Eye in Italy', *Museum* 2, 3–4 (1948): 204–7; Gordon Mirams, Francesco Monotti, et al., 'The Use of Motion Pictures in Museums of the Present Day', *Museum* 2, 3–4 (1948): 208–9.

43 N.N., 'The Film and the Art Museum', *Museum* 2, 3–4 (1948): 196.

44 Film Unit Projects Division, *Report of the First Conference on Art Film*, 8 (UNESCO/ MCF/Conf. 1/1, Paris, 15 September 1948).

45 René Huyghe, 'Changes in the department of paintings and the Grande Galerie; Le Remaniement du département des peintures et la Grande Galerie', *Museum* 1, 1–2 (1948): 94.

46 See Huyghe, 'Changes in the department of paintings', 11–18; René Huyghe, 'The Louvre Museum and the problem of the cleaning of old pictures', *Museum* 3, 3 (1950): 191–206; René Huyghe, *Coordination of International Art Exhibitions, Report for the Second Biennial Conference of ICOM, London 17–22 July 1950* (Paris: ICOM, 1950).

47 René Huyghe, *Coordination of International Art Exhibitions*.

48 Film Unit Projects Division, *Report of the First Conference on Art Film*, 2.

49 Film Unit Projects Division, *Report of the First Conference on Art Film*, 8.

50 Film Unit Projects Division, *Report of the First Conference on Art Film*, 3.

51 Willem Sandberg, 'An Old Museum Adapted for Modern Art Exhibitions', *Museum* IV, 3 (1951): 155–60.

52 *Program of the first Conference of Art Critics in Paris – June 1948*, Archives de la Critique d'Art, ref. FR ACA AICAI THE CON001 01/03. More on UNESCO's project for a *Catalogue of Colour Reproductions of Paintings from 1860 to 1955*, see Rachel E. Perry, 'Immutable Mobiles: UNESCO's Archives of Colour Reproductions', *The Art Bulletin* 99, 2 (2017): 166–85.

53 Willem Sandberg, *Working Party on Catalogue of Colour Reproductions of Paintings from 1860 to 1955* (Paris: UNESCO, 1954).

54 Sandberg, *Working Party*.

55 See *Statutes de la Fédération Internationale du Film d'Art, 1950* (Paris: UNESCO: 1950); and Correspondence between S. Gille-Dellafon and René Huyghe (18 March 1958), FIFA Archives Stedelijk Museum, Amsterdam.

56 See the correspondence between Willem Sandberg and an unknown person and the announcement of the 3rd international festival of films on art (20 May 1951), FIFA Archives, EYE Film Museum, Amsterdam, as quoted in Leon Duyck, *FIFA: Fédération Internationale du Film d'Art Onderzoek naar de samenstelling, doelstellingen, werking en activiteiten van de FIFA en de ondersteuning van de kunstdocumentaire na WOII tot en met de jaren '60* (Ghent University, MA diss., 2014), 25.

57 N.N., *Rapport de UNESCO de l'Assemblée Générale de la Fédération Internationale du film sur l'art 13 février 1959* (Paris: UNESCO, 1959), FIFA Archives Stedelijk Museum, Amsterdam.

58 Francis Bolen, 'Federation Internationale du Film d'Art, F.I.F.A', in *Le Film sur l'art*, 14.

59 John Read, 'The Film on Art', article for the *Enciclopedia universale dell'arte*, 7. Document at The Getty Research Institute, Collection title 'Art on Film 200080, Articles by John Read'.

60 Director unknown. Information found online at the French Film Library archive of the CNC, http://www.cnc-aff.fr/internet_cnc/Fiches/Oeuvre/ResultatRechercheSimple. aspx

61 Jean Cassou, 'Notes et Commentaires: L'art de l'accorchage', *Les Arts Plastiques* 5, 6 (June–July 1952): 454–5.

62 Francis Bolen, 'Per il film sull'arte', *Selearte* VI, 31 (iuglio–agosto 1957): 26–34.

63 N.N., *Rapport sur l'activité de la Fédération 1958*, UNESCO Archives, Paris.

64 IIFA: Institut International du Film sur l'Art, formerly CIDALC, under direction of art critic Carlo Ludovico Ragghianti, and the *International Film and Television Council*. Correspondence between S. Gille-Delafon and Carlo L. Ragghianti (15 January 1959), FIFA Archives, Stedelijk Museum, Amsterdam.

65 Henri Lemaître, 'La culture artistique et les moyens audiovisuels. Problèmes du film sur l'art au cinéma et à la télévision', in *Dix ans de films sur l'art (1952–1962): Peinture et sculpture* (Paris: UNESCO, 1966), 6.

66 First International Congress of Art Critics, Agenda, https://www.archivesdelacritiquedart. org/wp-content/uploads/2016/12/AICA48-Programme-eng.pdf

67 Film Unit Projects Division, *Report of the First Conference on Art Film*, 8.

68 *Communication 3 de René Huyghe, 1951* (Paris: AICA, 1951), Archives de la critique d'art, Paris.

69 Paul Haesaerts, 'La critique d'art par le Cinéma', *Communication au Congrès de l'AICA Hollande, 1951* (Paris: AICA, 1951), Archives de la critique d'art, Paris, https://www. archivesdelacritiquedart.org/wp-content/uploads/2016/12/AICA51-Com-Paul_ Haesaerts.pdf

70 *IIe Congrès et 1ère Assemblée générale AICA. Paris. 27 juin–3 juillet 1949* (Paris: AICA, 1949), Archives de la critique d'art, Paris.

71 Film Unit Projects Division, *Report of the First Conference on Art Film*, 2.

72 With *Daguerre ou la naissance de la photographie*, Leenhardt would also make a film on the early days of photography, featuring works by Louis Daguerre, Joseph-Nicéphore Niepce and Henry Fox Talbot.

73 Jean Brismée, *Cinéma: 100 ans de cinéma en Belgique* (Liège: Mardaga, 1995), 94–6.

74 Paul Haesaerts, 'Les arts plastiques: Notes et commentaire', *Les Carnets du Seminaire des Arts* 1, 1 (March 1945): 35.

75 N.N. 'La vie du Séminaire des Arts', *Les Carnets du Séminaire des Arts* 1, 4 (May 1945): 187.

76 The periodical ran between 1947 and 1954, edited by Editions de la Connaissance, Brussels.

77 Jean Cassou wrote on Vincent Van Gogh, Paul Fierens on Jean Vanden Eeckhout, English Painting, Claude-Nicolas Ledoux and Hiëronymus Bosch, while Herbert Read published several articles on Henry Moore. Painter Albert Dasnoy, who would later figure in Paul Haesaerts' *Quatre peintres belges au travail* (1952), wrote on Rubens, while Paul Haesaerts himself published an article on recent developments in Belgian painting. René Huyghe wrote on Flemish art, Lionello Venturi on Henri de Toulouse-Lautrec, and René Micha wrote on Olivier Picard. Finally, Gaston Diehl reported on the reopening of *La Grande Galerie du Louvre*. For a complete survey on all the articles published in *Les Arts Plastiques,* see http://agorha.inha.fr/inhaprod/servlet/Document FileManager?source=ged&document=ged:IDOCS:319750&resolution=MEDIUM&re cordId=musee:MUS_BIEN:141204

78 Paul Haesaerts, 'Caméra et spectateurs devant les Rubens de Munich', *Les Arts Plastiques* 2, 3–4 (1948): 146–50.

79 Lionello Venturi wrote on Italy, Arthur Knight on the USA, Gaston Diehl on France. Other articles included 'Musique et tableaux filmés' by composer André Souris on his composition for Storck's film *Le Monde de Paul Delvaux* (1946), a couple of excerpts of the screenplay of Haesaerts and Storck's 1948 film on *Rubens* and articles by Paul Davay en René Micha. See special issue: 'Le Film sur l'art', *Les Arts plastiques* 3,1–2 (1949).

80 N.N., *Films on Art: A Specialized Study and International Catalogue* (Brussels: Editions de la Connaissance, 1949).

81 See special issue 'Le Film sur l'art', *Les Arts Plastiques* 4, 5–6 (November–December 1950).

82 Film Unit Projects Division, *Report of the First Conference on Art Film*, 2.

83 The conference was held on 3–7 July at the Stedelijk Museum in Amsterdam. See *Communiqué 3e internationale festival van de film over kunst, 3–7 juli 1951, 357 FIFA 'Grootboek Film d'Art' (1953–1956)*; and the press review 'Congres: film over kunst verwacht 300 gasten', *Vrije Volk* (13 April 1952), FIFA Archives, EYE Film Museum, Amsterdam.

84 *Fédération Internationale du Film Artistique, 'Projet de statuts'*, FIFA Archives, EYE Film Museum, Amsterdam.

85 *Réunion du conseil de direction de FIFA à Bruxelles, 19 février 1958* (Paris: UNESCO, 1958), UNESCO Archives, Paris.

86 Henri Lemaître, 'La culture artistique et les moyens audiovisuels', 34–5.

2

American art comes of age: documentaries and the nation at the dawn of the Cold War

DIMITRIOS LATSIS

Today American art has captured public interest. Thousands are flocking to museums and exhibits. There is a new nationwide art movement, which critics say is greater in scope, greater in public interest than anything since the Italian Renaissance. Is it just another fad? Or is there a deeper more fundamental reason for America's new-found interest in art?

Americaness and *Art Discovers America*

This confident voice-over, coloured with hope and hyperbole, boosterist spirit and enthusiasm introduces the 1943 documentary *Art Discovers America*. Billed as 'an American commentary', the film embodies the can-do spirit of the early wartime years, but in a domain where Americans had not previously felt that much confidence: American art.

For many decades leading up to the Second World War, American art was considered a poor cousin to continental modernism.[1] The same was arguably true of American cinema's own claims to its status as an art form, rather than a form of commercial entertainment. More specifically, American directors and producers of non-fiction films had very rarely (even within educational contexts) dealt with the visual arts as a subject. That all changed during the mid-1940s when a number of factors converged to make American art a prominent player on the global scene and a significant topic for documentaries produced in the United States.

The process through which this came about at the outset of the Cold War can be traced using two key documentaries as primary evidence: the government-produced *Art Discovers America* (1943) and the omnibus film *Pictura: An Adventure in Art* (1951). Meant as a piece of propaganda to be screened primarily for foreign audiences, *Art Discovers America* was part of a series that 'portrayed the artistic, musical and literary background of the United States, the talents of its people, further counteracting Axis propagandists who characterize us as a nation of businessmen and industrialists'.[2] The leading ally in the fight against fascism had – or so the argument for a distinctive American aesthetic in art went – long cultivated a native tradition in intellectual and artistic pursuits that could rival, if not surpass, that of Europe. Emerging from the Great Depression, re-energized by the ascendant nationalist spirit of the war years and purged of a suspect 'internationalism', American art was ready to conquer the world. Conversely, the second film placed European and American films about art side-by-side, packaging them in a format that merged education and entertainment. Its comparative structure implicitly argued for the international stature of American art, pairing regionalist artists such as Grant Wood with Leonardo Da Vinci and Paul Gauguin. Seeking to define what was truly 'American' about American art while simultaneously claiming cinema itself as the New World art form par excellence, these documentaries actively participated in the larger political, cultural and social debates around nationhood and cultural imperialism that dominated the years following the Second World War.

The debate about the 'American-ness' of native-born art permeate the first film's references to the improved social status of artists (their works no longer sold 'for a few dollars, another meager meal') and the shift away from 'alien modernisms' ('no longer dreaming wistfully of Paris and the Left Bank')

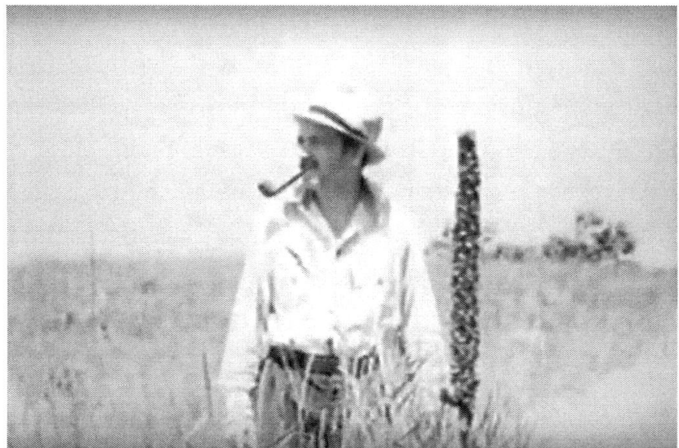

Figure 2.1 *Thomas Hart Benton in* Art Discovers America *(1943). Digital still.*

towards 'subjects which Americans understood in life'. As a suitable spokesperson of this latter tendency, the film presents the dean of the 'American Scene' movement, Thomas Hart Benton.

He is shown outdoors on one of his walks in search of subject matter, *painting en-plein-air* or modelling his scenes in plaster before 'transferring' them onto a two-dimensional canvas, a technique that the narrator praises for its fidelity to rural life: 'typically Benton and unmistakably American'.

Other artists represented as 'quintessentially' American range from John Sloan (as a representative of 'The Eight') to Reginald Marsh, to American modernists like Abraham Walkowitz, Charles Burchfield, Eugene Speicher, Max Weber, Alexander Brook and Grant Wood. The narrator finds a way to rhetorically redeem the 'native modernists' as distinct from European models ('they are painting New York cityscapes, or portraits of typical American figures like a farmer's wife'), but there is no mistaking where his preferences lie: when *American Gothic* (1930) comes on screen he heralds Wood as 'among America's best'. The artists of the time, the voice-over continues, have 'an enthusiasm for everyday American life', which he proclaims to be 'the subject matter of a *true* national art'.

Moreover, American art had become big business: 'it can be sold, it *is* sold'.[3] The film thus directly links the narrator's assertion about 'a *true* national art' with what sells and what the public is interested in; the role of the press is highlighted as a popularizer alongside cinema. In this populist context, it is primarily international reception and public acceptance that can in the final analysis realize 'American's destiny in this war-torn world: to assume cultural and spiritual leadership to the end that the pursuit of beauty shall not die'. This Lincolnesque adage is spoken over a sunset that elegiacally brings the film to a close.

Soft power and Pictura Films

The way the film was promoted to audiences can cast an additional light on its function as cultural propaganda and instrument of so-called 'soft power diplomacy'.[4] An article entitled 'Films Reinforce Hemispheric Ties', written by officers of the Office for Inter-American Affairs for *Foreign Commerce Weekly*, provides a useful overview of the wartime use of non-theatrical films produced or sponsored by the government for the purposes of external propaganda and cultural diplomacy. With respect to art documentaries, the authors proclaim that, 'These are closely allied to pictures showing the respect in this country for family life, pioneer ideals, inventive genius, social progress and interests of the people of the United States in the welfare of other republics'.[5] This remark, as well as the fact that a print of the film was found among the papers of art collector, dealer and cultural administrator Alfredo Valente, indicates the lengths to which the federal government went to forge a 'unified national aesthetic front' to present to the world, one that involved artists, producers, film studios, diplomats and the military.[6] The activities of motion picture departments across the various agencies of the federal government and the collaboration of Hollywood during the war years directly presage similar efforts during the Cold War years when propaganda was undertaken by the newly minted US Information Agency.[7]

Given this atmosphere of aesthetic propaganda and Americanist discourse in the arts, what was the standing of the film on visual art as a separate mode of filmmaking in America at the end of the War? In his article 'Art films in America', published as part of an international study of 'Films on Art' sponsored by UNESCO in 1949, film critic and MoMA film curator Arthur Knight addressed the fundamental confusion that plagued this subgenre's emergence in the United States: 'What is an art film? To many in America – perhaps to most – it means any foreign film, a picture shown in a cinema that in the trade is actually called an "art house".'[8] While it is true that most films on the visual arts that Americans might have encountered up to that point were produced abroad, this fact still does not account for the identification of the 'art house' movie (or the experimental film) with the documentary on subjects related to the fine arts. In fact, Knight found the crop of films on art in the United States quite wanting in matters of aesthetics, labelling them 'invariably pedestrian', 'often crude' and 'oversimplified classroom demonstrations'.[9] This in his estimation stemmed from the need felt by producers to 'sugar-coat' the pill of visual instruction with a bit of Hollywood glamour. While he concedes that American films on the subject cannot begin to compare 'with the work we have been seeing from Europe', he attributes this to the semi-professional status of the filmmakers who are overshadowed by the art critics and the artists themselves.[10] This comparison to European filmmakers like Resnais, Emmer and Storck would become all the more evident, he claimed, since audiences were now able to see films by these directors, re-edited with an English voice-over for distribution in the American market. The company that was almost exclusively responsible for bringing such documentaries to a wider American public was the newly formed Pictura Films.

After the Second World War, films played an increasingly central role in the 'visual instruction movement', culminating with the advent of educational television. Several distributors of non-theatrical features and shorts emerged during those years when marketing documentaries to schools, churches and other groups became a viable profit-making proposition. The catalogues of these distributors (Films Incorporated and Encyclopaedia Britannica Films among many others) are filled with films on every aspect of art appreciation and technique. Many of these were 'repackaged' from foreign producers, often with an added English-language voice-over, as by this time European producers (especially French, Belgian and Italian) had almost two decades of experience in what was commonly called the '*film sur l'art*'.[11]

This seems to have been the strategy of Pictura Films Corporation, founded in New York in the early 1950s by Leonid Kipnis and Herman Starr who were also credited with planning the distributor's first feature film.[12] In 1949, Kipnis brought a short film by Alain Resnais and Robert Hessens on the life and work of Vincent Van Gogh from France and had it dubbed with an English language commentary spoken by Martin Gabel. *Van Gogh* was acclaimed at public showings for cultural groups and art museums, and in 1949, it received the Academy Award for Best Two-Reel Short Subject. Based on the success of the short, Kipnis and Starr planned a feature-length film.[13] An advisory committee (called the 'committee on educational art films'), comprising the directors of all the major art museums and prominent curators in the country, met in February 1951 in New York: artists were selected, scripts were developed, commentaries prepared, musical scores written and performed, in a trilateral (France, Italy and the US) collaboration.[14]

Pictura: An Adventure in Art

Pictura: An Adventure in Art was the first 'omnibus' (or compilation) documentary on art produced anywhere in the world, although its genesis might have had more to do with commercial considerations than a desire to innovate. It represented a new concept in documentary feature films, consisting of six episodes based on the lives and works of Hieronymus Bosch, Vittore Carpaccio, Paul Gauguin, Francisco Goya, Henri de Toulouse-Lautrec and Grant Wood. Not surprisingly, since his passion for art collecting was well known by 1950, actor Vincent Price signed on to contribute the voice-over narration for one of the segments.[15] He was also featured on-screen, talking about art with young listeners in the framing scenes.[16] Price's sequences were filmed in Hollywood by E.A. DuPont who had several German silent films – including *Variety* (1925) – to his credit. With this overarching structure (consisting of Vincent Price's discussions with eager young art students) to hold the vignettes together, the feature was ready for distribution.

Pictura was shown widely and had a very positive reception by the art world and film press, as well as by museum professionals.[17] The director of the Metropolitan Museum of Art, Francis Henry Taylor, wrote a letter to producer Herman Starr, commenting: 'I found myself completely entranced with the wonders of this picture [. . .] Your discriminating selection of famous stage and screen stars as narrators and the wonderful music scores especially composed for it have made *Pictura* a production which provides fascinating entertainment and real excitement for every movie goer. Your company should be congratulated for its courage and accomplishment.'[18] *Variety* also praised the film for 'exploring a new field for motion pictures in combining visual displays of painting masterpieces by famous artists with explanatory narrative of the creators and suitable mood music for the subjects presented'.[19] Apart from Price, the film featured other well-known actors providing the voice-overs, including Gregory Peck, Henry Fonda (who narrated the segment on Grant Wood)[20] and Lilli Palmer, while the individual segments were directed by, among others, Alain Resnais, Luciano Emmer and Robert Hessens – all prominent European representatives of the *film sur l'art*.

What went largely unremarked at the time, however, was the film's contextualization of these individual segments, the larger narrative in which it sought to frame the 'story of art'. This was symptomatic of the boosterist rhetoric of the New Deal whose influence was still actively felt in the public discourse – especially concerning cultural matters. As art historians have demonstrated, during the first few decades of the twentieth century, American art and culture went through an intensive period of self-questioning in search of 'the Great American thing' – a native-grown version of modernism that would be free of European influence and represent the social and historical makeup of American society.[21] To achieve this goal, representational art dealing with national or historical themes and landscapes was particularly encouraged by the government's Federal Art Project and regionalist artists like Benton and Wood became very prominent in this effort during the 1930s and 1940s. Exhibitions like 'Three Centuries of American Art' staged in Paris in 1938 sought to present US artistic production as both a culmination of an entire tradition stretching back to classical times and as a new, democratic vision rising out of the fertile soil of the New World.[22]

It is thus not surprising that *Pictura*, which is structured precisely as a chronological tour of great figures in the history of art, would adopt this evolutionary template for its suitably American spin on the *film sur l'art*.[23] Following the film's narrative, from Bosch to Van Gogh to Gauguin and finally to Grant Wood, the implication seems to be that the US had come into its own in the cultural arena, its painters forming a legitimate link in this cultural chain. It is also particularly apt that such a history would be presented in moving pictures rather than dusty old books, since cinema was considered to be the artistic medium par excellence of the twentieth century, and largely an American invention at that. Indeed, from Thomas Edison to poet and critic Vachel Lindsay early commentators had envisioned that the primary use of cinema would eventually be for visual instruction, in what Lindsay imagined would be a 'universal film museum'.[24] Instead of a stroll through a museum (which came to be a dominant narrative trope in art documentaries later on), *Pictura* is framed as an informal lecture set in the verdant premises of an American university campus.

Further touting the intellectual capital of the already economically dominant superpower, higher education was seen as the great equalizer in the post-war, GI-bill era. In the place of a professorial lecture, however, the more approachable instructor played by Vincent Price adopts a genuinely American, more interactive approach to teaching more usually associated with 'art appreciation'. He actively engages the students in the subject matter, which is in fact set up as a story, a grand narrative of art through the centuries, 'a moving panorama of paintings', as the reviewer for the *New York Times* described it.[25] Although it is difficult to ascertain today, since the introductory and intermediate sequences have not been seen in more than sixty years, Price's role was to introduce the students to 'a strange and interesting voyage into the world of art', as exemplified

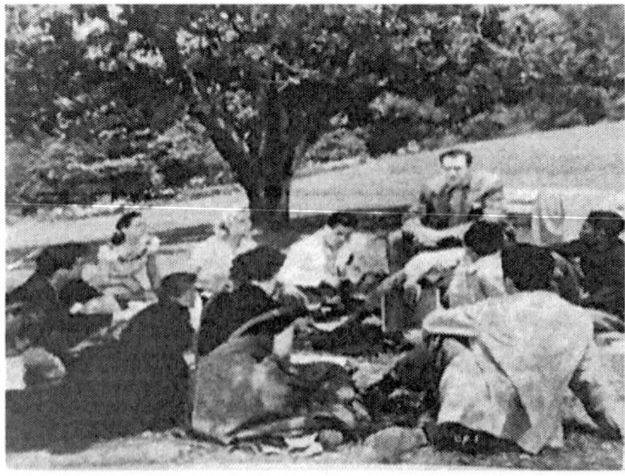

Figure 2.2 *Vincent Price as art professor in a production photograph of one of the intermediate scenes in* Pictura *(1952). Digital still.*

by six noted artists from the fifteenth century to the present time.[26] Instead of dwelling on the formal or technical characteristics of the paintings, he emphasizes their narrative and historical aspects and thus it is only natural that the familiar Midwestern scenery and episodes of American 'types' and folklore as depicted by Grant Wood are placed at the conclusion of the trajectory traced by *Pictura*.

This last segment was the only one produced especially for the movie, in addition to being one of the earliest films dedicated to the work of an American Artist.[27] It presents a multi-strand story involving Wood's own life as well as the stories behind several of Wood's most famous paintings, including *John B. Turner, Pioneer* (1929), a portrait of a Midwestern undertaker; *Woman with Plants* (1929) a study of his mother; and the famous *American Gothic* (1930), in which his sister and his dentist were the models for the corn farmers. Using an Aaron Copland-inflected score and with Henry Fonda's stentorian voice-over repeatedly referring to Wood as a 'quintessentially American artist', the film features a multitude of symbols and imagery connected to the idea of the region and the nation: maps situating the 'Middle-West', the rolling hills of Iowa in Wood's paintings, his humorous portrait of the fabled cherry tree episode from George Washington's life, and others of his 'masterpieces of Americana'.

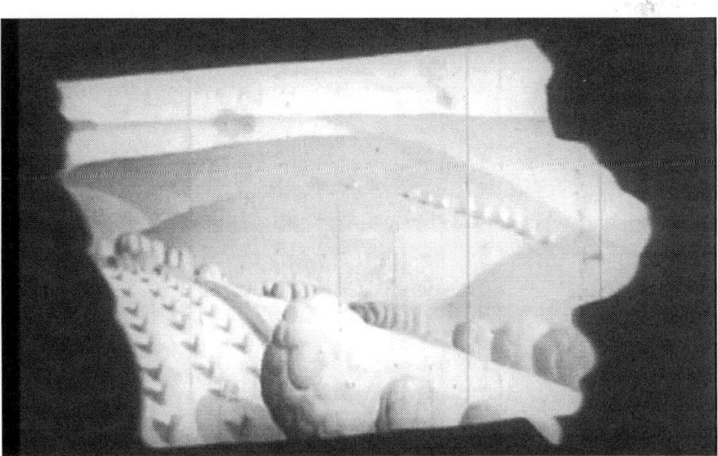

Figure 2.3 *One of Grant Wood's landscape paintings seen through an outline of a map of the state of Iowa in* Pictura *(1952). Digital still.*

Wood finally comes across as a gentle, self-taught 'man of the people' with his artful hand on the pulse of the nation.[28] He is quoted at the conclusion, which also marks the end of *Pictura,* in a remark that neatly summarizes the film's overall intentions and place in history: 'I had in mind a picture of the country rich in the arts of peace, homely, lovable, and infinitely worth any sacrifice.' The place of American art at the outset of the Cold War would be as the guardian of Western values and as a democratic (and even populist) counterbalance to modernism, at least of the varieties associated with European pre-war elite culture.[29]

For all its warm initial reception and wide exhibition, the film's acclaim was rather short lived – only some of its constituent parts have been screened since 1952. In fact, one of its shortcomings was evident to *New York Times* critic Bosley Crowther who opined that 'as a photographed recording of works of art, rather than a real creation of cinematic art on its own, it is essentially a transcript'.[30] As a transplantation of an essentially European film genre on American soil, *Pictura* embodied an expository slide-show approach to its subject matter. But to those expecting to see an art film as well as a film on art, the lack of formal innovation in the Grant Wood segment was obvious. The style of painting foregrounded in it was also on the wane in public tastes at the time, with the mix of old masters and contemporary figurative and quasi-didactic painting, being fast replaced by abstract expressionism.

American art documentaries

More generally, the art documentary in the United States underwent a transition during the later 1940s and early 1950s that took it away from a focus on educational narratives on representational art towards an embrace of modern abstraction, beyond the narrow focus on regional and national themes towards a more international orientation, and beyond the homely values of tradition and community towards a style and rhetoric that more closely mirrored the politics of the Cold War. Films on art became more and more experimental, escaping their initial placement in newsreels and educational features and aspiring to become works of art in their own right.

It is perhaps useful to pause here and reflect on what a typology of these earliest documentaries on American Art would look like. Several subgenres can be identified and the gradual shift in approach and style during the early 1950s is helpful in understanding the parallel but quite independent development of this mode of documentary in the United States. A list of titles from the period is evocative of this transition in both subject matter and style: from folksy titles like *Art Discovers America* (1942), *Grandpa Called it Art* (1944) and *The Making of a Mural* (1947) – all three prominently dealing with the work of Thomas Hart Benton – via *Pictura* (1952), to films like Marie Menken's *Visual Variations on Noguchi* (1945), the equally experimental *Works of Calder* (1950) and *Jackson Pollock 51* (1951). More specifically, four main strands can be traced.[31]

First, films with an anthropological or ethnographic focus recording the arts and crafts of indigenous American or folk artists. This includes some of the earliest examples of films on art made in America, often framed as travelogues and rarely if ever dwelling on individual artists, preferring instead to look at their subjects as examples of 'local colour' and tribal practices viewed from a touristic or scientific perspective. The Human Studies Film Archives of the Smithsonian Institution preserves a plethora of such films, many of which were made for non-theatrical audiences and would thus not have, ordinarily, come into broad public notice. Expedition films like Joseph K. Dixon's *The Romance of a Vanishing Race* (1916) – sponsored by department store magnate Rodman Wanamaker, *The Vanishing Indian* (c. 1920) produced by Super Sioux Films and Grover T. Sanderson's *American Indian Footage* (c. 1926–32), all include lengthy sections on traditional crafts like basket-weaving and pottery in addition to covering the vernacular architecture of the Southwestern United States. This trend continued into the 1940s and 1950s and the titles of such films manifest a greater focus on art and artists (including folk artists) and a greater geographic range: Robert Flaherty's *The Pottery Maker, An American Episode of the 19th Century* (1925) produced by the Metropolitan Museum of Art, *The Last of the Wood Engravers* (1930) on artist Timothy Cole, Bryson Jones' travelogue *The Lure of the West* (c. 1935), *Maria and Julian [Martinez]'s Black Pottery* (1938), *Patterns of American Rural Art* (1943), *Tempera Painting by Quincy Tahoma* (1945), *Hopi Indian Arts and Crafts* (Coronet, 1947), *One*

Hundred Years of Art and Artists in Indiana (Indiana University, 1949) and *Grandma Moses* (Film Images, 1950). As the list of producers and distributors indicates, these short documentaries were the first to be disseminated to a wider public for educational purposes.

Secondly, films focusing on art appreciation, art technique and visual art instruction. Museums, universities and independent filmmakers were all engaged in the production of instructional film for further education audiences (e.g. through university extension departments). As Richard Barsam has observed, 'the beginnings of the American tradition of films on art are found in the more functional context of the educational film'.[32] This category is by far the largest and it includes Encyclopaedia Britannica's *Painting Reflections in Water, Brush Techniques: The Language of Watercolor, The Making of a Mural* (all from 1947). *Don Kingman Paints a Watercolor* (1946) and *Painting an Abstraction* (1950) are also representative of this trend, as is *Etcher's Art* (1930), a demonstration by Frank W. Benson, and Lewis Jacobs' film on the woodcarving technique of Chaim Gross, *From Tree Trunk to Head* (1939). The Museum of Modern Art-produced *What is Modern Art?* (1948) and *Art in Our World* (Paul Bunforth and Virginia Purcell, 1950) are examples of films that were meant as visual aids in art appreciation classes.[33] Quite a few films were produced on sculpture, including *Making of a Bronze Statue* (Metropolitan Museum of Art, 1922) on A. Phimister Proctor's equestrian statue of Theodore Roosevelt, *Lorado Taft, Sculptor* (1930), *Stone and Sculptor* (1931), *Sculpture Today* (1935), and *Men of Our Age: The Sculpture of Jo Davidson* (1946). Many of these films are hybrid artist profiles (see below) and technique demonstrations.

Thirdly, broad overviews of the development of American art and biographical films on individual artists. This category is the closest one to the 'mainstream' of art documentaries in Europe as they emerged in the period following the Second World War. That said, their tone, discursive framing and reception differed significantly from the paradigm of the European *film sur l'art*. These films did not set out to use the visual arts as raw material for cinematic experimentation, as was the case with European directors like Luciano Emmer, Robert Hessens and Alain Resnais. The names of American pioneers of the genre, Robert Coffin, Stewart Moss, Kenneth Bloomer, Elias

Katz, Lewis Jacobs, Evelyn Brown, Arthur E. Baggs and Francis Thompson are not usually found in the annals of documentary history. Their aim was to provide the audio-visual equivalent of a textbook or an entry in an encyclopaedia – descriptive and concise, adopting the format of an illustrated slide show guided by voice-overs and occasional interviews. Their films include: *Wayman Adams* (1933), *Childe Hassam Artist: A Short Personal Sketch* (1933), *Alexander Calder: Sculpture and Constructions* (1945), *Fernand Léger in America* (1945), *The Photographer* (1948) on Edward Weston, the self-produced *Sierra Journey* (*c.* 1947) by Western landscape painter Edgar Alwin Payne, *Frank Lloyd Wright: California Architecture* (1948), *Introduction of Architecture* (1949), *Meet the Artist* (1949) on illustrator Stevan Dohanos, *Franklin Watkins* (1950) produced by the Philadelphia Museum of Art, *Jefferson the Architect* (1950), *America: The Artist's Eye* (1950), *American Art from the Gilded Age to the Armory Show, 1865–1913* (*c.* 1950) and *Birth of a Painting: Kurt Seligmann* (1950). These films mark the institutionalization and entry of the art documentary into the mainstream of non-fiction filmmaking in the United States and would have very likely been the first examples of the genre that most audiences experienced in cinemas and/or museums.[34] Even more significant at this early stage is the distribution of documentaries that singled out the work of minority and underrepresented artists, as seen in the Harmon Foundation's *A Study of Negro Artists* (1935), *Creative Hands* (1945), *The Negro and Art* (1947) and *Portrait of a New York Waterfront* (1949), among others. Quite a few films belonging to this category were produced by or on behalf of the various agencies of the federal government (like the Works Progress Administration), especially during the boom of government-sponsored art in the 1930s. Special mention should also be made of early National Film Board (NFB) of Canada documentaries on the visual arts that form an integral part of the flourishing of the genre in North America. Although the genre was already represented in government-produced films made during the silent period, productions like *Canadian Landscape* (1941) on painter A.Y. Jackson, *Eskimo Arts and Crafts* (1943), *West Wind* (1944) on painter Tom Thomson, and *Klee Wyck* (1946) all of which were part of the NFB's 'Canadian Artists' series, marked what is likely the earliest state-sponsored series of art documentaries anywhere.

Fourth, films on art as 'Art Films'. This last category represents a radical departure (rather than an outgrowth) from the previous three. It marks the maturation of the genre of the documentary on the visual arts in America and was accompanied by a shift to works that could qualify as 'art' in their own right, irrespective of their subject matter. This represents a belated turn to modernism in style as well as content, of the kind that *Anemic Cinema* (1926) and *Entr'acte* (1924) had marked in European cinema. Douglass Crockwell's *Glenn Falls Sequence* (1941), James and John Whitney's series of *Film Exercises* (1943–4), Marie Menken's *Visual Variations on Noguchi* (1945), *Works of Calder* (1949) and *Jackson Pollock 51* (1951) share the aesthetic ambitions of two nascent American avant-gardes: the rise of abstract expressionism as a quasi-national aesthetic in the visual art of the United States and the development of an experimental film culture that flourished in New York (and elsewhere) after the end of the Second World War. These films accomplish to a much greater extent than previous attempts Arthur Knight's wish for films on art that would be 'a *new* experience, a *new* work of art [...] the film itself developing with the same excitement and fervor as the original work of art'.[35] The nationalist discourse of earlier documentaries returns here, but in a markedly formal way, while the films are also indirectly imbricated in the cultural rhetoric of the Cold War, with lines drawn on aesthetic as much as geopolitical grounds.

Lastly, a development of equal importance was a newfound emphasis on cinema itself as an art form worthy of preservation, documentation and inclusion in museums. The Museum of Modern Art, an early leader in these fields, sponsored an episode of the well-known newsreel *The March of Time* that was in production at the same time as *Art Discovers America*.[36] Entitled *The Movies March On*, it provided an overview of the museum's activities related to the seventh art, prefaced with words that simultaneously anticipate the emergence of the art documentary in America and encapsulate the role that cinema, 'the liveliest of all arts' and a legitimate art form in its own right, occupied in an American context:

> No dusty storehouse for old Masters, this museum is a showroom for Art in Our Time. Painting, Sculpture, Architecture and Still Photography, and ... the Motion Picture.

Notes

1 Serge Guilbaut, *How New York Stole the Idea of Modern Art: Abstract Expressionism, Freedom and the Cold War* (Chicago, IL: University of Chicago Press, 1983) and contributions to the 2006 symposium 'American Art in a Global Context' available at https://americanart.si.edu/research/symposia/2006

2 Jean A. Miller and Chauncey O. Rowe, 'Films Reinforce Hemispheric Ties', *Foreign Commerce Weekly: Journal of International Economy* (2 June 1945): 9.

3 Several of the paintings shown in the film, by Marsh, Walkowitz, Birchfield, in addition to those by Benton, are also landscapes. Even the cover of the book prominently displayed in a bookstore (Peyton Boswell's *Modern American Painting*, first published in 1939) features a landscape painting: Benton's *Tornado Over Kansas* (1929) which must have looked particularly evocative to audiences in 1939, the year when *The Wizard of Oz* was released in cinemas. The idea of representations of landscape as 'valuable' or mirroring the monetary value of the land itself has particular potency within American art history, from topographic drawings of prospects to paintings of the West, to the railways' sponsorship of artists, but it became most explicit within modernism. For instance, the painter Ralph Blakelock late in his career did a series of small oil and watercolour paintings entitled *Landscape Money* that adopted the shape and colouring of dollar bank notes. One should remember that this is also the shape of widescreen cinematography that was so significant later on in the dissemination of landscape to a wide public through the movies.

4 For a recent history of American cultural diplomacy see Michael L. Krenn, *The History of United States Cultural Diplomacy: 1770 to the Present Day* (London: Bloomsbury Academic, 2017).

5 Miller and Rowe, 'Films Reinforce Hemispheric Ties', 9.

6 Alfredo Valente papers, 1941–78, Archives of American Art, Smithsonian Institution, Washington DC.

7 See Richard Dyer MacCann, *The People's Films: A Political History of U.S. Government Motion Pictures* (New York: Hastings House, 1973); and David Holbrook Culbert, Richard E. Wood and Lawrence H. Suid (eds), *Film and Propaganda in America: A Documentary History*, 4 vols (New York: Greenwood Press, 1990).

8 Arthur Knight, 'Art Films in America', in *Films on Art: A Specialized Study and International Catalogue* (Brussels: Editions de la Connaissance, 1949), 44. The original French edition was published by the journal *Les Arts Plastiques* and UNESCO's Film Section, and was 'the first attempt at a factual and critical introduction to a particularly interesting and comparative new branch of the cinema'.

9 Knight, 'Art Films in America', 45. Another very enlightening appraisal of the status quo of the 'educational art film as a subdivision of the documentary' in America is to be found in a 7 February 1951 letter by Frank Stauffacher (filmmaker and curator of the

pioneering 'Art in Cinema' series) to museum director Grace McCann Morley – Office of the Director Records 1935–58 (ARCH.ADM.001), San Francisco Museum of Modern Art Archives. Stauffacher also deemed that 'Art films must be better made, more interesting, more dynamic, even more entertaining' and take a purely 'filmic approach to documentary material'. For a later, more scholarly appraisal of the emergence of the American art film see Richard M. Barsam, 'Beginnings of the American Film Art', in 'Chapter 7: American Nonfiction Film: 1930–1939', in *Nonfiction Film: A Critical History* (Bloomington: Indiana University Press, 1992), 137–9.

10 Knight, Art Films in America, 46.

11 See Steven Jacobs, 'Camera and Canvas: Emmer, Storck, Resnais and the Post-war Art Film', in *Framing Pictures: Film and the Visual Arts: Film and the Visual Arts* (Edinburgh: Edinburgh University Press, 2011), 1–37.

12 The company has long ceased to exist and prints of most of its films have not been screened in more than sixty years, with 'film prints lost somewhere in limbo'; Joel Eisner, *The Price of Fear: The Film Career of Vincent Price, In His Own Words* (Antelope, CA: Black Sheet/Diverse Media, 2013), 61. *Pictura* was just one of a number of producers and distributors that sprang up during this time and which specialized in films on art. A.F. Films Inc. is another example of such a short-lived venture. For a fuller listing see Robert Goldwater (ed.), 'Directory of Film Sources Listed', in *Guide to Art Films* (Washington DC: American Federation for the Arts, 1995), 28–31.

13 For more information on the history of the company (which is also a history of the development of the art documentary in the United States), see the prospectuses 'The Pictura Story', 'Pictura – Adventure in Art', and the catalogue 'The Pictura Portfolio' in San Francisco Museum of Art, Women's Board Records, 1934–77 (ARCH.ADM.003), Film Department records (ARCH.ADM.008), and Office of the Director Records 1935–58 (ARCH.ADM.001). The director of the San Francisco Museum of Art (as it was then called), Dr Grace McCann Morley, was instrumental in the conception and promotion of *Pictura*. I would like to acknowledge the help of SFMoMA's archivist Peggy Tran-Le in reconstructing this history.

14 Letters of 16 January and 22 January 1951 between Leonid Kipnis and Grace Morley, Office of the Director Records 1935–58, San Francisco Museum of Modern Art Archives.

15 Price later wrote a popular book on the subject entitled *The Vincent Price Treasury of American Art* (New York: Country Beautiful Corporation, 1972).

16 In 1954, Price's segment on Bosch was also released as an 11-minute stand-alone short. Plans were also made by Pictura to produce films on Edward Hopper and a short called 'American Processional' although it's not clear that these were ever realized.

17 The film premiered in several major American cities, each time sponsored by the local art museum, including the Metropolitan, the Los Angeles County Museum of Art, the Art institute of Chicago, and the San Francisco Museum of Art under whose aegis it premiered at the Clay theatre on 8 February 1952. Promotional materials featured

quotes by major museum directors and film director John Huston praising the film for its innovations. It should be noted that by this time almost all major American museums had inaugurated film screenings as part of their regular programming. See Suzanne Elizabeth Regan, *The Utilization of the Film Medium by American Art Museums* (PhD Thesis, University of Massachusetts, 1981).

18 Quoted in 'Metropolitan Museum Supports Art Feature' (press release of 27 March 1951) in *Women's Board Records*, 1934–77, San Francisco Museum of Modern Art Archives.

19 'Pictura' (review), *Variety* 186, 4 (2 April 1952): 22.

20 Wood and Benton's work was collected by another Hollywood star of the time, Edward G. Robinson, as Erika Doss has documented. See Erika Doss, Regionalists in Hollywood: Painting, Film, and Patronage, 1925–1945, 2 vols, (PhD thesis: University of Minnesota, 1983).

21 Wanda M. Corn, *The Great American Thing: Modern Art and National Identity, 1915–1935* (Berkeley, CA: University of California Press, 2000) and Erika Doss, *Benton, Pollock, and the Politics of Modernism: From Regionalism to Abstract Expressionism* (Chicago, IL: University of Chicago Press, 1991).

22 Regionalist artists were particularly well represented in exhibitions organized or sponsored by the Works Progress Administration (WPA). For more on 'Three Centuries of American Art', see Dimitrios Latsis, 'À la Recherche de Yankee Art Franco-American Exhibition Diplomacy between the Wars', *Transtlantica: Revue d'Études Américaine* 2 (2004).

23 For a similarly structured documentary see *Grandpa Called it Art* (MGM/NBC, 1944) where Benton and Reginald Marsh are similarly touted as representing a home-grown American art while older artists are dismissed as part of an older 'artistically challenged' period of American history.

24 Peter Decherney, *Hollywood and the Culture Elite: How the Movies Became American* (New York: Columbia University Press, 2005), 13–40.

25 Bosley Crowther, 'At the Little Carnegie' (review), *The New York Times* (8 April 1952): 35.

26 As a witty review in the *LA Daily News* put it, 'Price, as a kind of garrulous Sunday painter given to park bench disquisitions before a cluster of young students, agreeably etches the transitions between the several episodes and, with his unseen but audible thespian colleagues, provides an entertaining narrative account of the temper and circumstances that conditioned the several palettes.' Review quoted in 'The Pictura Portfolio' in *Women's Board Records*, 1934–77, San Francisco Museum of Modern Art Archives.

27 The segment on Grant Wood was one reel (14 mins) in length and was produced by Leonid Kipnis. The director was Mark Sorkin, the music was composed by Lan Adomian and it was photographed by John Lewis.

28 Implicit comparisons with acknowledged artists like Van Gogh (the subject of one of the previous episodes in the film) are also made, as when a pair of shoes painted by a young Wood pans across the screen.

29 For more on the cross-pollination between American painting and American cinema during this period (including the brief collaboration between Grant Wood, Thomas Hart Benton and John Ford during the production of *The Long Voyage Home* (1940)), see Christiane Viviani, 'Promenade dans une tradition réaliste: Peinture et cinéma américains, quelques pistes', *Ligeia: Dossiers sur l'Art* 20, 77–80 (July–December, 2007): 196–205.

30 Crowther, 'At the Little Carnegie', 35.

31 These strands include only films on American artists, craftsmen and architects. In the aforementioned article 'Art Films in America' from 1949, Arthur Knight arranged films in three categories: 'films about art technique, films about individual artists, and films that seek to interpret a work of art'. Other films on visual art were, of course, produced in the United States during the 1940s and 1950s, but they would be more properly dealt with in the context of the contemporaneous flowering of educational and visual instruction films. The American Federation of Arts' *Guide to Art Films* (1950) lists no fewer than 353 such titles, more than 100 of which had been produced in the preceding year alone. Fifty-eight of those films dealt with some aspects of American visual art and art instruction.

32 Barsam, 'Beginnings of the American Film on Art', 138.

33 *What is Modern Art?* was based on MoMA director Alfred Barr's booklet of the same name published in 1947. Additional films in this category saw a more limited distribution, including: *The Making of a Fresco* (n.d.) produced by the Legion of Art Museum in San Francisco on the making of Diego Rivera's mural of the same name, the series of instructional films on 'Art Techniques and Appreciation' produced by Walter O. Gutlohn Inc. in 1944–5 and the 'Artists at Work' series produced by Elias Katz, including films on Lynd Ward, George Grosz and William Gropper.

34 Some of these films were made to accompany related exhibitions. MoMA was a pioneer of such productions dating to its early days with films on architecture (*Evolution of the Skyscraper*, 1938) and art (*World of Calder*, 1949). To these must be added films about American museums that were produced as early as the 1920s, including the Metropolitan Museum's *Behind the Scenes: The Working Side of the Museum* (1928), *Your National Gallery* (1948) about the National Gallery of Art in Washington DC, and *The American Wing* (1935) on the newly inaugurated wing of the Metropolitan Museum. A number of additional documentaries focused on public art with *New York Heritage* (1950), sponsored by the New York City Art Commission, being a notable example.

35 Knight, 'Art Films in America', 47 (my emphasis).

36 Another early film on cinema and its preservation is *The Film that was Lost* (1942) that was also produced for a popular newsreel (MGM's *Film Parade*). The film is preserved at the UCLA Film and Television Archive.

3

Art history with a camera: Rubens (1948) and Paul Haesaerts' concept of cinéma critique

STEVEN JACOBS AND
JOSÉPHINE VANDEKERCKHOVE

In the 1940s and 1950s, prominent art historians such as Roberto Longhi, Lionello Venturi, Giulio Carlo Argan, Henri Focillon, Pierre Francastel, Carlo Ludovico Ragghianti and Gaston Diehl among many others showed an outspoken interest in art documentaries. Occasionally, they were also involved in the production of such films. For these art historians, cinema was not only capable of bringing art to wider audiences, it also made it possible to compare, analyse and investigate artworks in original ways.[1] Art documentaries, consequently, became tools of the art historian, generating new art historical methods and paradigms. This notion was crucial for Belgian critic and art historian Paul Haesaerts (1901–74), who would become a leading filmmaker specialized in art documentaries in the late 1940s and 1950s.

After his studies in painting, architecture, and philosophy, Haesaerts did not only become a painter, illustrator, etcher, designer and architect, he also developed into an accomplished art critic and writer. From the 1930s onwards he was a principal member of the Belgian art scene and he published several books on Belgian artists such as on George Minne (1939), Constant Permeke (1940), James Ensor (1957, 1973), as well as on illustrious international artists such as Pablo Picasso (1938), Ossip Zadkine (1939) and Pierre-Auguste Renoir (1947).[2] In addition, Haesaerts regularly curated exhibitions such as the 1938 show of *Les Compagnons de l'Art* at the Palais des Beaux-Arts in Brussels and he often gave lectures at museums and universities.[3] Shortly after the Second World War, he started exploring a new way of practising art criticism by experimenting with the medium of film.

Unlike most of his colleagues who collaborated with filmmakers, Haesaerts went beyond the traditional role of advisory expert or author of the voice-over text, taking the full responsibility of the film's form and content. With his first film *Rubens* (1948), which was made in collaboration with filmmaker Henri Storck (1907–99), Haesaerts brought the art documentary into the domain of art analysis.

Through various cinematic devices such as camera movements, split screens, dissolves and animation techniques, *Rubens* went beyond an art

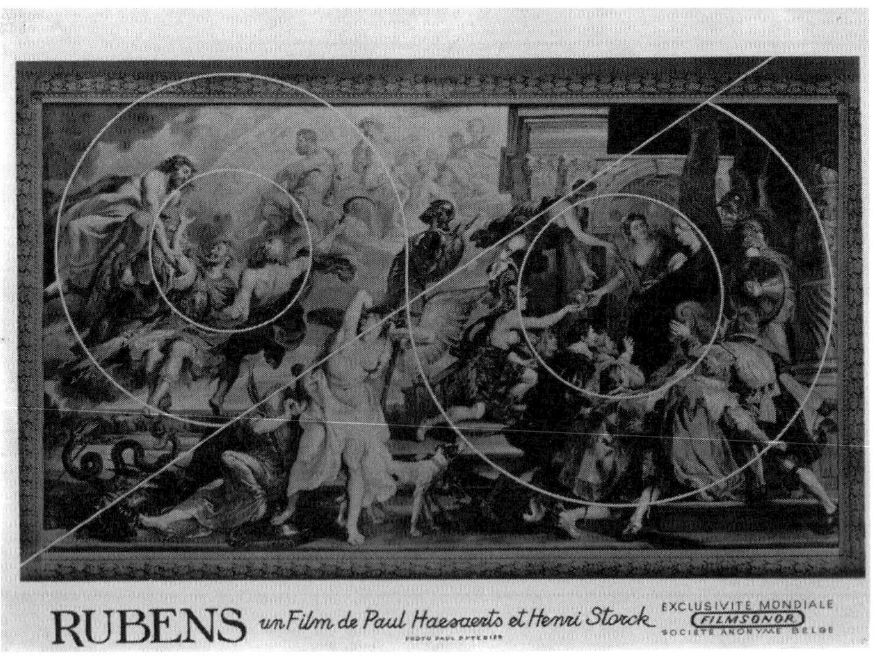

Figure 3.1 Rubens *(Paul Haesaerts and Henri Storck, 1948). Still by Paul Bytebier.*

historical reading of the work of the baroque painter by also providing a formal analysis of his artworks. Following his concept of 'cinéma critique', Haesaerts attempted to let images speak for themselves, presenting the medium of film as an analytical tool capable of constructing a discourse based on the succession and montage of images. Followed by art documentaries such as *Visite à Picasso* (*Visit to Picasso*, 1950), *De Renoir à Picasso* (*From Renoir to Picasso*, 1950) and *Quatre peintres belges au travail* (*Four Belgian Painters at Work*, 1952), *Rubens* would become a landmark film, screened and praised all over the world.

Haesaerts and the illustrated art book

The Golden Age of the art documentary of the late 1940s and early 1950s coincided with interesting experiments and innovations in the field of the illustrated art book, epitomized by André Malraux's *Musée imaginaire* (*Museum without Walls*, 1947), which was based on the juxtaposition of artworks of divergent styles, periods and cultures.[4] Already in the early 1930s, Haesaerts was aware of the fact that the perception and knowledge of art had changed drastically through the ubiquitous availability of mechanical reproductions. More than a decade before Malraux's *Musée imaginaire*, Haesaerts published *Flandre: Essai sur l'art flamand depuis 1880* (*Flanders: Essay on Flemish Art since 1880*) together with his brother Luc in 1931.[5] This book on Flemish impressionist painting was striking as it developed its arguments first and foremost by means of illustrations, every left page only showing a combination of reproductions. Even their method seems to prefigure that of Malraux, who was famously presented by photographer Maurice Jarnoux amidst a collection of reproductions scattered over the floor of his room, as painter Jean Milo remembered how the Haesaerts brothers were preparing their book by spreading out pictures on the floor of their room.[6]

Haesaerts was highly conscious of his method as the book also included a preface entitled 'un critique par la photographie', in which he praises the ability of the mechanical eye of the photo camera to surpass human vision by revealing the touch, technique, and material aspects of paintings.[7] According to Haesaerts, combinations of photographic reproductions do not only demonstrate certain assertions of the text, they also enable the art critic to surpass textual discourse and to dissect, analyse, reconstruct and situate artworks. By means of juxtapositions, successions and a diversity of combinations of photographs, an art book could tell a different, and often more accurate, story than one primarily based on texts.[8] Furthermore, photographic reproductions, and close-ups in particular, could stimulate the formal analysis of works of art.[9] In addition, the book of *Flandre* contains a variety of techniques that anticipate Haesaerts' approach of dealing with paintings in his films.[10]

Although the medium of photography supplied the materials for the art book, it was cinema that provided its organizational model.[11] According to Malraux, the art book was, just like a film, a succession of images arranged on the basis of montage.[12] Strikingly, in his praise of the mobile eye, Haesaerts, too, refers to film in his introduction on the use of photographs in art books: 'Let us take inspiration from the experiments in the cinema, which, for a long time, has recognised its capabilities and did not resist to attach cameras to the shoes of pedestrians, reaping scythes and crashing airplanes.'[13] According to Storck, with whom Haesaerts would make his first film, the confrontations and successions of images in the *Flandre* book evoked a kind of cinematic montage. Storck described the book as 'a cinematic exercise', which was inspired by the framings and close-ups of the cinema.[14] In its turn, Haesaerts' book inspired Storck to make his innovative art documentaries of the late 1930s and 1940s. Following his conviction that reproductions of artworks make the accompanying text complete and generate new reflections in the reader's mind, Haesaerts kept on publishing art books throughout his career, in which the role of illustrations remained important. However, it was with his 1948 film *Rubens,* that Haesaerts would develop this concept of art criticism even further, when he introduced his ideas into the practice of film.

Preparations, production and awards

Although Haesaerts and Storck only released their film in 1948, already before the war there were intentions to produce a film dedicated to Peter Paul Rubens (1577–40).[15] In 1936, the script of Storck's *Regards sur la Belgique ancienne*

(*Views of Ancient Belgium*) included a part devoted to Rubens, a part that never made it into the final film.[16] However, Storck stated that while filming Rubens' works in Antwerp Cathedral, he realized that 'paintings come more to life when you move the camera and take close-ups', since the works of art 'are no longer part of the architecture' and therefore the subjects of the paintings come to life and they become more meaningful.[17] Afterwards, Storck began discussing the idea of a film on Rubens with Kamiel Huysmans, then mayor of the city of Antwerp, who was very eager to start this project.[18] Subsequently, in 1939, the city council of Antwerp launched the idea to commemorate the 300th anniversary of the death of Rubens and it even gave some guidelines for the realization of a 20-minute black-and-white film.[19] Serving as a glorification of Antwerp as the city of Rubens, they wanted the film to be 'as dynamic, fascinating and varied as possible',[20] with different versions in Dutch, French, English and German.[21] Soon after the request of the city council of Antwerp was released, Storck started working on *Rubens*, commissioned by the Ministry for Public Education (Cinema Department) and the Ministry for

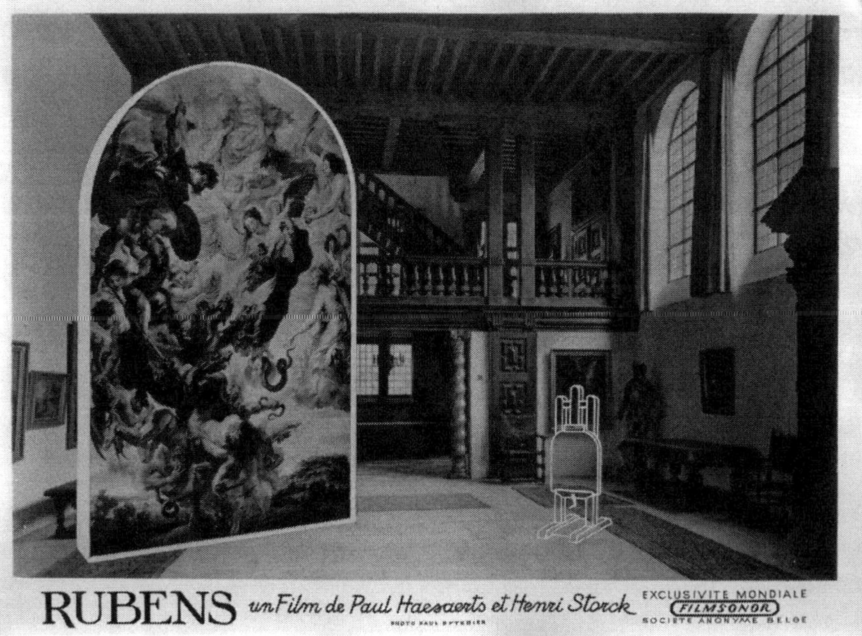

Figure 3.2 Rubens (*Paul Haesaerts and Henri Storck, 1948*). *Still by Paul Bytebier.*

Communication (State Tourism Commission).[22] Eventually, after the interruptions of the production process caused by the war, Paul Haesaerts joined Storck, signing a contract in 1947, stating that Haesaerts was responsible for the screenplay and the all-round assistance with the montage, the sound, the commentary, and all other artistic and technical problems that might occur.[23] In addition, Haesaerts spent months creating a script that covered the rich oeuvre of Rubens, which he divided thematically into five chapters: the gothic and the sublime, Rubens and his environment, Rubens' technique, Rubens as a painter of abundance, the history of Christ evoked by Rubens, and his paintings on music and dance.[24] Extensive preparations in the Haesaerts archives show that this thematic classification was already made at an early stage.[25]

In the press release for the film, Haesaerts and Storck proclaimed that the means of cinema in seeing works of art are far greater than the human eye, since film 'can go quickly from one museum to another'.[26] They consequently considered *Rubens* as a grand cinematic exhibition, presenting the art documentary as a 'tour du monde', containing works from museums in Madrid, Paris, London, Munich, Vienna, etc., all coming together on the silver screen thanks to photographic reproductions.[27] In a 1949 interview, Storck declared that in order to collect all the images of Rubens' paintings, he had to (re-)photograph almost everything on-site.[28]

To translate Rubens' works into cinema, Haesaerts and Storck called in a wide variety of cinematic techniques, including camera movements, split screens, overlap dissolves, multiple exposures, parallel editing and animation techniques. Apart from the titles of the works that are included in the film and the museums where they are situated, the elaborated script also contains the voice-over texts and instructions on the use of these 'special cinematic movements'.[29] The script also comprises notes and handwritten clarifications by Haesaerts himself, emphasizing that, for example, 'the movements of the diagrams are only momentary visual indications quickly coming to underline this or that characteristic of a painting on which we want to focus the attention of the spectator'.[30] In addition, together with two technical teams of twenty-five collaborators, Storck worked for six months trying to make these images 'come to life'.[31] Due to the grand scale of Haesaerts' screenplay and the experimental character of the film, the originally intended length of twenty minutes for *Rubens* was extended to one hour of film.

After working on the film for over a year, *Rubens* premiered in May 1948 at the Venice Biennale, where Storck and Haesaerts won the Golden Medal in the category of films on visual arts. They also won the prize for best documentary of an artistic character (shared with Alain Resnais' *Van Gogh*), awarded by CIDALC (Comité International de Diffusion de l'Art et de la Littérature par le Cinéma).[32] Also in Belgium, where *Rubens* premiered in October 1948 in Antwerp, the film was an immediate success. In the following months, it was screened in galleries, museums and local cinemas all over the country, often accompanied by a brief introduction by Haesaerts.

Furthermore, *Rubens* also found its way to several other European countries: it was screened at the Edinburgh Film Festival;[33] Roger Manvell discussed the

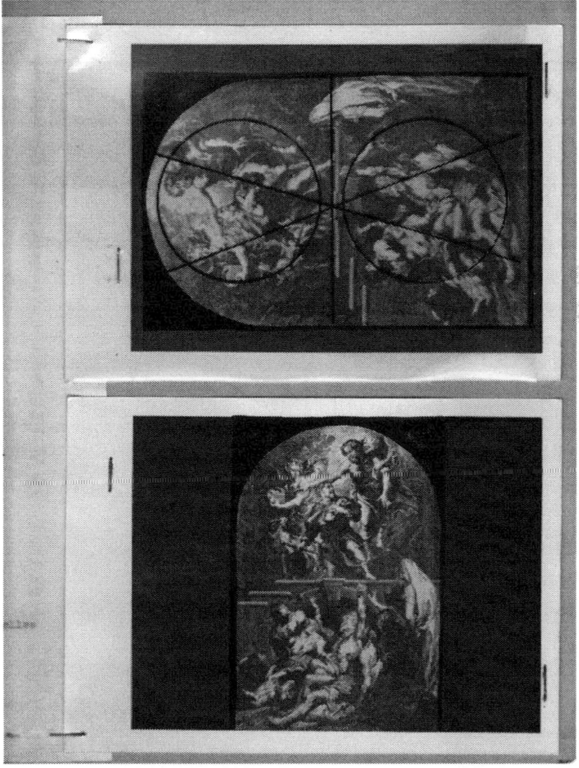

Figure 3.3 Rubens *(Paul Haesaerts and Henri Storck, 1948), Scenario. Henri Storck Papers, Cinematek, Brussels.*

film in a *Sight and Sound* article tellingly entitled 'And Finally a Great Film';[34] and Storck's production company CEP (Cinéma Edition Production)[35] planned to screen the film in Canada and the USSR.[36] Also in the United States, where *Rubens* was distributed by Brandon Films Inc. in New York,[37] the film was screened in art galleries such as the Museum of Modern Art in New York and at several universities.[38] As a result, the film became a landmark art documentary that was often discussed in film and art journals, surveys and books on the topic by authors such as Theodore R. Bowie and Siegfried Kracauer among others.[39]

Rubens as art criticism without words

For Haesaerts, conventional art criticism was outdated and unadjusted to its objects. Cinema, by contrast, offers a 'new instrument of investigation and thinking', that enables us to comprehend artworks in a new way.[40] Developing his concept of 'cinéma critique', Haesaerts considers cinema a superior art critical tool because written criticism can be separated from its subject, which, according to Haesaerts, is not the case with film: 'When a mistake is used in a comparison, in a description of a form, in the nature of a confrontation or an influence, the film will display this mistake and the viewer will see it immediately. The succession of images compels the author to keep constantly in contact with the images.'[41] Additionally, Haesaerts distinguishes three types of 'cinéma critique', which correspond to the possibilities of written criticism: the anecdote, the technical analysis and the lyrical representation.[42]

In a 1951 lecture, Haesaerts presents cinema as the culmination of a process of juxtaposing images that was earlier developed in lectures and art books, while also emphasising film's power to enable a close and intimate confrontation with works of art: 'Writing distances us from the object. Film brings us closer to it. The beauty of a phrase, the eloquence of an affirmation may distract us easily from the quality of the artwork, whereas a harmonious movement of the camera or successful lighting can never distance our judgment from the real value of the filmed object.'[43] 'Writing can now be abandoned,' he states, and 'commentary is made by the voice and music, criticism is first and foremost achieved by the movement of the camera.'[44] In addition, Haesaerts advocates for images replacing words, to let discourse become 'an eloquent succession of images.'[45]

Already in the first and introductory part of the Rubens film, which deals with the transition from a gothic to a baroque style, Haesaerts and Storck use several innovative cinematic strategies to support the narrative of the voice-over commentary. For example, instead of explaining Rubens' concept of a universe in motion and a fertile nature with words, a dissolve between paintings and footage of water, clouds and flames is used to evoke these ideas. At other times, Rubens is presented as a master of ultimate flexibility and movement by means of animated circles and ovals that point out the characteristics of Rubens' compositions – his focal points, divisions, and the sweep of his movements. These animated lines also share a striking resemblance to the linear structures drawn by Picasso in the film *Visite à Picaso*, showing the famous artist at work. However, in *Rubens*, this use of linear patterns to emphasize or reveal Rubens' compositions is somewhat remarkable, as the art of Rubens is generally positioned against classicist tendencies favouring line over colour.[46] According to André Thirifays, Haesaerts used 'a technique which is perfectly adapted to the film medium, and which, moreover, in this case, is more efficacious than the written word. By using graphs, pointing quick contrasts, or introducing music, he succeeds in giving forceful expression to his critical opinions, whilst at the same time, with a few swift touches, he indicates various influences and successive trends in the realm of art and dwells on the dramatic aspects of the works mentioned.'[47]

However, it is in the second, and more experimental half of the film, that this cinematic language is used to its fullest potential and that the lyrical representation of Rubens' artworks is fully accomplished. Specially in the sequence on Rubens' representation of the life of Christ, the importance of the voice-over commentary diminishes and sometimes even disappears completely, whereas the shots of the paintings perfectly match the score by Belgian composer Raymond Chevreuille, gradually intensifying as Christ's death on the cross approaches.[48] This specific part was also praised by the local press as one of the highlights of *Rubens*, calling it 'a moment of pure cinema,'[49] of an 'almost unbearable dramatic intensity',[50] and lyricism at its best because it's 'not bound by any comment'.[51] Haesaerts, however, argues that technically, the first half of *Rubens* is the best part, while also recognizing that 'as for the most moving passage, it is obviously the reel dedicated to Christ'.[52]

The emphatic presence of the voice-over commentary in the first segment of *Rubens* was often the target of criticism in reviews, accusing the film of being too didactic, stating that for example 'nothing is in fact more disturbing than the teachers-tone of voice coming to tell us what to think about Rubens or even what we can see with our own eyes'.[53] André Bazin, too, used this argument against the film, but he also stated that because of *Rubens'* didactic potential, Haesaerts and Storck were able to 'seriously shorten the long path of culture that only a privileged few can walk'.[54] Likewise, Paul Davay stated that *Rubens* has the ability to reach a wider audience, because 'Storck and Haesaerts oblige us to remain in front of the picture, to see it, with *their* eyes, but they give us the right to protest, to disagree, and to join in a discussion which is always open to *our* intelligence'.[55]

Rubens and the formalist tradition

In contrast with some other landmark art documentaries of the 1940s, Storck and Haesaerts present cinema as an analytical tool to dissect artworks. They do not use film to re-tell the story of a painting's subject, as in several of Luciano Emmer's films. In addition, only to a certain extent do they attempt to enter the biographical or mental world of the artist, as in Storck's *Le Monde de Paul Delvaux* (*The World of Paul Delvaux*, 1946) or Alain Resnais' *Van Gogh* (1948). First and foremost, *Rubens* consists of a formal and stylistic analysis of the works of the baroque painter, facilitated by the use of a variety of cinematic techniques in which the camera is presented as an instrument that enables us to compare the artworks. In so doing, Haesaerts and Storck present themselves as modernists – in one of his essays, Haesaerts refers to the famous formalist definition of art by French painter Maurice Denis stating that 'a picture, before being a battle horse, a nude, an anecdote or whatnot, is essentially a flat surface covered with colours assembled in a certain order'.[56]

In *Rubens*, for example, Haesaerts and Storck frequently isolate a fragment of a painting through the device of an iris, sometimes even a shifting iris, the subsequent shot showing a close-up of that fragment for a more detailed analysis. At other instances, a moving camera and rapidly rotating images reveal Rubens' predilection for spiral-shaped movements. Furthermore, the omnipresence of animated lines highlights the compositions and rhythm of Rubens' paintings. In addition, Haesaerts unmistakably situates himself in the formalist tradition of art history, reaching back to the writings by Heinrich Wölfflin in the late nineteenth and early twentieth centuries. Usually considered as one of the first art historians using parallel slide projections in his lectures, Wölfflin also based his method on a visual analysis of artworks, implying that art operates as a visual language.[57] Wölfflin's famous *Kunstgeschichtliche Grundbegriffe* (*Principles of Art History*, 1915) is based on a series of formal oppositions in order to discuss the differences between renaissance and baroque art.[58] On the one hand, echoing Wölfflin's juxtapositions, Storck and Haesaerts frequently use split-screens to compare Rubens with earlier painters such as Van der Weyden, Van der Goes, Van Eyck, Bosch or Bruegel. On the other hand, split screens are invoked to demonstrate Rubens' influence on later artists such as Jordaens, Watteau, Delacroix, Wiertz and Renoir. Furthermore, they also make comparisons between similar details from a number of works by Rubens himself. For instance, a sequence juxtaposes a series of hands painted by Rubens and investigates their significance in the construction of a narrative, a topic already present in preparation sketches by Haesaerts, trying to create an order in which the details of these hands could appear.[59]

Haesaerts continued to use the technique of split-screens in other films such as *De Renoir à Picasso* in 1950, to make statements about the development of modern art in general, attempting to trace three inspirational sources of modern art – the so-called sensual or carnal (Renoir), the cerebral (Seurat) and the instinctual or passionate (Picasso). Self-evidently, such confrontations, which also structured Malraux's *Musée imaginaire*, became only possible and were even fostered by the availability of the mechanical reproduction of images. In one of his texts on the film on art, Haesaerts asserted that the discipline of art history and the practices of art analysis and art criticism are no longer conceivable without mechanical reproductions.[60] Furthermore, reproductions made it possible to 'investigate, understand, compare, and explain artworks' by means of 'anything other than visual perception'.[61] Just like Malraux, Haesaerts does not use a chronological framework in *Rubens* but he juxtaposes works of art in a 'temps esthétique', comparing them stylistically.[62]

Another idea that was important to Haesaerts is that the film has to adopt the style and rhythm of the artworks being filmed: 'The camera has to borrow its gestures and demeanour from the subject it is talking about. The camera has to be *trecento* with Giotto, impressionist with Renoir, classical and Poussinesque with Poussin, baroque and Rubensian with Rubens.'[63] Storck and Haesaerts' hectic camera movements, swift editing and curling animated lines evoke the dynamic compositions, the vertiginous spaces, the muscular power of the figures, the vivid brush work, and the rich colour contrasts that characterize Rubens' paintings.

Because of the varying light and the falling and turning movements of the camera used in the film, Rubens' art is even presented as a proto-cinematic spectacle. Storck and Haesaerts present Rubens as a precursor of cinema in a scene in which the interior of a Jesuit church with an altarpiece painted by Rubens is almost transformed into a cinema theatre. Suddenly, the image is underexposed apart from the altar, which illuminates as a cinema screen showing details of several Rubens paintings. With his staged spectacles on large formats and compositions characterized by movements and spatial depth, Rubens is perfectly fit for the film camera – Anne Hollander tellingly described Rubens as an artist with 'a cinematic understanding'.[64]

Haesaerts and Storck presented *Rubens* as a highly autonomous work of cinema and they were often praised for the experimental character of their film. For example, in a lecture on Haesaerts, Francis Bolen stated that with *Rubens* 'we were far away from the "clichés" which had begun to appear in the ordinary brand of films on art'.[65] Furthermore, H.W. Janson, author of a well-known and popular survey of art history, wrote that:

> ambitious and successful films such as the Belgian-made *Rubens* and *Le Monde de Paul Delvaux* have demonstrated how effectively the moving camera can guide the beholder's eye so as to focus his attention and heighten his perceptions. There is a strange excitement about viewing paintings thus spread out upon the movie screen. A new dimension, we feel, has been

added to our experience, and we find ourselves in a state of visual alertness that makes the forms speak to us with particular eloquence and intensity.[66]

Rubens as a film on art versus an art film

Rubens is, in some ways, a typical art documentary of the late 1940s and 1950s, in the sense that it is a didactic film on art but, at the same time, it is an art film that self-consciously touches upon the boundaries between painting and film, oscillating between art and reality, stillness and movement, and two and three dimensions. Thanks to the illusion of Rubens' paintings, a new cinematic illusion is created. In addition, its didacticism is developed thanks to cinematic techniques and devices. Consequently, *Rubens* was not conceived as an educational project, nor as pure cinema, but rather as something in between. This ambiguity was also noted by Siegfried Kracauer, who wrote that:

> *Rubens* combines cinematically brilliant camera penetrations of the painter's world with an attempt to drive home his predilection for gyrational movements. Note that this film is neither pure cinema nor merely a teaching instrument. It is a glamorous hybrid.[67]

Because of the experimental character of *Rubens*, however, Haesaerts and Storck were also often criticized by art critics and historians, arguing that they attempted to realize effects that sometimes had little to do with the original work of art or showed it completely out of context. Furthermore, according to Beatrice Farwell, art documentaries are confronted by a dilemma by definition: 'The more a film on art succeeds as a film, the less likely it is to increase one's understanding of painting.'[68] Alluding to the film by Storck and Haesaerts, Farwell deals with the example of Rubens, which, at first sight, seems like a natural for film treatment because his art is full of movement. The point, however, is that Rubens was capable of creating this movement in a static medium. When a painting is set in motion by means of cinematic devices, the illusion Rubens skilfully created is lost. A new filmic illusion is constructed, which, according to Farwell, falsifies Rubens' art and which can even lead to a misinterpretation of the art of painting in general. Haesaerts, however, contradicts the notion that cinema goes against the nature of painting as an immobile art form. For Haesaerts, the art film is the expression of the filmed artwork but also the expression of the spectator looking at it. Furthermore, he denies the idea that by introducing movement to still paintings, cinema betrays the intentions of the artists represented. Far from doing harm to the painter or the sculptor, Haesaerts states, the filmmaker-critic can help the artists in revealing their expression. For this purpose, filmmakers can employ an entire cinematic toolkit. André Bazin, too, recognized this conflict inherent to the art documentary, stating that these filmmakers use 'an already completed work sufficient unto itself'.[69] But, he asserted:

> it is precisely because it substitutes for the painting a work one degree removed from it, proceeding from something already aesthetically formulated, that it throws a new light on the original. It is perhaps to the extent that the film is a complete work and as such, seems therefore to betray the painting most, that it renders it in reality the greater service.[70]

Likewise, Theodore R. Bowie emphasizes that Haesaerts uses film as 'an instrument of interpretation', and it is precisely this interpretative aspect that holds the critical potential of the art documentary.[71] This discrepancy between the educational on the one hand and the artistic on the other did not only result in divided opinions on the film, it also created disagreements between Storck and Haesaerts. Letters from the Haesaerts archives indicate that the division of tasks stipulated in the contract in 1947 – Haesaerts being responsible for the analytical-didactic part of the script and Storck for the technical-artistic part of the camerawork – also caused doubts regarding the authorship of *Rubens*.[72] Consequently, this raises questions about to what extent the educational or the creative ability determines the value of the art documentary, a topic which was often at the centre of discussions at international conferences and in professional film and art journals at the time. However, with *Rubens*, Haesaerts managed to break down the boundaries between an educational document on the one hand and an independent work of art on the other. In doing so, he created a new model of art historical scholarship, which, decades later, certainly still amazes us by its attempts at developing new ways of analysing artworks in cinematic ways.

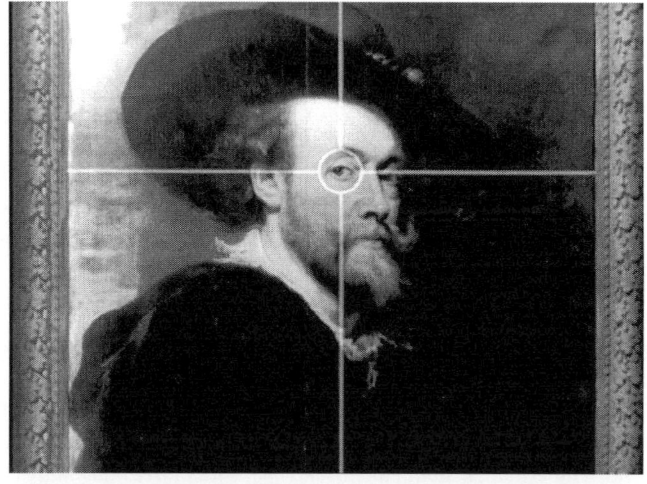

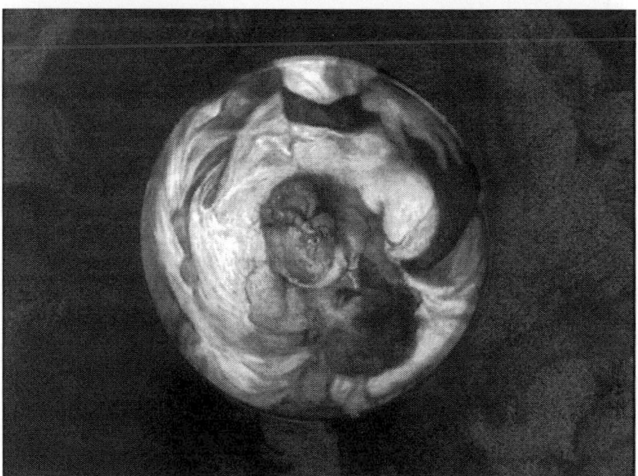

Figure 3.4 and 3.5 *Rubens* Paul Haesaerts and Henri Storck, 1948). Digital Stills.

Notes

1   See for instance: *Carpaccio* (Umberto Barbaro and Roberto Longhi, 1947), *Michelangelo* (Carlo Ludovico Ragghianti, 1964), and *Van Gogh* (Alain Resnais, Gaston Diehl and Robert Hessens, 1948).

2   Of Haesaerts, see *Beeldhouwwerken en tekeningen van George Minne* (Amsterdam: De Spiegel, n.d.); *Permeke of de drang naar grootheid* (Amsterdam/Antwerp: De Spieghel/Het Kompas, 1940); *James Ensor* (Brussels: Elsevier, 1957); *Picasso et le gout du paroxysme* (Antwerp/Amsterdam: De Spieghel/Het Kompas 1938); Renoir: Sculptor (New York: Reynal and Hitchcock, 1947), and *Ossip Zadkine* (Amsterdam: De Spieghel, 1939).

3   In 1938, Paul Haesaerts, together with his brother Luc and artists René Magritte, Paul
    Delvaux and Léon Spilliaert, founded the group *Les Compagnons de l'Art*, which
    organized a landmark exhibition at the Palais des Beaux-Arts in Brussels that same
    year including artists such as James Ensor, Valerius de Saedeleer and George Minne.
    Forty years later, in 1978, the Palais des Beaux-Arts paid tribute to the brothers
    Haesaerts with the exhibition *Art in Belgium from Ensor to Jeune Peinture Belge*, with a
    focus on the 1938 exhibition of *Les Compagnons de l'Art*. See Karel Geirlandt,
    introduction to *Kunst in België 1880–1950: Hulde aan Luc en Paul Haesaerts* by Karel
    Geirlandt (ed.) (Brussels: Paleis voor Schone Kunsten, 1978), 5.

4   Malraux's *Le Musée imaginaire* was originally published in 1947 as the first volume of
    Psychologie de l'art (Genève: Skira) and was later adapted to become a part of *Les Voix
    du silence* (Paris: Gallimard, 1951). In 1965, the text was republished as *Le Musée
    imaginaire* (Paris: Gallimard). See also Walter Grasskamp, *The Book on the Floor: André
    Malraux and the Imaginary Museum* (Los Angeles, CA: Getty Research Institute, 2016);
    Georges Didi-Huberman, *L'Album de l'art à l'époque du musée imaginaire* (Paris: Hazan,
    2013); and Angela Dalle Vacche, *Film, Art, New Media: Museum Without Walls?* (New
    York: Palgrave Macmillan, 2012).

5   Paul and Luc Haesaerts, *Flandre: Essai sur l'art flamand depuis 1880. Vol. 1:
    L'Impressionnisme* (Paris: Lazzaro, 1931). Dealing with impressionist art, the book of
    more than 700 pages was originally intended to be part of a trilogy, the other parts
    dedicated to Symbolism and Expressionism respectively. See Sofie Neuckermans,
    'Organization and Inventory of the Paul Haesaerts Archive' (Masters diss., Vrije
    Universiteit Brussels, 2006), 40.

6   Jean Milo, 'Wij waren jong . . ', in Geirlandt (ed.), *Kunst in België 1880–1950*, 40.

7   Haesaerts and Haesaerts, 'Un critique par la photographie', introduction to *Flandre*, 13.

8   Haesaerts and Haesaerts, 'Un critique par la photographie', 17.

9   Haesaerts and Haesaerts, 'Un critique par la photographie', 21. Haesaerts also refers
    to the inventions of cubist and constructivist painting that enabled us to see pure
    forms.

10 For example on page 46, split screens of photographic reproductions are used to compare
    different ways of portraying the female body in the work of nineteenth-century artists
    Louis Gallait and Henry Leys, a technique Haesaerts would frequently use in several of
    his art documentaries such as *De Renoir à Picasso* (1950) to exemplify stylistic differences
    in certain paintings. Or on pages 186–95, a succession of fragments of James Ensor's
    painting of *Christ's Entry into Brussels* of 1889 are used to emphasize the attention of
    detail versus the grandeur of the entire painting. This approach shows clear similarities to
    the use of montage in Haesaerts' later films on Ensor: *Masques et Visages de James Ensor
    (Masques and Faces of James Ensor*, 1952) and *Ik, Ensor* (*I, Ensor*, 1972).

11 See also Douglas Smith, 'Moving Pictures: the Art Documentaries of Alain Resnais and
    Henri-Georges Clouzot in Theoretical Context', *Studies in European Cinema* 1, 3
    (2004): 167.

12 Smith, 'Moving Pictures', 167

13 Haesaerts and Haesaerts, 'Un critique par la photographie', 15.

14 Henri Storck, 'Paul Haesaerts est mort', *Le Soir* (2 February 1974).

15 Jean D., 'Les Mystères de la cathédrale ou toute l'œuvre de Rubens a la clarté des sunlights', *Hebdo* (13 December 1947): 21.

16 *Regards sur la Belgique ancienne* is divided into two parts: 'The Treasures of Faith' and 'Communal Freedom'. The script also included two additional parts: 'Rubens and his Time' and 'Leopold the First, the Creation of Present-day Belgium'. See http://fondshenristorck.be/en/henri-storck/filmography-hs/films-alphabetically/insights-into-the-former-belgium/

17 Johan Swinnen, 'Paradoxale sferen: Interview met Henri Storck', in Johan Swinnen and Luc Deneulin (eds), *Henri Storck: memoreren* (Brussels: VUB Press, 2007), 83–4.

18 Swinnen, 'Paradoxale sferen: Interview met Henri Storck', 84.

19 See the correspondence between Oscar Leemans and Leo Delwaide (Secretariat of the sub-committee for the Rubens film) and Head of the 'Soc. An. Belge. C.E.P', *Commemoration of Rubens 1940* (25 July 1940), Henri Storck Papers, Cinematek, Brussels.

20 Correspondence Leemans-Delwaide.

21 Before the film was finished, several copies were ordered from all over the world. Jean D., 'Les Mystères de la cathédrale', 21.

22 Henri Storck, *Academie des Beaux-Arts d'Anvers: Entrevue avec Messieurs Wappers et Opsomer* (13 September 1939), Henri Storck Papers, Cinematek, Brussels. See also http://fondshenristorck.be/en/henri-storck/filmography-hs/films-alphabetically/rubens/

23 However, the division of tasks between Haesaerts and Storck during the production process of the film remains unclear. This ambiguity also caused later problems regarding the question of authorship of the film. Correspondence between Henri Storck and Paul Haesaerts, *Contract Paul Haesaerts* (20 March 1947), Henri Storck Papers, Cinematek, Brussels.

24 This thematic classification with an emphasis on the sublime, the cosmic and the musicality in the works of Rubens is in line with the general Rubens scholarship. Around the time of the film's production, there was a tremendous interest in the oeuvre and the life of Rubens exemplified in the research of German art historian Ludwig Burchard from the 1930s onwards, resulting in the *The Corpus Rubenianum Ludwig Burchard Catalogue Project*; the restoration and the purchase of the *Rubenshuis* by the city of Antwerp in 1948; the founding of the Research Institution *Centrum Rubenianum* in 1963; and numerous monographs such as *Rubens et son temps* (René Huyghe, 1936), *Rubens* (Jakob Christoph Burckhardt, 1940), *Rubens und sein Werk: Neue Forschungen* (Hans Gerhard Evers, 1943) and *Les vies multiples de Rubens* (Jef Crick, et al., 1946), which all focus on the same 'themes' as the Haesaerts and Storck film. See also Frans Baudouin and Roger d'Hulst, 'Foreword', in *The Ceiling Paintings of the Jesuit Church in Antwerp. Corpus Rubenianum Ludwig Burchard, vol. 1,* John Rupert Martin (New York: Phaidon, 1968), vii–xiv, and Paul Huvenne and Hans Nieuwdorp, *Het Rubenshuis Antwerpen* (Brussels: Gemeentekrediet, 1990).

25 This division already marked the very first version of a script as indicated in the guidelines by the Antwerp city council. See the correspondence between Oscar Leemans, Leo Delwaide and Head of the 'Soc. An. Belge. C.E.P', *Commemoration of Rubens 1940* (25 July 1940), Henri Storck Papers, Brussels, Cinematek. These different chapters contain minor changes compared with the final version of *Rubens*. The idea was that these chapters could be shown and sold separately. See Paul Haesaerts and Henri Storck, *Script Rubens,* 3.10.2, 504–6: 'Rubens', 1948, Scenario, Haesaerts Papers, The Archives for Contemporary Art in Belgium, Brussels.

26 Paul Haesaerts, 'Art Criticism and Art History by the Kinema: The Work of Rubens on the Screen', press release for the film *Rubens* (1948), Haesaerts Papers, The Archives for Contemporary Art in Belgium, Brussels.

27 Jean D., 'Les Mystères de la cathédrale', 21.

28 Storck stated that some of the works of Rubens hadn't been photographed for over fifty years. Th. De Coster, 'Une heure avec Henri Storck', *Jeunesse et Vie* (3 March 1949): 10.

29 Haesaerts, *Script Rubens*, part I, 10.

30 Haesaerts, *Script Rubens*, part I, 10.

31 Th. De Coster, 'Une heure avec Henri Storck', *Jeunesse et Vie* (3 March 1949): 10.

32 Marc Turfkruyter, 'Een Belgische triomf op het Venetiaans filmfestival: *Rubens* van Henri Storck en Paul Haesaerts', *ABC Weekblad* (17 October 1948).

33 Forsyth Hardy, 'The Edinburgh Film Festival', *Film Quarterly* 4, 4 (1950).

34 Roger Manvell, 'And Finally a Great Film', *Sight & Sound* 17, 67 (1948).

35 CEP was founded in 1934 by Henri Storck (as the artistic director), in collaboration with Belgian business manager René-Ghislain Le Vaux and attempted to obtain governmental protection for Belgian productions. Vincent Geens, 'Een tijd van begoochelingen: Le temps des utopies. L'ambition cinématographique d'Henri Storck, de 1907 à 1940', in Swinnen and Deneulin, *Henri Storck: memoreren*, 285–6.

36 Correspondence between Paul Haesaerts and Henri Storck, *Resultats de l'exploitation du film 'Rubens'* (10 January 1951), 3.10.2, 508: 'Rubens' (1948), letters between Rispoloulos/Haesaerts/Van Raemdonck/Storck, Haesaerts Papers, The Archives for Contemporary Art in Belgium, Brussels.

37 William McK. Chapman, *Films on Art 1952* (New York: American Federation of Arts,1952), 133. Katerina Loukopoulou mentions Brandon Films, Inc. as a distributor of *Rubens* and emphasizes that advertisements for European films on art like *Rubens* addressed a wide-ranging audience of teachers, artists and film enthusiasts. See Katerina Loukopoulou, 'Museum at Large: Aesthetic Education through Film', in *Learning with the Lights Off: Educational Film in the United States*, Devin Orgeron (ed.) et al. (New York: Oxford University Press, 2012), 364.

38 Marc D., 'De film *Rubens* gaat de wereld door. Paul Haesaerts en Henri Storck ter ere', *Weekblad Cinema* (5 March 1949).

39 *Rubens* was discussed in journals such as *Sight & Sound, College Art Journal, Film Quarterly* and *Documentary Film News,* among many others.

40 Paul Haesaerts, 'Arts plastiques et caméra', *Festival* (Cahier 4) (Brussels, 21 June 1947). Also published in *Arts de France* 23–4 (1948): 25–31.

41 Haesaerts, press release for the film *Rubens* (1948), n.p.

42 The anecdote being the place, the time, the character, the friends, etc. of the artist, the technical analysis being the scientific research of the different elements of a work of art and, according to Haesaerts the most important one, the lyrical representation being the expression of a personal message through a work of art, a style or time. Press leaflet of *Rubens,* n.p.

43 Paul Haesaerts, 'La Critique par le cinéma' (Lecture at the third congress of the Association international des critiques d'art (AICA) (1951), 3.10.2, 510–11, Haesaerts Papers, The Archives for Contemporary Art in Belgium, Brussels.

44 Haesaerts, 'La Critique par le cinema', 26.

45 Haesaerts, 'La Critique par le cinema', 26.

46 The fact that Rubens was shot in black and white was often a subject of criticism, since Rubens is usually considered a great colourist. This, however, should be situated in a context in which the vast majority of art reproductions were in black and white. Nevertheless, already in 1938 French art historian René Huyghe made a 35mm film in colour on the baroque painter: *Rubens et son temps* (*Rubens and his Time,* 1938), which can also be considered one of the first art documentaries in colour.

47 André Thirifays, 'The Potentialities and Limitations of Films about Art', in *Films on Art* (Paris: UNESCO and Brussels: Editions de la connaissance, 1951), 9.

48 Haesaerts' script also contains indications for the musical score written by Belgian composer Raymond Chevreuille. Haesaerts, *Script Rubens.*

49 Armand Bachelier, 'La Critique d'art par le cinéma: *Rubens*', *Le Phare* (20 October 1948).

50 Bachelier, 'La Critique d'art par le cinéma'.

51 'Rubens', *De Standaard* (22 October 1948).

52 Armand Bachelier, 'Quand un esthète-cinéaste rêve à haute voix', *Le Phare* (15 December 1948).

53 The didactic character of the voice-over commentary is often part of a more general criticism of the 'traditional' *film sur l'art* which persists to the present day. H. Vandersteen, 'Film als reproductie en expressie', *De Spectator* (29 October 1948).

54 André Bazin in *Le Parisien libéré* (10 June 1949), see 'Rubens' http://fondshenristorck. be/nl/henri-storck/filmografie-2/filmsalfabetisch/rubens/

55 Paul Davay, 'Compelled to See', in *Films on Art* (Paris: UNESCO/Brussels: Editions de la connaissance, 1949), 17, emphasis in original.

56 Paul Haesaerts, 'Art plastique et cinéma', *L'Amour de l'art* 29, 37–9 (1949): 39.

57 According to Thomas Hensel however, Bruno Meyer, professor of Art History at the Polytechnic Institut in Karlsruhe, was the first art historian who used side-by-side projections and superimpositions in his classroom in 1880. Also Aby Warburg was using parallel slide projections in his lectures at the same time as Heinrich Wölfflin. See Thomas Hensel, *Wie aus der Kunstgeschichte eine Bildwissenschaft wurde: Aby Warburgs Graphien* (Berlin: Akademie Verlag, 2011), 144.

58 Heinrich Wölfflin, *Kunstgeschichtliche Grundbegriffe: das Problem der Stilentwicklung in der neueren Kunst* (München: Bruckmann, 1915).

59 Haesaerts, *Script Rubens,* part IV, n.p.

60 See also: Helene E. Roberts, *Art History through the Camera's Lens* (London: Routledge, 1995); Costanza Caraffa (ed.), *Fotografie als Instrument und Medium der Kunstgeschichte* (Berlin: Deutsche Kunstverlag, 2009); Costanza Caraffa (ed.), *Photo Archives and the Photographic Memory of Art History* (Berlin: Deutscher Kunstverlag, 2011); and Thomas Hensel, *Wie aus der Kunstgeschichte eine Bildwissenschaft wurde: Aby Warburgs Graphien* (Berlin: Akademie Verlag, 2011), among others.

61 Paul Haesaerts, 'Sur la critique par le cinéma', 18.

62 Haesaerts, *Flandre,* 45.

63 Paul Haesaerts, 'Kunstkritiek en kunstgeschiedenis door de kinema: Het werk van Rubens op het scherm', press release for the film *Rubens* (1948).

64 Anne Hollander, *Moving Pictures* (Cambridge, MA: Harvard University Press, 1991), 112.

65 Francis Bolen, 'The "critofilm d'art" as developed by Paul Haesaerts and Carlo Ragghianti' (Lecture at the 1951 congress at The Metropolitan Museum in New York), Haesaerts Papers, The Archives for Contemporary Art in Belgium, Brussels.

66 H.W. Janson, 'College Use of Films on Art', in William Mck. Chapman (ed.), *Films on Art 1952* (New York: The American Federation of Arts, 1953), 40.

67 Siegfried Kracauer, *Theory of Film: The Redemption of Physical Reality* (Princeton, NJ: Princeton University Press, 1997), 198.

68 Beatrice Farwell, 'Films on Art in Education', *Art Journal* 23, 1 (Autumn, 1963): 39–40.

69 André Bazin, 'Painting and Cinema', in *What Is Cinema?* (Berkeley, CA: University of California Press, 1967), 169.

70 Bazin, 'Painting and Cinema', 169.

71 Theodore Bowie, 'The Third Art Film Festival', *College Art Journal* 17, 1 (1957): 70.

72 See the correspondence between Paul Haesaerts and Henri Storck (16 September 1948), 3.10.2, 508: 'Rubens' (1948), letters between Rispoloulos/Haesaerts/Van Raemdonck/Storck, Cinematek, Brussels.

4

Carlo Ludovico Ragghianti's critofilms and beyond: from cinema to information technology

EMANUELE PELLEGRINI

His contribution to the development of film studies is one of the most investigated aspects of the multifaceted biography of the Italian art historian Carlo Ludovico Ragghianti (1910–87). Ragghianti played a pioneering role in film studies in Italy and particularly in the field of the art documentary. He named his art documentaries 'critofilms', standing for a form of art criticism carried out through film. Ragghianti considered his critofilms not simply as art documentaries but as a true form of art criticism. The twenty-one critofilms he produced between 1948 (*La Deposizione di Raffaello*) and 1964 (*Michelangiolo*) represent an attempt to interpret works of art through their own visual language. Ragghianti was so committed to this goal that his films initially did not include spoken commentary. The producers insisted on adding narrative voice-over in an effort to reach a broader audience. The diversity of subjects addressed by these critofilms – individual artists (*L'arte di Rosai*, 1957), individual artworks (*Cenacolo di Andrea del Castagno*, 1954), individual monuments (*Certosa di Pavia*, 1961), specific urban contexts (*Pompei urbanistica*, 1958; *Canal Grande*, 1963) – and their chronology (spanning from ancient to modern times) perfectly reflect Ragghianti's scholarly activities, which were characterized by multiple interests and supported by meticulous research methods.[1]

Considering the rich bibliography dedicated to critofilms and the different kind of analysis already carried out, this chapter instead concentrates on two aspects of Ragghianti's work as an art documentarian, which are connected to two specific phases of his critofilms, the initial and the final one. The initial phase, which took place in the aftermath of the Second World War (from around 1948, when the first critofilm on Raphael was made), reveals the reasons for taking up a camera and presenting documentaries as a tool for critically analysing artworks. The final phase, in the 1960s, allows us to understand why he ceased to proceed with this project. In particular, this last phase represents a highly important moment both theoretically and experimentally. Ragghianti's decision to stop writing and producing art documentaries was not the result of a lack of creative impetus but rather of his move to information technology as a means for reading artworks. Indeed, research in Ragghianti's archives enables us to confirm that he shifted from film to IT equipment, then in its early stages, as a tool for interpreting works of art. In so doing, Ragghianti prefigures the application of information technologies to the humanities that took place in the following decades.

Ragghianti's first two critofilms were made on two different occasions. The first one, realised in 1948 and dedicated to Raphael's *Deposition* (better known as *Pala Baglioni*, a painting currently on view in the Galleria Borghese in Rome), is closely connected to an essay Ragghianti had written the year before on the same subject. The second, made in 1949 (which unfortunately has been lost) concerns the personality of Lorenzo the Magnificent, to whom Ragghianti had dedicated an exhibition in Florence in 1949 on the occasion of the 500th anniversary of Lorenzo's birth.[2]

There may have been many reasons why Ragghianti decided to make an art documentary. From a more general perspective, however, two elements in particular deserve our attention. First, Ragghianti's critofilms were part of the flourishing of Italian art documentaries, which began in the 1930s.

As demonstrated in the introduction of this volume, in the 1940s, the art documentary was radically reconceptualized by Luciano Emmer as well as by the experiments by eminent art historians such as Roberto Longhi and Giulio Carlo Argan, both of whom were close to the young Ragghianti.[3] Second, Ragghianti's interest in film as a form of artistic expression was kindled at the beginning of the 1930s (when he introduced the idea of film as a visual art) and further developed after the Second World War. During this period, Ragghianti's interest in film broadened to encompass mass media – radio and television – as he believed that they would prove crucial for the popularization of (visual) culture.[4] Hence, Ragghianti's approach to critofilm stems from his intention to explore the technical possibilities of film as well as from his ambition to reform the field of the art documentary. The role of a film theoretician was not enough for him. Experimentation as a film maker was the only way to show directly his methodology as an art critic. One of his main objectives was to transform the art documentary into a device for disseminating visual culture, improving non-specialized audiences' ability to understand art.

It is clear that Ragghianti's work differed from traditional Italian art documentaries and especially the documentaries produced by the *Istituto Luce* to flaunt the country's artistic gems in an effort to attract tourists. However, Ragghianti's critofilms were not entirely against tourist promotion. Plenty of archival documents demonstrate Ragghianti's requests for financial support from the *Azienda Autonoma del Turismo di Firenze* (the official tourist office of Florence). Often involved in other Ragghianti initiatives during this period, the *Azienda Autonoma* was a leading partner in the production of documentaries that were of interest to the city of Florence and its image (beginning with the 1949 critofilm on *Lorenzo il Magnifico*). Not only did the *Azienda Autonoma del Turismo* agree to provide funding, it also suggested using the critofilm on Lorenzo the Magnificent to promote tourism in the city and its surroundings, which were slowly recovering from the disasters of the war.[5] It is no coincidence that, a few years later, Ragghianti made a similar request to the *Azienda Turistica* for Lucca to make a critofilm about the city. This film was not produced until 1955, following a fierce debate over measures to safeguard Lucca's historic city centre.[6]

Yet Ragghianti did not only distance himself from the traditional format of the art documentary. First and foremost, he sought to differentiate his activity as 'critofilm maker' from the experimental documentaries made by other art historians such as Roberto Longhi. Thanks to the collaboration with film critic and essayist Umberto Barbaro, Longhi produced several films dedicated to painters such as *Carpaccio* and *Caravaggio*, which were shot in 1948, the same year as Ragghianti's *La Deposizione di Raffaello*. While Longhi's documentaries focused on his exclusive area of interest, i.e. painting, with a rich verbal commentary guiding the eye of the observers into the artwork's hidden details, Ragghianti's critofilms evoked a broader theoretical aim, that of being able to interpret images from different arts (painting, sculpture, architecture, etc.) through images. His work was the culmination of a long philosophical research process based on the axiom that visual language could and should be wholly independent of verbal language.[7]

A critofilm is thus the concrete result of the application of his methodology to investigate the visual arts, using Benedetto Croce's philosophy as a starting point. Artistic creation is a process based on freedom and autonomy, and visual language is a language per se, with its own rules. Cinema, as a visual art, will offer the unique opportunity to investigate images not through words but through other images. Indeed, it is an active exercise of art criticism, not a different way of presenting art to the public. Ragghianti's essay on Raphael's *Deposition*, published at nearly the same time as the critofilm on the same painting was released, allows us to follow the theoretical process that gave rise to this body of work. His choice of subject was guided by the nature of the artwork. It might be the 'painting that most effectively enables the ultimate proof of our ability to critically understand or, in other words, to retrace – by following the shapes, regardless of any pattern or frame – a pictorial process in which prose and poetry are inextricably connected, the living drama of artistic creation'.[8]

This statement must be re-interpreted in light of the document that introduced the first critofilm, focusing on precisely this painting. Instead of reducing the film vision of an artwork to a static contemplation of a sequence of fixed frames and details on the screen, connected and explained only by verbal commentary, Ragghianti relied upon the authentic expressive resources of film. The transition from one idea to another, artistic influences and references are clearly explained through the deliberate use of fade-outs, mattes, cuts, etc. All of what the artwork can teach us is truly enlightened by this technique, showing that film can be persuasive and produce instant evidence which, by virtue of being absolutely objective, is superior to that provided by verbal commentary.[9]

Ragghianti must have judged the experiment as successful as he devoted himself with renewed energy to other film projects in the years to follow. He founded a 'Cinematic Office' as a part of the *Studio Italiano di Storia dell'Arte*, an institute based in the Palazzo Strozzi in Florence where he had been appointed commissioner in 1945, becoming 'the first to have included cinematic research and its relationship with the arts in its program'.[10] Moreover, in this specific period, the Italian government provided support for the production of documentaries: law no. 379 issued 16 May 1947 guaranteed 3 per cent of ticket sales from the feature film screened after the documentary. After being nominated president of the *Comité international pour le cinéma et les arts figuratifs* in 1952,[11] Ragghianti worked on his critofilms steadily for over a decade, experimenting with both the content of the films and their technical aspects.

It was during this period that Ragghianti developed an understanding of the crucial role television could play as a means of popularizing culture, a true bulwark against the return of dictatorships. Following the fall of the fascist Regime, Ragghianti was increasingly driven to improve and facilitate the process of spreading culture among wider strata of the population, beyond the inner circle of experts. Film undoubtedly offered the possibility to pursue this goal by significantly expanding potential audiences. The production of the critofilms was closely connected to the new journal *seleArte*, which appeared during this period (1952–66). It was the first Italian periodical focusing on art history which was able to capture the interest of a broad, non-specialized audience. The magazine was sponsored by Adriano Olivetti, who also funded the critofilms from 1954 onwards.[12] The popularization of visual arts through a visual language became perfectly clear in the introductory text to the first three critofilms funded by Olivetti (*Comunità millenarie*, *Cenacolo di Andrea del Castagno* and *Stile di Piero della Francesca*), a brief leaflet still preserved in

Ragghianti's archive, probably given as a handout before the screenings. To close the gap between art and popular culture, documentary films must be short and address the widest possible audience:

> Becoming aware of art, of this manifestation that is so important for the life of our spirit, does not only entail enriching and broadening our experience as civilized men. We are living in a century in which a truly great phenomenon is being unveiled everywhere: the aesthetic need, figurative art in particular, permeates every aspect of social and everyday life, from the household to the industrial sector, from urban planning and architecture to manufacturing and the most indispensable and common tools of practical life. [. . .] At present, film is without a doubt the most universal and immediate means of communication, a language that speaks to all with a more direct power of persuasion and no language barriers.[13]

Extensive documentation about the preparation of each critofilm preserved in the *Fondazione Centro Studi Carlo e Licia Ragghianti* in Lucca offers new insights into the complex mechanisms that lay behind the creation of each critofilm and reveals Ragghianti's interest in the experimental possibilities of cinema in visualizing art works. The documents include handwritten notes and comments on both paper and photographs. Illustrating the very origins and development of Ragghianti's ideas, these notes contain both words and images. The notes comprise descriptions of shooting plans, usually numbered and listed, first drafted in pen and then typewritten, along with camera movements and the soundtracks intended to accompany the footage. Rough sketches in pen or crayon provide vivid impressions of his meticulous method: they describe the way the camera had to move over the photographs or the original artworks, describing movements that follow the geometrical patterns emerging from the artwork itself. Having identified the patterns and forces within the shapes, Ragghianti then used the camera to highlight their trajectories, translating them into visual outlines to be projected onto a screen. These elements consisted of vectors, arrows, axes, and underlinings of the picture's structural elements (field lines, symmetry lines, geometrical shapes made of overlapping circles, squares, and isolated or intersecting rectangles coming together to form complex architectural graphics), which were often

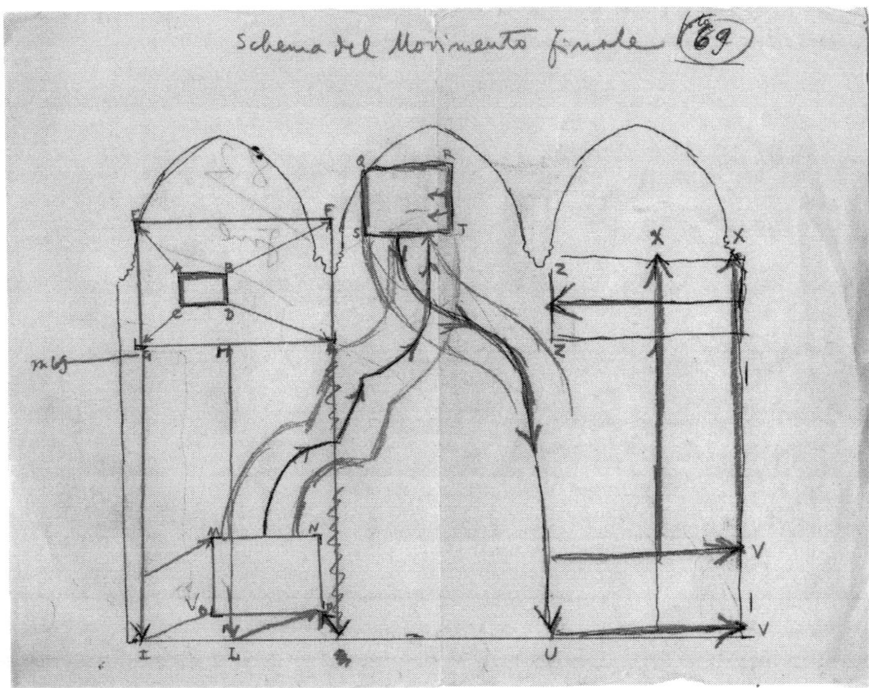

Figure 4.1 *C.L. Ragghianti. Sketch, Fondazione Centro Studi sull'Arte Licia e Carlo Ludovico Ragghianti, Lucca. Serie Critofilm.*

sketched on paper. In many cases they are clearly recognizable despite the hurried character of the scribbles.

Moreover, Ragghianti also carried out equally important work on the photographs he obtained from numerous museums around the world. Indeed, the use of the photographic medium as a point of departure and crucial supporting aid for these documentaries is striking. Like many art historians, Ragghianti left a very generous photographic archive featuring all kinds of images, from cuttings of mainstream magazines to copies of works purchased from professional reproduction photographers such as the firms of Anderson or Alinari. In so doing, Ragghianti's photographic archive contains fundamental evidence of the construction his critofilms. The majority of the artworks reproduced in Ragghianti's documentaries are, in fact, not original artworks but photographic reproductions over which the camera moves.[14] In countless cases, he drew graphic patterns directly onto photographs using a pen, tracing

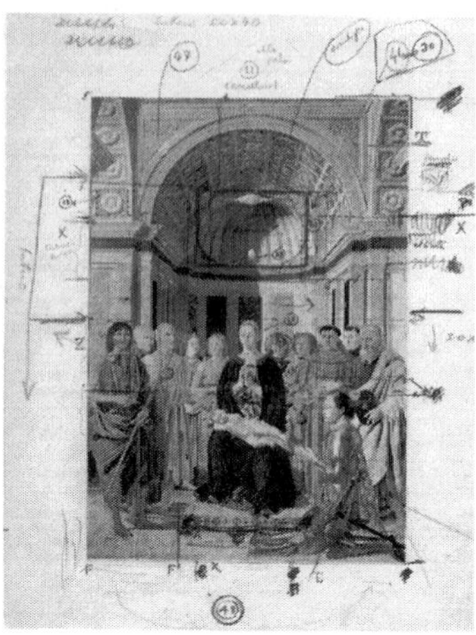

Figure 4.2 *C.L. Ragghianti. Visual and verbal notes on a photograph showing Piero della Francesca's* Pala di Brera, *Fondazione Centro Studi sull'Arte Licia e Carlo Ludovico Ragghianti, Lucca.*

continuous or dotted lines as well as vectors, arrows and three-dimensional solids, indicating his preliminary camera work.

In line with the paper sketches, the camera had to retrace the geometrical shapes drawn directly onto the picture. Furthermore, Ragghianti placed carefully cut clippings – many of which are, fortunately, still intact – directly onto the photographs, leaving the parts of the image that were to be shot uncovered.

He also applied this procedure to his critofilms addressing urban planning, where the drawing is constituted by the spatial capacity of the urban perimeter of cities such as Lucca and Venice, high viewpoints like spires and towers and the structure of a square (such as the Piazza dei Miracoli in Pisa), which Ragghianti traced from above. The drawing interacts with the written notes describing camera movements and soundtracks, and these two elements in turn intersect to give life to the documentary's task of telling a story through images. There are also diagrams on the maps indicating the movements the helicopter had to make while flying over historic city centres or the transparencies with geometrical constructions involved in planning *Michelangiolo* (1964).[15] This attempt to balance text, graphic sketches and images leads to the definitive preparatory documents, which were divided into two columns: a left column showing the critofilm's images described

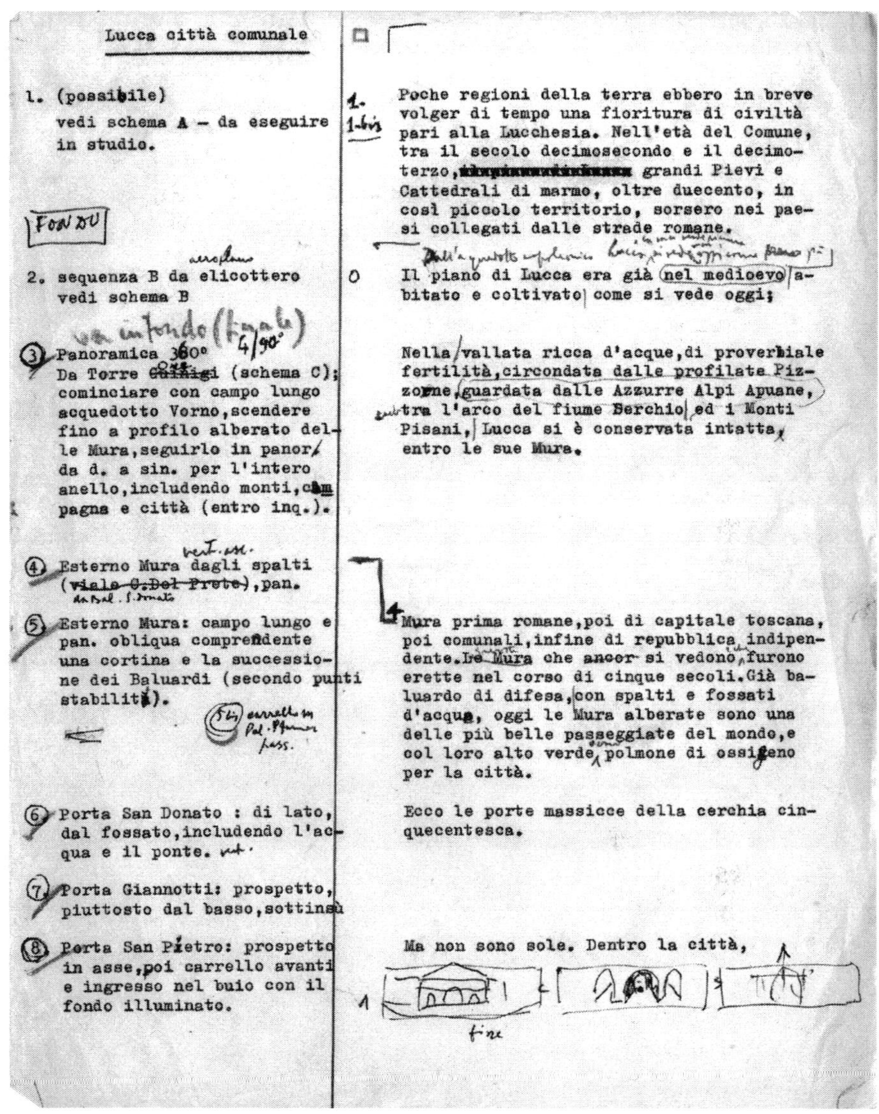

Figure 4.3 *C.L. Ragghianti. Draft scenario of the critofilm on Lucca città comunale, Fondazione Centro Studi sull'Arte Licia e Carlo Ludovico Ragghianti, Lucca.*

in words and a right one displaying the verbal comments that were to accompany these images.

The last critofilm, dedicated to Michelangelo on the occasion of the 400th anniversary of his death, was definitely the most elaborate and enjoyed great success, both nationally and internationally.[16]

When Ragghianti stopped producing critofilms in the mid-1960s, he began to experiment with computer technology, an encounter said to have taken place at the Euratom Centre at Ispra in 1968. There is no evidence of any direct relationship between Olivetti, critofilm producer and head of one of the leading companies in the field of computer manufacturing in Europe at the time, and Ragghianti's interest in information technologies. What is certain is that his research developed further by using the plotter instead of the movie camera. Only four years had passed between the last critofilm and the first experiments of Ragghianti with the computer. This fruitful relationship led to the creation of the specialized centre APAVOCA (Arts Processes and Visual Objects Computer Analysis) at the International University of Art in Florence (UIA), funded by Ragghianti in 1968, as well as the establishment of the periodical *Sound/Sonda* (1978–80), which presented the results of research by Ragghianti and some of his fellow students (Zanobini, Testi Cristiani and Bruno).[17]

However, Ragghianti's shift towards information technology was actually very gradual and, at least at the beginning, quite reluctant. As early as 1964, in an essay in *Critica d'Arte*, Ragghianti openly opposed the idea that machines might be able to express aesthetic judgement. This essay drew ironically on the title of an article about comprehending art through artificial intelligence by Silvio Ceccato, a philosopher expert on artificial intelligence, founder of the Centro di Cibernetica e di Attività Linguistiche at the University of Milan, and published in *Il Giorno*. His critique targeted the experiments carried out by the Politecnico di Milano (Institute of Scientific Cinematography), strictly related to Ceccato's research. Ceccato and his research group went through one of the first computer analyses of an art object, specifically an image of horn-blowing angels from the monastery of San Pablo de Casserras, now kept in the Diocesan Museum of Solsona.

According to Ragghianti, the weakest aspect of this attempt, which can be considered one of the first true experiments in reading an artwork with a computer in Italy, was the proposed double interpretation that re-traced the trajectory of the eye along two different paths, which the research group of the Centro di Cibernetica in Milan called 'chronicle observation' ('a cronaca', i.e. more detailed) and 'aesthetic observation' ('estetica', i.e. eye movements free to run along the artworks). On the contrary, in his own critofilms, Ragghianti was

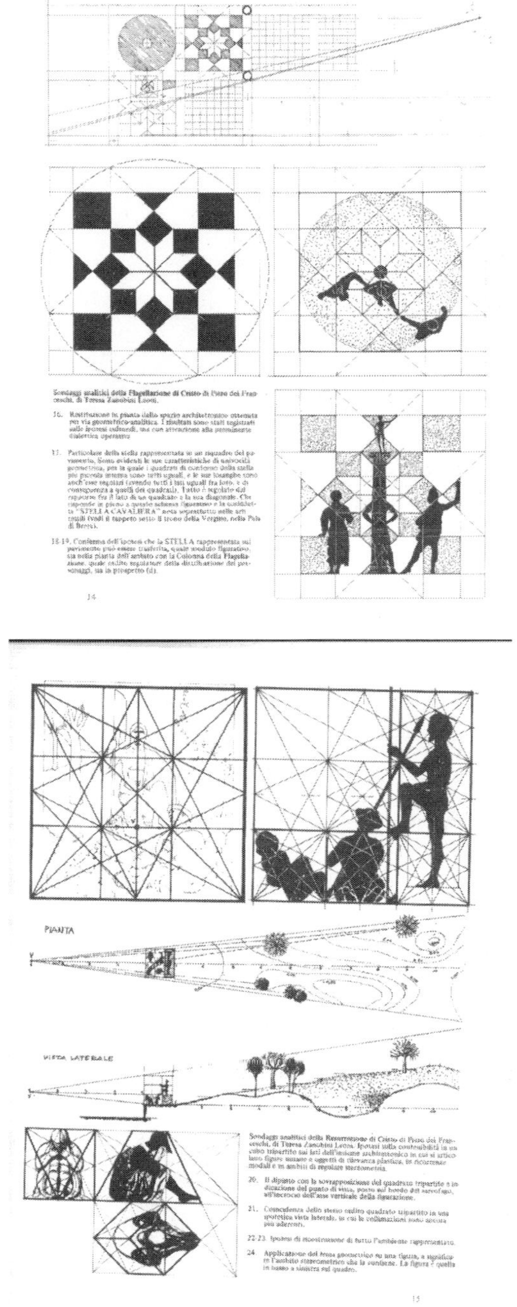

Figure 4.4　*Plotter experiments on Piero della Francesca paintings, in* Sound/Sonda, *1, 1978.*

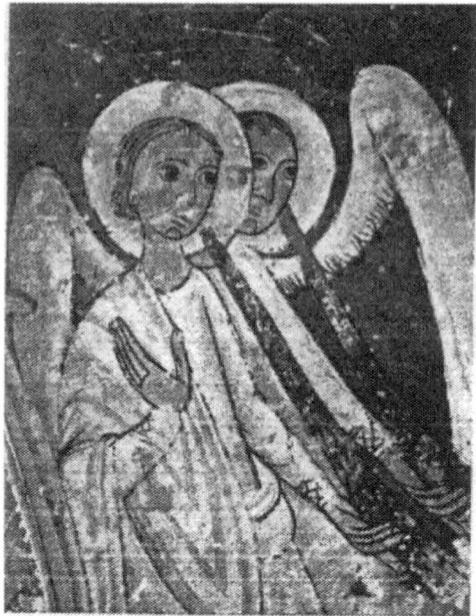

Figure 4.5 Angels with musical instruments *(from San Pablo di Casseras), Museo Diocesano y Comarcal de Solsona.*

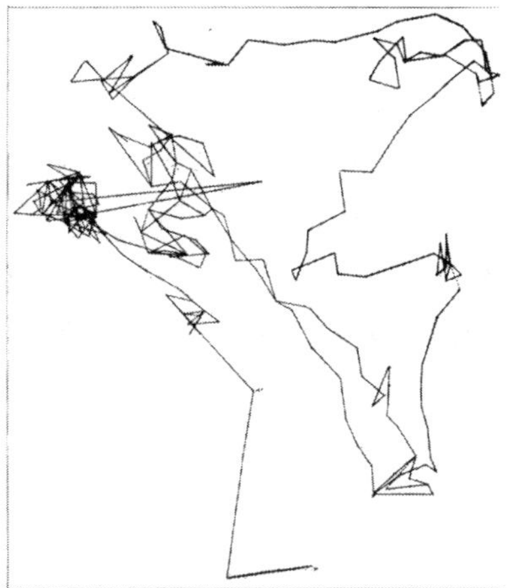

Figure 4.6 Chronicle reading on the angels with musical instruments *from San Pablo di Casseras (an experiment led by Silvio Ceccato, Milan).*

trying to prove that it is the artwork itself that guides the eye of the observers over it, and that the duty of art historians, as experts in the field of visual arts, is to recreate the intimate images using camera movements. Thus, there is only one possible way of seeing an image correctly.

However, Ragghianti did not reject the idea that a machine might be able to carry out an analytical reading of formal languages or visual processes (still associated with human capacities). But this would be possible only if the machine in question applied a 'capacity to see, a linguistics, aesthetics and method that was more mature and modern', and which certainly did not use beauty as the selection criterion. In Ragghianti's opinion, this machine 'capable, obviously if operated properly, of conducting a fitting visual interpretation of visual or figurative processes' already existed: 'it is the film camera'.[18]

The situation changed quickly with the development of the plotter, digital printers able to translate the output of data into a graphic form. Through a 1968 article on the possible applications of the plotter by engineer Roberto Favero, published in *La Stampa*, Ragghianti once again came into direct contact with the computer. In the same year, he visited the above-mentioned Euratom Centre in Ispra, which also included a computer graphic information centre. It is also worth noting, emphasizing the cyclical character of this engagement, that in this period it was Bruno Munari who showed Ragghianti the hypercube rotating in space, a computer program written by Michael Noll, one of the pioneers of computer technologies applied to the visual arts.[19] It did not take Ragghianti too long to begin testing ways to use this new tool to interpret works of art. Indeed, his first attempts were inspired by geometric forms, such as a projection of the well from Piero della Francesca's *De Prospectiva pingendi*, an arch by Serlio and Dürer's *machina humana*. It is not

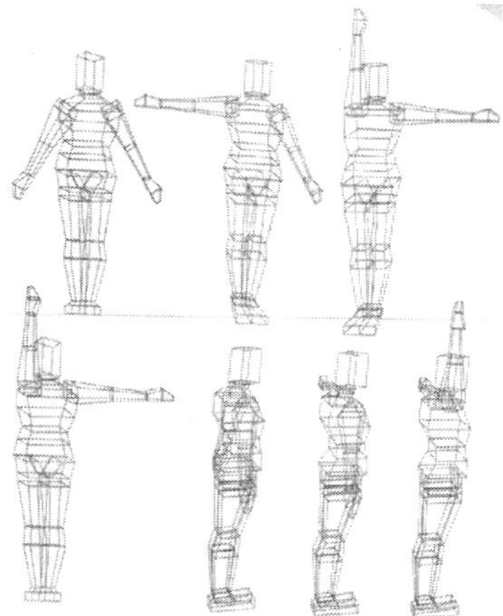

Figure 4.7 *Plotter experiments on Dürer's* Machina Humana, *in* Sound/Sonda, *1978.*

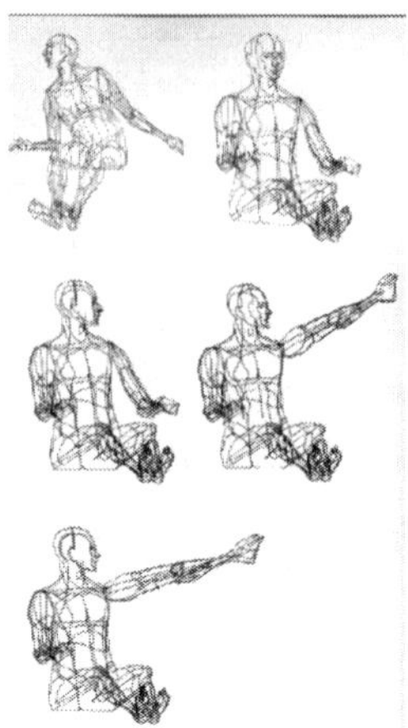

Figure 4.8 *Ford graphic design on passengers, from* Cybernetic Serendipity, *catalogue of the exhibition, London 1968.*

a coincidence that, in the same period, two major industries such as Ford and Boeing were carrying out graphic representation of experiments of a body rotating in space whose visual results were quite similar to Dürer's *machina humana*.

Even though these experiments belonged to a completely different context and were created with quite different objectives, the resulting visual renderings, and the idea of using information technologies to let drawings rotate in space, are remarkably similar.

According to Ragghianti's interpretative lens, works of art, especially ones with 'imaginary' depth such as paintings, can be considered 'upside-down orographies', from the foreground to the background.

This is even possible when there is no perspective or when differences in depth, according to the ideal or constructible stratigraphy of paintings are rendered through optical or numerical references. Ragghianti referred to it as an 'artisan' interpretation of artwork. The computer thus becomes a tool capable of providing us with an objective analytical survey that is scientifically verifiable, thereby delving into the compositional structure of the artwork. This IT experimentation was based on two specific foundations: the first was cultural, inherent in the philosophical premises of this technological application, and the second technical. Norbert Wiener's studies in cybernetics

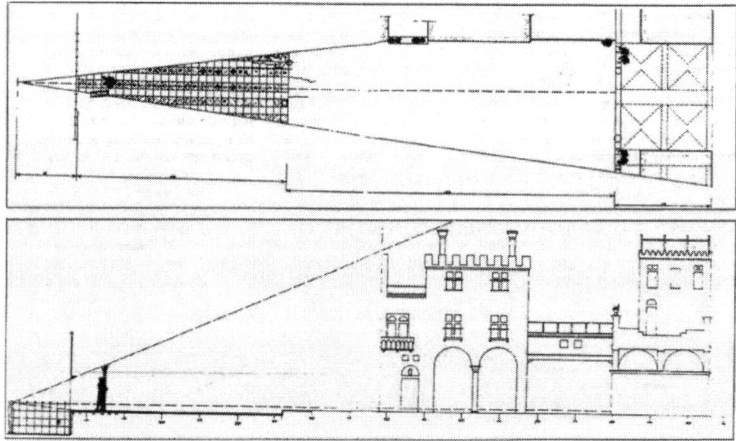

Figure 4.9 *Plotter experiments on Antonello da Messina's* Saint Sebastian, *in* Sound/Sonda, *1978.*

addressed this former aspect: as a matter of fact, Ragghianti dedicated several publications to cybernetics and clearly understood the possible applications of this science.[20] His familiarity with cybernetics probably dates from the early 1950s when Wiener's works were first published in Italian. However, in a 1978 article, Ragghianti once again engaged with Wiener's work at exactly the same moment that he once again became interested in applying information technology to works of figurative art.[21]

Analysing the methodological premises for reading artworks, Ragghianti highlighted the close relationship between critofilm and computers, almost as if the one naturally followed the other. What plotters and IT machines are able to accomplish is exactly what was being asked of the film camera. While Bell Laboratories in New Jersey attempted to program a machine able to decode artworks as tools of communication, Ragghianti sought rather to exploit the potential of the computer as a sophisticated viewing device to explore works of art. These experiments primarily generated graphics, geometric structures and virtual reconstructions of the spaces inside works of art.

It was precisely the computer's ability to delve into the space of an artwork that was recognized as an entirely innovative step compared to film. In Ragghianti's view, this was different from cinema by virtue of the fact that, while the camera lens is only able to move on the surface or what we might call the epidermis of the image, thus establishing a two-dimensional relationship with the image, the computer is able to probe into the work of art, reconstructing its interior spaces. In so doing, the computer provided a range of additional information about the artist's creative process. The plotter, a 'planimetric-volumetric sensor and tracer, that is, a tool for transforming two-dimensionality into three-dimensionality', thus entered the 'universe of the artwork'. Ragghianti compared the plotter to an 'explorer' travelling through the planetary system and recording the dimensions and distances of celestial bodies.[22] The drawings produced by the plotter displayed a striking similarity to the purely visual analysis he had carried out by hand and recorded in the notebooks. This use of the computer remained closely linked with the use of the camera lens on artworks, although the move to enter into the space of paintings can be considered the forerunner of 3D analysis of cultural heritage. In a sense, Ragghianti's visual ideas and methodology were cinematic even if the relevance of these primary efforts in applying information technology to artworks remains a major landmark in history of art criticism and film studies.

Notes

1 Tiziana Tommei, *Ut pictura pellicola: dissolvenze incrociate. Ragghianti, cinema e arti figurative* (Lucca: Fondazione Ragghianti, 2014); Marco Scotini (ed.), *Ragghianti e il carattere cinematografico della visione* (Milan: Charta, 2000). Information concerning the history of each critofilm can be found in Valentina La Salvia (ed.), *I critofilm di Carlo L. Ragghianti. Tutte le sceneggiature* (Lucca: Fondazione Ragghianti, 2006). See also the bibliography in Andrea Costa (ed.), *Carlo L. Ragghianti, I critofilm d'arte* (Udine: Campanotto, 1995).

2 Carlo Ludovico Ragghianti, 'La Deposizione borghesiana di Raffaello', *Critica d'Arte* 157–9 (1978): 152–61 (first published in 1947). See also Ragghianti's introduction to *La Deposizione di Raffaello Sanzio* (Milan: Bompiani, 1957), a volume containing full-scale representations of the painting's details. See also Carlo Ludovico Ragghianti, *Lorenzo il Magnifico e le arti* (Florence: Studio Italiano di Storia dell'Arte, 1949).

3 Lionello Venturi, 'I documenti d'arte in Italia', in *Le Film sur l'art* (Brussels: Unknown, 1950). Venturi emphasizes that many documentaries made before 1943 were produced by the *Istituto Luce* and focused on Italy's beautiful works of art. From 1940 onwards, Luciano Emmer and Enrico Gras transformed 'tourist' documentaries into art documentaries. See also Lionello Venturi, 'Le Film sur l'art en Italie depuis le premier congrès du film sur l'art', *Les Films sur l'Art* (Brussels: Unknown, 1950), 1. For a

discussion of the Italian context, see also *Rassegna nazionale del film documentario. Catalogo* (published at the occasion of a festival held in Vicenza, 14–18 September 1953); in particular see G. Carancini, *Breve storia del nostro documentario*, 9–15. On Longhi, see A. Uccelli, 'Due film, la filologia e un cane. Sui documentari di Umberto Barbaro e Roberto Longhi', *Prospettiva* 129 (2008): 2–40; Tommaso Casini, 'Critica d'arte e film sull'arte: una convergenza difficile', *Annali di Critica d'Arte* 1 (2005): 431–57. See also *Longhi, Ragghianti e il documentario d'arte* (http://storiedellarte. com/2013/03/longhi-ragghianti-e-il-documentario-darte.html).

4   Carlo Ludovico Ragghianti, *Cinema arte figurativa* (Turin: Einaudi, 1952); Valentina La Salvia, 'L'esercizio della cultura come responsabilità sociale: Ragghianti e lo strumento televisivo', in Emanuele Pellegrini (ed.), *Studi su Carlo Ludovico Ragghianti* (Ghezzano: Felici Editore, 2010), 245–60.

5   Archivio Fondazione Ragghianti di Lucca (hereafter AFRL), Serie Critofilm, faldone 1, letter written by President Tancredo Tancredi to Ragghianti (8 August 1948).

6   AFRL, Serie Critofilm, faldone 1, letter written by Ragghianti to Giulio Mandoli, President of the Ente prov. Turismo of Lucca (7 September 1948). Regarding the debate on Lucca's historic centre, see Monica Naldi and Emanuele Pellegrini (eds), *Carlo Ludovico Ragghianti. Il valore del patrimonio culturale. Scritti dal 1935 al 1987* (Ghezzano: Felici Editore, 2010), 129–30, 138–41.

7   On Ragghianti's method see in particular Carlo Ludovico Ragghianti, *L'arte e la critica* (Florence: Vallecchi, 1980); Carlo Ludovico Ragghianti, *La critica della forma* (Florence: Baglioni & Berner, 1986). For a general overview see also: Maria Teresa Filieri (ed.), *Carlo Ludovico Ragghianti. Pensiero e azione* (Lucca: Fondazione Ragghianti, 2010); Emanuele Pellegrini (ed.), *Studi su Carlo Ludovico Ragghianti* (Ghezzano: Felici Editore, 2010).

8   Ragghianti, 'La Deposizione', 161.

9   AFRL, Serie Critofilm, faldone 1: this folder also contains all the documents related to the film framings, editing and text. An article in the press understood this critical need: N.,V., 'L'opera d'arte spiegata dal cinematografo', *La Nazione italiana* (21 October 1948), 3.

10 AFRL, Critofilm. Studio italiano di storia dell'arte – Ufficio cinematografico (1947–51). This folder is full of practical information, regarding, for example, costs and promotional methods. The archival documentation about Ragghianti's critofilms consists of eight folders. In 1949, *Raffaello* was screened together with the film *La Città Magica* (*Magic Town*) by William A. Wellman (1947); *Lorenzo il Magnifico* received first prize at the Biennale d'Arte Cinematografica of Venice in 1949. In 1951, the critofilm *Lorenzo il Magnifico* still existed and was conserved in the Studio Italiano of Florence. In a letter dated 30 September 1949, Ragghianti requested the Biennale of Venice to sponsor a festival dedicated to art documentaries to be held in Florence: a letter by Luigi Chiarini (dated 5 October 1949) mentions the preparation of a 'Settimana del Film documentario d'arte' (AFRL, Critofilm. Studio italiano di storia dell'arte – Ufficio cinematografico (1947–51)). Venice hosted the same art documentary festival the following year.

11 All these aspects are documented in *seleArte*; see *seleArte* 20 (1955) for an account of
the second Film and Arts International Congress and the constitution of the Istituto
internazionale del film sull'arte, whose executive committee included Paul Haesaerts,
Réné Jullian, Carl Lamb, Theodore Bowie, Mario Verdone and Ragghianti as president.
Beginning in issue 21 of 1955, *seleArte* started a new column called 'Selezione del film
sull'arte', edited by François N. Bolen, author of an art film repertoire commissioned by
UNESCO.

12 Ragghianti himself put *seleArte* and the critofilms on the same footing. See Carlo
Ludovico Ragghianti, 'Informazione sul critofilm d'arte', *seleArte* 23 (1956): 1–6. As
Ragghianti writes, critofilms 'separate artwork from the normality of static and fixed
observation (and even more so from the perception of figural matter), repositioning it
along its true path'. Furthermore, 'every effect or variation of the shooting, editing and
production (intersections, overlappings, cross-fades etc.) are strictly dependent from its
critical goal, as they cinematographically express the analysis of the artwork's inner
structure and inner dynamics' (4). See Maria Adriana Giusti, 'Autre chose que le
massacre du paysage. Costruzione e ambiente nella visione di Le Corbusier, Olivetti,
Ragghianti', in Susanna Caccia, Maria Grazia Eccheli, Mecca Saverio and Emanuele
Pellegrini, *Ragghianti e Le Corbusier. Architettura, disegno, immagine* (Florence: DIDA,
2015), 163–83; and Silvia Bottinelli, *seleArte (1952–1966) una finestra sul mondo.*
Ragghianti, Olivetti e la divulgazione dell'arte internazionale all'indomani del Fascismo
(Lucca: Fandazione Ragghianti, 2010).

13 AFRL, Serie critofilm, faldone 2, fasc. 4. For a discussion of cultural popularization,
see Silvia Bottinelli, 'Carlo Ludovico Ragghianti e il concetto di divulgazione della
cultura storico-artistica', in Pellegrini (ed.), *Studi su Carlo Ludovico Ragghianti*,
231–43.

14 AFRL, Serie Critofilm, Faldone n. 7, Carteggio Mortara A. Romor Film (1943–85);
AFRL, Serie Critofilm, faldone n. 8, carteggio (1954–75), 8.

15 See AFRL, faldone 2 and 3, the monographic folder concerning the work material of
each critofilm (for the city of Lucca see faldone 3, fasc. 1); for the *Michelangiolo* see
AFRL, Serie Critofilm, faldone 5, fasc. 1. There are also notebooks, not bearing
Ragghianti's handwriting, including descriptions of the framings through words and
images (for the case of the city of Pisa see faldone 3, fasc. 3; or Rosai, Faldone 4, fasc. 1).
For the work on the city maps see, in particular, *Terre alte di Toscana* – winner of the
prize at the 'IV Bergamo Internazionale del Film d'Arte', under the category of 'film on
architecture', where many documents can be found (AFRL, Serie Critofilm, faldone 4,
fascicolo 4), see also *Canal Grande* (AFRL, Serie Critofilm, faldone 4, fasc. 4).

16 AFRL, Serie Critofilm, faldone 6. This critofilm, directed by Marco Chiarini, was
successfully shown in Italy and abroad, starting from the Festival in Venice in 1964. In
a letter (22 April 1966) to Ragghianti, Dorothy Macpherson from the *Centre canadien
du film sur l'art* described the great success of the screening of the *Michelangiolo* in
Ottawa: 'more than three thousand people were turned away': FRL, Serie Critofilm,
faldone 6, fasc. 4.

17 Elisa Bassetto, 'Sound Sonda. Carlo Ludovico Ragghianti e gli esordi dell'approccio informatico all'analisi dell'opera d'arte', *Luk* 22 (2016): 60–3; Carlo Ludovico Ragghianti, 'Capire l'arte col computer', *Critica d'Arte* 160–2 (1978): 3–13.

18 Carlo Ludovico Ragghianti, 'Professore, me la fa questa macchinetta?' *Critica d'Arte* 67–8 (1964): 3–8. All the articles written by Silvio Ceccato, one of the first Italian philosophers interested in cybernetic and its application to the Humanities, were collected in Silvio Ceccato, *Cibernetica per tutti* (Milano: Feltrinelli, 1968).

19 Michael Noll, 'Human or Machine: A Subjective Comparison of Piet Mondrian's *Composition with Lines* (1917) and a Computer-Generated Picture', *The Psychological Record* 16 (1966): 1–16; Michael Noll, 'The Beginnings of Computer Art in the United States: A Memoir', *Leonardo* 1 (1994): 39–44; Jon Gertner, *The Idea Factory: Bell Labs and the Great Age of American Innovation* (New York: Penguin, 2012).

20 Carlo Ludovico Ragghianti, *Norbert Wiener: i principi della cibernetica*, in *Arti della visione. Il linguaggio visivo* (Turin: Einaudi, 1979), 83–102; Carlo Ludovico Ragghianti, 'Lettura cibernetica delle opere d'arte', in *Arti della visione. Il linguaggio visivo* (Turin: Einaudi, 1979), 287–94.

21 Michael J. Apter, 'Cybernetics and art', *Leonardo* 3 (1969): 257; Norbert Wiener, 'Cybernetics', *Bulletin of The American Academy of Arts and Sciences* 7 (1950): 2–4.

22 Ragghianti, 'Capire l'arte', 10–11; Cristiani Testi, Maria Laura, 'Carlo Ludovico Ragghianti: umanesimo e informatica', in Raffaele Bruno (ed.), *Ragghianti critico e politico* (Milan: Franco Angeli, 2004), 182–91.

5

André Bazin's art documentary in Saintonge

ANGELA DALLE VACCHE

French film critic André Bazin (1918–58) reviewed many art documentaries before embarking on his own production in this genre. Bazin's very first essay, 'The Ontology of the Photographic Image' in *What is Cinema?* and his very last, 'Les églises romanes de Saintonge' (1958) deal with his preference for the Romanesque style over Renaissance perspective.[1] In his critical biography of Bazin, Dudley Andrew clarifies why Bazin's Saintonge essay proposes a film-making project which was financed and researched, but never fulfilled due to the critic's death:

> Early in 1957, after some conversations with Pierre Braunberger, the man who produced so many of the New Wave's first efforts, Bazin contracted to make a short documentary on the Romanesque churches of the Saintonge district in France, the area in which he had grown up.[2]

Between 1957 and 1958, Bazin knew that he did not have much time to live or much energy to work with. He was aware that every single day made a difference. This intimation of death might explain his renewed interest in the Saintonge region of his youth. After all, his engagement with this topic and location date back to when he studied in La Rochelle and possibly rode a bicycle in his free time, exploring the nearby countryside. Furthermore, the unexpected decision to become a filmmaker suggests that he was eager to experience the cinema in front of as well as behind the camera before dying. Of course, Bazin knew very well that the ancient stones of Saintonge make visible the destructive passage of time and the persistence of human emotions. Most importantly, this project offered Bazin the opportunity to summarize for his readers the major coordinates of his film theory. Thus, his essay on Saintonge is like an intellectual testament, written in the form of a preliminary treatment or scenario.

Notwithstanding the proximity of the Saintonge region to La Rochelle, Bazin's attachment to the Romanesque architecture may look suspicious to some readers unfamiliar with his work. As Sarah Wilson explains:

> The Romanesque and medievalist revival of the late 30s was accentuated during the occupation of France, and was not, of course, unrelated to the general return to artisanal and pre-industrial values that were being promoted under Vichy.[3]

In regard to this reactionary movement back to the 'blood-and-soil' of the Middle Ages, Bazin's political record is crystal clear: in his critical biography, Dudley Andrew mentions that the young critic constantly avoided Catholic collaborators.[4] Besides staying away from all political affiliations, Bazin shunned intellectual elites and upper-class circles. After all, realism and narrative are as essential as the gospels for the illiterate poor. Given this perspective, it is worth mentioning that Bazin's foray into religious art had nothing to do with the *Art Sacré* movement centred around Père Marie-Alain Couturier (1897–1954), who sponsored works by Henri Matisse and Fernand Léger in the immediate post-war period.

Bazin wanted his Saintonge documentary to celebrate contemporary life over the vestiges of the past, focusing on the daily life around the abandoned ruins in a ready-made mise-en-scène. Eager to reach a new and larger audience beyond the written page, Bazin focused on an ethnography of spontaneous vitality. His ideal plan was to shoot the film in the spring, after the pruning of the linden trees which typically grow on the roads to these churches. This timing was already a gesture in favour of new life, the present and the future, since more 'art historical' photographs of this site were usually taken in the winter. At that time, the trees are so barren that artistic detail is easier to grasp from a distance, and in context with the rest of the architecture.

Despite the fact that Bazin engaged in all the preparatory art-historical research necessary for this documentary, art history was not his major focus. Besides preferring spring over winter, he avoided the specialized architectural and sculptural language which Henri Focillon (1881–1943) expected from one of his Yale students in a thesis on Saintonge.[5] As usual, Bazin's prose was fluid and precise, but, most of all, brimming with details from daily life woven with the rural dimension of the location.

The Saintonge region became geographically important during the eleventh and twelfth centuries, because this period saw the development of a pilgrimage route to Santiago de Compostela in Spain, passing through the town of Saintes. Despite the common association of medievalism with mysticism, an attentive reading of Bazin's Saintonge essay discloses that his orientation was more existentially spiritual than traditionally Catholic or institutionally religious. Although he wrote in a lyrical way, Bazin was no mystic.

Despite the Middle Ages' reputation for darkness, fear of suffering in the flames of Hell, and belief in a punitive God, Bazin points out that Saintonge's terrifying bestiary comes up against a deeply-rooted rural wisdom based on serenity and moderation.[6] Bazin's approach was more anthropological and meteorological than theological or political. Far away from powerful castles and wealthy towns, Saintonge's little churches sit in a fabric of farms, cemeteries, open land and small villages. Their presence is barely noticeable, while their modest size makes them look like barns turned into pilgrims' shelters or roadside reliquaries. The ambition behind Bazin's film was to document an anti-conformist and down-to-earth kind of spirituality. He cared to show how the human element is only one among many aspects of life in motion. The film's anti-anthropocentric protagonists are the wind and motion itself, embodied in the symbiotic encounter between wild vegetation and worn-out stones that is provoked by the weather.

Through this project, Bazin returned to a place whose century-old weathering he could transfigure into 'the charm of the stones'.[7] Still, he avoided all nostalgic and picturesque temptations. The Saintonge region charmed Bazin so much that he wanted his camera's lens to soften the white stones and move like a caress over the 'white gown of the churches'. Innumerable microscopic churches punctuate the countryside. Their overall effect is comparable to a blanket of white pebbles spread across the land. It is as if Bazin were planning an aerial view. The exceptional frequency and humbleness of these churches strike a note of contrast with more famous places of worship in the Burgundy area or with the important centres of Poitiers and Angoulême.[8] In these much bigger towns, the Romanesque churches have a triangulated space on top of the central entrance with enough room for a causal narrative with climax, dénouement and resolution.

By contrast, in Saintonge, small façades cannot sustain such an imposing threshold. Without an architectural tympanum, they limit themselves to a few series of sculptures. At the same time, these churches – often as large as a private chapel – retain the round shape of the Roman arch. Characterized by curvy domes outside, with low ceilings and billowy naves inside, the typical little Saintonge church looks young and feminine. By contrast, the thickness of its interior walls strikes a note of contrast with the harrowing decay of its heavily punctured stones, devoured by sea salt.

In mixing sacred and profane elements, the sinuous sculptures of Saintonge feature not only acrobats, musicians, comedians, craftsmen, farmers, centaurs, sirens, virgins, madmen, fools and kings, but also Adam and Eve, Samson and Delilah, Cain and Abel. In a word, just as Bazin spelled out the social mythologies of different filmic genres in his film theory, Saintonge's art relied on a religious and mythological, vernacular and fantastic potpourri. Saintonge's sculpture freely drew from famous characters and stereotypes of human behaviour, by reinventing old and well-known Biblical tales.

The sculptors in charge of decorating these churches became the equivalent of oral storytellers wandering from village to village. The decorations resemble a pre-Darwinian disorderly picture catalogue, the plant, the beast and the human intertwine their extremities in a chain of mutual support, but also of constant fear and destabilization. The anthropocentric humanism of the Renaissance was still far away into the future. In Saintonge, all living creatures need each other, while different species constantly battle with one another. Altogether, interdependence, competition, mixed breeding and supernatural occurrences explain why the farm animal can morph into a dragon with sharp teeth, or a peasant can drop his plough and take St Peter's keys to Paradise. Mouths spew out flames and birds acquire fishlike fins. Any modern understanding of science is still impossible, since magic and alchemy cultivate the bizarre, the occult, the monstrous and the hybrid.

Unravelling like a comic strip, these sculptural reliefs bear witness to a humankind adrift in superstition. The world of Saintonge is so ancient and steeped with magic and so strangely modern due to its sensorial overload that it becomes a roller coaster of tears and laughs, cruelty and rebellion, blissful joy and horror. These sculptures are based on metamorphosis, while their serial unleashing of miracles and catastrophes invokes early medieval chronicles called 'annals'. In these texts, each event is uncontrollable and, therefore, absolutely equal in importance to every other; the frequency of horny angels and winged devils reminds the viewer that contingency and witchcraft rule; medieval chronology is nothing but a flat list without any causality.

Just as neorealist cinema privileged a quasi-documentary approach to daily life, likewise the sculptures of Saintonge specialized in the chores, skills, objects and tools of nearby farms, cemeteries, hostels, artisanal spaces and merchants' shops.[9] At the same time, these sculptures chronicled the drinking, burials, lust, music, feasting and dancing of the nearby inhabitants. By choosing the Saintonge area over other locations, Bazin privileged local activities over the picturesque and the monumental:

> The sculptor of Saintonge rejects grand dramatic subjects. He's an observer of daily life, treating sacred themes and profane life with the same realism. This is undoubtedly true of all Romanesque sculpture, but perhaps nowhere other than in Saintonge has the artist restricted himself to that zone of familiarity, far removed from the great terrors and the grand mystical symbolisms that enliven so many Romanesque capitals and tympanums. It could be said that a sort of rural wisdom, combined with serenity and moderation, emerges from Saintonge, in harmony with its history and its landscape, and has humanized and tempered the medieval religious soul here.[10]

The characters of this elementary mise-en-scène smile, cry, scream and frown with their protruding eyes, teethed or beaked mouths, triangulated faces and round bellies. Hats and shoes tell stories dealing with profession, trade, poverty and wealth. These sculptures are filled with missing limbs, eroded cheeks, wild beards. The typical and initially white Saintongese stone is malleable as well as friable. These sculpted figures on their way to abstraction look like photographic negatives in a state of progressive decomposition. In both sculpture and photography, time is allegedly frozen when everything remains indoors. However, due to their constant outdoor exposure, these chains of polymorphous beings slowly disappear into nooks and crannies. The stones crumble into dust. In a similar way, when photographic glass plates spend too much time in the sun, their transparent skin-like images peel off and shrivel into waste.

In contrast to the fully three-dimensional Gothic style, so seriously devoted to transcendence, apocalypse and punishment, Bazin praised the curvy, Romanesque placidity. Boredom is not an issue in these isolated dwellings: any accidental visitor can look at a church façade and experience amusement in front of tongues sticking out, leaping shapes and grotesque couplings. In these cases, the realist component is minimal, but the expressive power is at a maximum.

By referring to a specific cultural group discussed by art historian Paul (le chanoine) Tonnelier (1886–1977), called *Combat des Vertus et des Vices*, Bazin lingered on how wavy folds of dress sit on top of flat arms and legs.[11] Strange flowers and leaves interrupt the animal menagerie typical of the Romanesque style. Fancy peacocks, ominous bats and repulsive lizards run around portals and down little columns. Without Renaissance perspective to establish hierarchy inside an imaginary, mathematical space, any figure can become independent and float into abstraction, as if a spiritual *élan* or an inspirational encounter were a banal matter of fact.

Openly didactic rather than deceptively illusionistic, within the Romanesque style each emotional state is experienced as if for the first time. Horror, joy, pain, fear pierce every stone with an abstract intensity of motive and sincerity of expression. Instead of triggering superficiality and condescension, the local sculptors' naïve skills guaranteed depth and seriousness.

While the passions stored in these sculptures may seem to challenge photography's indifferent automatism, Saintonge's church façades can become comparable to a cinematic screen. All around these little churches, a multiplicity of forces takes over: scorching sun, frantic downpours of rain, blizzards of snow, and thick layers of fog or mist. No matter the season, a special breed of

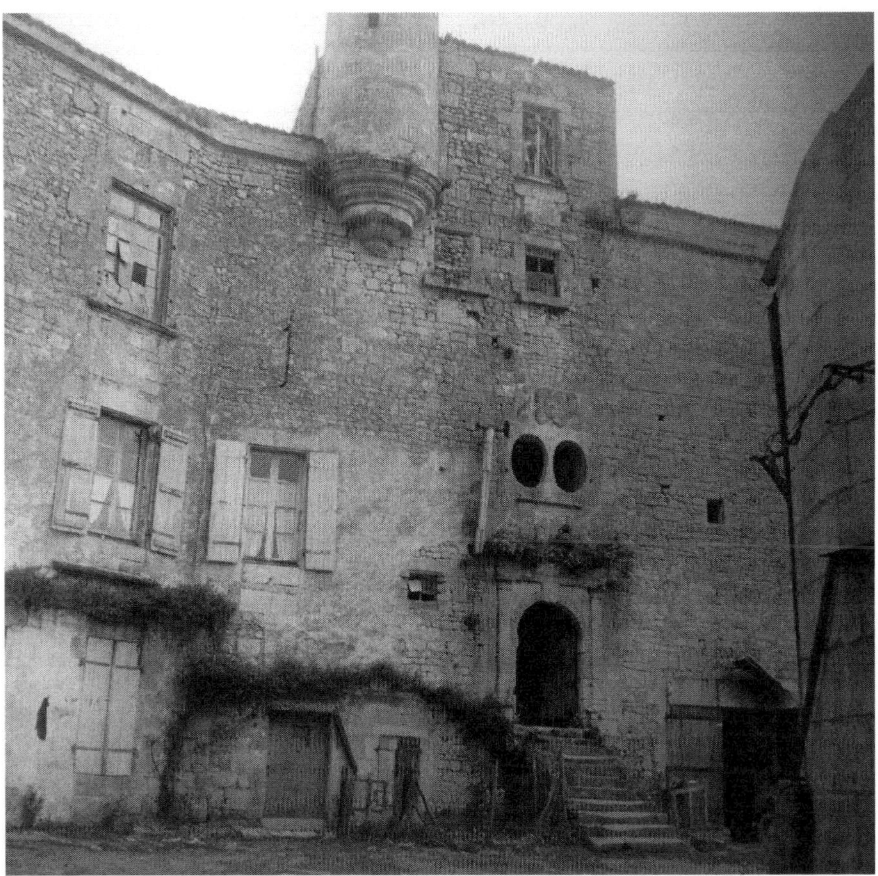

Figure 5.1 *André Bazin. Photograph taken in the Saintonge region. Courtesy of Dudley Andrew.*

wild and tenacious grass, Bazin's lowest and most stubborn level of botany, behaves like a moving image:

> Asleep for centuries in the villages, but not dead, they have become a part of and absorbed by the life and the vegetation around them. Many of the churches have been invaded by the greenery – even penetrated by it, like the chapel at Saint Ouen whose stones are held in place only by the roots of ivy and new vines.[12]

In a state of semi-abandonment and quasi-anonymity that protects them from ill-advised contemporary restorations, the churches surrender themselves to a new form of random or experimental architecture.

The famous French, nineteenth-century architect Eugène Viollet-le-Duc (1814–79) would scorn any assignment in the region of Saintonge. In front of the unruly greenery running all over the walls inside and outside, Viollet-le-Duc would enforce a drastic cleaning. No weeds would interfere with his preservationist aesthetics. In the Saintonge region, villages are too ordinary and unadorned to justify landscape design and architectural restoration at any level. Within this general state of calm disarray, seeds and spores can find cracks in the stones. Thus, they begin a new level of vegetative life in systematic defiance of time and weather.

Bazin called all this wild grass '*l'herbe folle de l'espérance*' (the wild grass of hope).[13] Unexpectedly, the monopoly on narrative action reverses itself from sculpture to weeds, sprouts and roots. The emphasis switches from art to nature. Nothing could be more photographic in method, since, in his famous 'Ontology' essay, Bazin declared that nature through light becomes an artist.[14] Similarly, Bergson's erratic and discontinuous *élan vital*, along with Bazin's preference for contingency over coincidence, are the undisturbed rulers of Saintonge.

Usually associated with stillness, plants evoke origins, grounding, passivity and lack of action unless water, air, wind and fire take over and make the vegetation move. Here, this rule does not apply. All by itself, wild grass travels as fast as burning fire or flowing water. In addition, the sounds and cries of farm animals may disturb the search for a museum-like sterile setting. The most timid flowers, such as daisies, lavender and dandelions, have just enough colour to look rebellious by sticking out of a few grey tombstones. Occasionally, a tabernacle with a few votive candle stubs replaces a traffic sign.

Animals may dominate Saintonge's sculptures, but botany looms large due to Bazin's appreciation of contingency. The co-dependence of architecture and vegetation strikes Bazin, because the relentless spreading of wild grass amidst the stones keeps these buildings' physiognomies constantly changing and lifelike. Although Bazin is adamant that his film would underline how these churches integrate themselves into the local human geography of farms and cemeteries, he does not stop there. He is so keen on movement, randomness and change that he describes how the very profane local poultry takes over a sacred space reserved only to saints inside the abbey of Trizay, where the chickens nest in the niches of saints, where the multi-lobed arches are covered with wire netting to serve as chicken coops, where wood is stored in the magnificent little apses as if next to the oven, where the chapter house has become a hay barn. Meanwhile, from one column to another the green beans are drying on wires.[15]

In this universe of domestic animals and green beans, Bazin's technical and ironic exactitude with '*polylobes*' and '*absidioles*' leaves no doubt that modest agriculture is as important as religious architecture.

Possibly thinking of what his filmmaking crew might need to know in advance for working in this location, Bazin hinted at the fact that the smallest

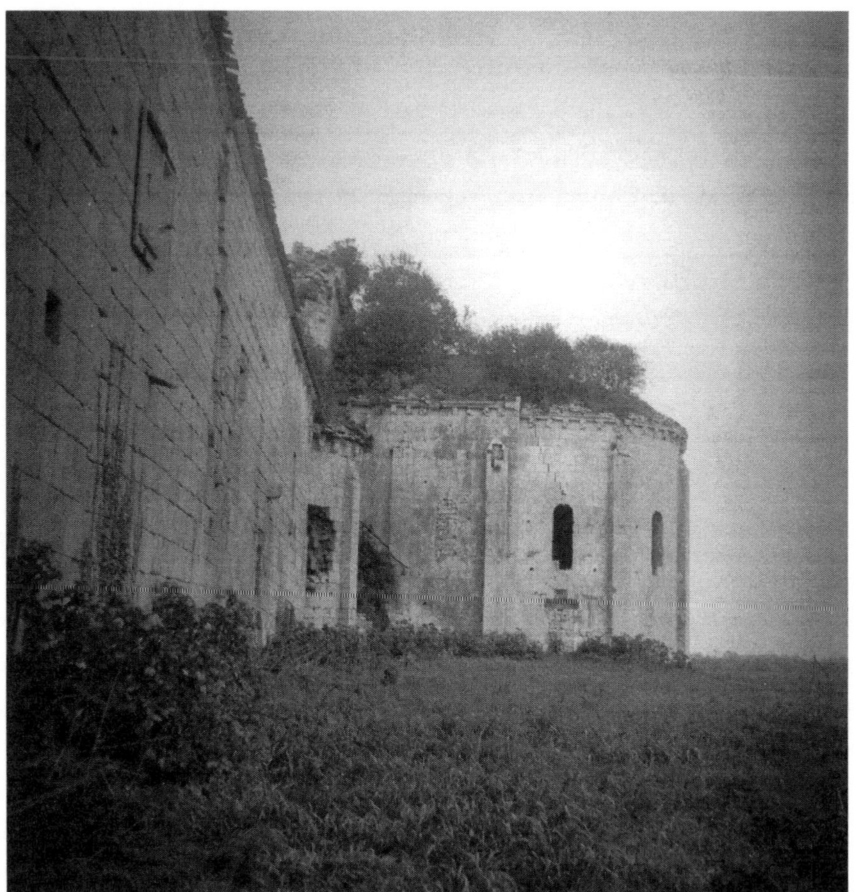

Figure 5.2 *André Bazin. Photograph taken in the Saintonge region. Courtesy of Dudley Andrew.*

churches look like abandoned private homes. Thus, contemporary visitors may get a key from some neighbour, either the owner of a nearby farm or the guardian of the adjacent cemetery.

Although Bazin did not go into this degree of detail, as soon as one opens the door of a small church, a wave of century-old dust, a sort of physiochemical micro-storm, rushes out of this airtight time-capsule and clouds their vision. Inside, wooden religious figures made of straw and rocks, as well as shells and worn-out candles, overwhelm one's expectations with their pagan, irreverent colours, so well preserved under seal. Protected inside an undisturbed container, a chromatic wealth of saturated reds, yellows, blues and greens survived with the defiance of gaudy crayons for young artists' picture books.

Besides his personal familiarity with the Saintonge area, the film critic's relationship to this geography was based on art historical research. Bazin's readings on the Romanesque style go back to his 1937–8 school year in the École Normale d'Instituteurs in Versailles. At the time, this institution was considered to be the best preparation for the entrance examination at the École Normale Supérieure de Saint-Cloud. According to Ludovic Cortade, one section of Bazin's written exam gave the following instructions:

> Gothic Art in France (Candidates are urged to visit and study one or more monuments in their region. They can bring to the oral exam postcards of these monuments.)[16]

Cortade also tells us that the reading assignment was a chapter from Louis Réau's (1881–1961) *L'art primitif, l'art medieval* (1955). French art historian Réau owed his reputation to his research exploring the dialogue between Western and folkloric Eastern European art. The transnational slant of Réau's work prepared Bazin for the early medieval 'universalism' hovering over the Saintonge region.

A resting point for pilgrims walking from France to Spain, the town of Saintes was most cosmopolitan around the year 1000. It was the unavoidable crossroad of adventurous and determined travellers who walked from Northern to Southern Europe. Back in those days, the time such a trip took might coincide with a whole lifespan. Bandits and thieves, pregnancies and plagues were foils to the healthy independence and the communal support required by such a long adventure. The Asian sculptural references included in the churches' facades lend Bazin the opportunity to further highlight his film theory's universalist bent:

That diabolical big-mouthed figure, devouring the column, [...] where the Marquis de Chasseloup-Loubat seemed, rightfully, to see a resemblance to Tao Tie, the Chinese glutton. It's not only from [...] the Middle East via the Crusades, with the manuscripts, ivories, and fabrics, but even from the Far East.[17]

Just as the moving image travels and links different cultures, likewise the Romanesque style involved a vast geography which, through merchants and soldiers, monks and pilgrims, spread all over Christian Europe. Its range of action absorbed images and themes from far-away countries such as China and the Arab world.

So wary was Bazin of elitist models that he explained the Romanesque style through parallels between cinema's mass appeal and the shared official language of the Middle Ages. The result is that cinema, just like Latin, becomes the lingua franca of the twentieth century:

We are at the dawn of a sort of artistic technocracy comparable to that of the Greco-Roman world, or the Christian era when, in the Middle Ages, a renowned theologian could teach equally (depending on the facilities offered him) in Ghent, Frankfurt, Paris, or Perugia.[18]

Besides percolating in his mind between 1938 and 1945, the Romanesque art of Saintonge reappeared when Bazin reviewed Amédée Ayfre's book *Dieu au Cinéma* (1953). Prompted by Ayfre's choice of examples, Bazin latched on to a sequence from a little-known Swedish film. Concerned with witchcraft, greed and forgiveness, Alf Sjöberg's *Himlaspelet* (*The Heavenly Play/Le Chemin du Ciel* (1942)) suggests a meta-textual definition of cinema as a medium capable of turning itself towards the irrational, Otherness, and the unknown:

I would have chosen, at the beginning of *Chemin du Ciel*, that curious travelling shot along a wall pierced by grilled openings behind which we follow the hesitant steps of a man with a lantern, as he seeks to find traces of God in a series of naively religious paintings on the wall opposite.[19]

Sjöberg's man with a lantern made an impression on Bazin, because he looks like an imaginary director or hypothetical spectator. For either one the cinema can turn to a lamp or a flashlight for secrets, or to a chandelier for spectacles.[20] While art itself will never reveal the origins of human creativity, the cinema, at least, can shed different kinds of light on reality's darkness.

Furthermore, cinema's penchant for a suspension of disbelief speaks to the medium's emotional power to inspire love. Even if God is love, for those who believe, God remains 'hidden', namely inaccessible to any lantern. This theme of the 'hidden' God sets up a resonance between Bazin and the eponymous title of a book published in 1955 by Marxist literary critic, Lucien Goldmann (1913–70). He underlined how the tragic nature of the human experience results from a condition of quasi-blindness.[21] Interestingly, Bazin's film theory argues that, on one hand, cinema's light can distort; on the other, the non-human eye of the camera enjoys a heuristic or revealing potential; it objectifies everything. This dialectic between human creativity and technology can lead to moments of illumination that bypass the blindfolding of human perception.

In *Le Chemin du Ciel*, the travelling shot explores a discontinuous layout of openings and obstacles that reveal glimpses of 'naively religious paintings' on a pockmarked wall. This scene enables Bazin to comment on how the chalky stones of the Saintonge area crumble into Romanesque ruins:

> But some of those harmonies, or at least the material of that stone, will come through in black and white. I'm thinking especially of the manner in which the stone has been eaten away, hardening in places, falling into dust in others, and thus curiously superimposing on the original sculptural ornamentation the hazardous tracery of wear and wind.[22]

A mixture of abstraction and figuration, the Romanesque style anticipates the arabesques of Art Nouveau surrounding cinema's invention and the grotesque combinations of Surrealism sustaining photographic ontology.

Bazin's essay on Saintonge starts with a quote from Émile Mâle (1862–1954): 'Nowhere else in France has Romanesque art found greater appeal.'[23] Possibly

Bazin was exposed to writings on the Romanesque by Mâle and by Focillon through Réau's familiarity with these two towering scholars.

Here Bazin's choice of Mâle stems from how the latter was the first to popularize St Augustine's proto-semiology of natural and cultural signs. In his introduction to *On Christian Doctrine*, translator D.W. Robertson remarks that for Mâle, 'the symbolic technique of medieval art' was 'essentially analogous with the symbolic techniques of Scriptural interpretations'.[24] In contrast to Mâle's allegorical reading of medieval iconography in the light of spiritual issues, Henri Focillon's influence on Bazin is more complicated to chart.

In 1924, Focillon succeeded Mâle as professor of medieval archeology at the Sorbonne. By 1931, he published his ground-breaking book *L'an 1000, l'art des sculpteurs romans*. Focillon argued that art forms change over time. In addition, since stylistic changes cannot be reduced only to external variables, he situated formal mutations within the changing use of materials and techniques. One thing is for sure: by the mid-1930s, when the discipline of film studies had not even been born, Erwin Panofsky (1892–1968) and Focillon agreed that 'cinema is the medium of reality'.[25] More specifically, according to Christophe Gauthier, Focillon is intrigued by how the cinema expresses itself through the documentary genre at the highest level: 'There are some admirable documentary films: *Nanook of the North* (1922) and *Moana* (1926) are examples. But the cinema as spectacle more often has recourse to fantasy'.[26]

In his essay, 'Evolution and Event in *Qu'est-ce que le cinéma*?' Tom Conley argues that Bazin's 'The Evolution of the Language of Cinema' (1951) and his 'Evolution of the Language of the Western' (1955) were influenced by Focillon's theories.[27] Without a doubt, Henri Bergson's *Creative Evolution* (1907) was, in turn, an important source for Focillon's *The Life of Forms* (1934) – a book published one year after the art historian started teaching six-week courses at Yale. By 1938, he received a Chair in Medieval Art. Even if the link between Bergson and Focillon is clear, a direct relationship between Bazin and Focillon cannot be easily established. One can only acknowledge that Bazin thinks of cinema as a living form that grows, matures and evolves. Bazin's appreciation of resilience and interconnections points to Bergson's *élan vital*. The wild grass growing within the stones of the Saintonge churches is the dominant figure of such a vital impulse. One could even argue that Bazin's wild grass stands for all the genre films ever made, never seen, or never discussed, a gigantic mass of looping celluloid that slowly disintegrates into a powder of assorted chemicals.

Of course, movement means time, space, change and chance, in a word: cinema itself, as soon as the elements of recording, editing and projection come literally into the picture. Thus, Bazin's focus on the wild grass is more than just a way to answer his famous question 'what is cinema?' By stressing the humblest roots of this medium, the theorist returns to how impure cinema oscillates among mass communication, popular culture and previous art forms.

Bazin is delighted with wild grass. Very difficult to uproot, wild grass thrives on specks of dust, the bits of soil and the ubiquitous seeds that the wind randomly deposits between one stone and the next. Wild grass points to an uncultivated origin that owes more to the earth, the rain and the sky than to the plough. Through the tenacity of weeds turning into chainlike roots, Bazin reminds his readers of the direct contact which binds model and copy, object and trace in photography. Finally, the appearance of wild grass as an unintended part of the architecture depends on the contingency of the wind, which is an energizing as well as corrosive force. Of all the elements, Bazin speaks of the wind most frequently.

A first example comes from his review of Georges Rouquier's *Farrebique* (1947). In the context of this quasi-documentary film, with nonprofessional actors, the passing seasons become characters on the screen, and an ethnography of farm life dominates the narrative. In dealing with *Farrebique*, Bazin brings up the most famous of all film anecdotes:

> 'Look,' shouted the first viewers of the Lumière cinematograph as they pointed at the leaves on the trees, 'look, they're moving.' The cinema has come a long way since the heroic days when crowds were satisfied with the rough rendition of a branch quivering in the wind![28]

As if the *Farrebique* example by itself were too uncouth, Bazin comes up with a second reference proving that cinema's wind circulates from the peasants to the intellectuals. This new meditation on the leaves rustling in the wind on the screen of early cinema emerges from Marc Allegret's documentary *Avec André Gide* (1952). There one can see the famous writer sitting in a garden with Jean-Paul Sartre:

The first aesthetic emotion ascribed to the cinema is that which moved the spectators in the Grand Café to cry out 'the leaves are moving'. Gide saw it and this simple spectacle overwhelms us.[29]

Just one year later, in one of his 1953 reviews, Bazin writes of 'the fresh wind that blows over the cinema. As long as such revelations are possible, the cinema will continue to live.'[30] As a source of motion and life, visible changes and revealing epiphanies, the cinema is as unpredictable as the wind, but the wind of history also pushes the cinema towards new creative adjustments and technological stages.

One wonders if Bazin's emphasis on the wind is his way of responding on behalf of the cinema to poet Paul Valéry's (1871–1945) famous line: 'The wind is rising, we must try to live!' from *Le Cimetière Marin* (1920). In *Le Cimetière Marin*, the illustrious polymath and incredibly popular Valéry meditates on human finitude by thinking of his parents buried in the cemetery of his native town, Sète. Unlike Valery, the ever-sickly Bazin, inflicted with tuberculosis and leukaemia, preceded his own parents to the grave. November 11, 1958 was Bazin's last day alive.

As for graveyards by the sea, one should keep in mind that in Bazin's Saintonge essay, two buildings stand out for their respective involvement with light and the sea. The first is the tower of Fénioux, made of stones cut like fish scales. This building is not a church or a lighthouse for ships adrift in the sea, but a 'lantern of the dead' standing out in an unmemorable rural area. Looking like a piece of art brut, it is an orientation structure with a small opening on top where a light shows the way towards a cemetery:

Also in the architecture, let's not forget those enigmatic lanterns of the dead, and especially the one at Fénioux, whose little scale-encrusted tower stands on a bundle of slender columns, erected in the middle of a field where the sheep graze.[31]

The second building mentioned by Bazin, Talmont, exemplifies an intriguingly fortified Romanesque church. It looks halfway between a lighthouse on the edge of the sea and a ship's prow ready to cast off from the earth. In this case, the whole planet is reduced to a spectacularly steep cliff. Religious architecture, here, becomes a leap into the unknown.

And how could Bazin not respond to the role assigned to the wind by the Gospel of St John. Once it is transported in the context of Bazin's film theory as a whole, this very same wind takes on a special trajectory. On the one hand, it links the cinema with wild grass, meteorological weather and cosmological time. On the other, it spells out the paradoxical combination of human free will and God's providence. There is still more to tell in regard to the wind as a spiritual trope and as a metaphor for the cinema in general. In Bazin's language, Bergson's *élan vital* becomes a 'souffle vital'.[32] In his anthropology of religion, Régis Debray (1940–), points out that the 'spirit' of spirituality is comparable to breath. Significantly, the verb 'to breathe' in Greek is *pneuma*. Yet *pneuma* also means soul, besides the scientific fact that energy or *energheia* depends on deep breathing and oxygen intake.[33]

We may never know for sure whether the universe we belong to is the one and only exception ever to have been born out of energy, time, space and matter. Perhaps different universes co-exist in the cosmos at large, in such a way that they, too, replicate the cinematic idea of parallel worlds. As far as this planet is concerned, the photographic cinema of the twentieth century is a spiritual mind-machine that allows for creativity and helps us to orient ourselves as ethically responsible human beings.

In the end, what matters is that the very last word of Bazin's essay on 'Les églises romanes de Saintonge' is *vent* (wind). For Bazin, the wind as such describes cinema's promising, yet volatile nature.[34] Wondering about the future of the medium to which he dedicated his entire life, Bazin's essay on the churches of Saintonge reads like a farewell to his readers and colleagues. Was Bazin thinking of his own imminent death or of the flight into dust of all living things? If so, his focus on the wild grass of innumerable genre films suggests that his legacy belongs entirely to his writings. No fancy tombstone is needed.

Notes

1   André Bazin, 'The Ontology of the Photographic Image', in *What is Cinema? Vol. 1*, trans. Hugh Gray (Berkeley, CA: University of California Press, 2004), 9–16; André Bazin, 'Les églises romanes de Saintonge: Projet de film d'André Bazin', *Cahiers du Cinéma* 100 (October 1959): 55–61. Bazin's piece was published posthumously.

Consulted at Yale André Bazin Archive (YABA). All translations are the author's unless otherwise cited.

2 Dudley Andrew, *André Bazin*, revised edition (New York: Oxford University Press, 2013), 204.

3 Sarah Wilson, 'Art and Politics of the Left in France: 1935–1955' (PhD diss., Courtauld Institute of Art, University of London, 1991), 3. See also: Romy Golan, *Modernity and Nostalgia: Art and Politics in France between* the *Wars* (New Haven, CT, and London: Yale University Press, 1995); Michele Cone, *French Modernisms: Perspectives on Art before, during, and after Vichy* (Cambridge: Cambridge University Press, 2001).

4 Andrew, *André Bazin*, 41.

5 Elizabeth Lawrence Mendell, *Romanesque Sculpture in Saintonge* (New Haven, CT: Yale University Press, 1940). The author of this monograph studied at Yale with Henri Focillon. On Henri Focillon and the *Life of Forms* in relation to Henri Begson, one of Bazin's philosophical influences, see Andrei Molotiu, 'Focillon's Bergsonian Rhetoric and the Possibility of Deconstruction', *In Visible Culture: An Electronic Journal for Visual Studies* 3 (1 January 2000).

6 Bazin, 'Les églises romanes de Saintonge', 58. For a cinematic overview of the French regional landscapes, see: André Bazin, 'Le Tour de France', *Écran Français* 209 (26 June 1949): n.p.

7 Bazin, 'Les églises romanes de Saintonge', 61.

8 For Bazin, the early medieval church of Torcello is comparable to the humble, but resilient atmosphere of a small church in Saintonge: *Parisien Libéré* 1543 (30 August 1949): n.p. YABA.

9 Even though his preference for the Romanesque is unique, André Bazin is not the first to relate the Middle Ages to the cinema. For example, Élie Faure, inspired by Erwin Panofsky, compares a film's complex organization to a medieval cathedral. On this point, see Eva Kuhn, 'La cinéplastique d'Elie Faure ou du cinéma et de la plasticité des arts', *Regards Croisés* 5 (2016): 69; Muriel van Vliet, '"L'esprit des formes est un" – Élie Faure: Pour une esthétique révolutionnaire', *Regards Croisés* 5 (2016): 74–85.

10 Bazin, 'Les églises romanes de Saintonge', 58.

11 Bazin, 'Les églises romanes de Saintonge', 57–8.

12 Bazin, 'Les églises romanes de Saintonge', 59.

13 André Bazin, 'Les nuits de Cabiria', *Parisien Libéré* 4073 (16 October 1957): n.p. YABA.

14 Bazin, 'The Ontology of the Photographic Image', 15.

15 Bazin, 'Les églises romanes de Saintonge', 60.

16 E-mail from Ludovic Cortade (12 September 2012).

17 Bazin, 'Les églises romanes de Saintonge', 58. On universalism, see André Bazin, 'Le
    Tour de France', *Écran Français* 209 (27 June 1949): n.p. YABA: 'L'immense audience du
    cinéma exige que le singulier y prenne valeur d'universalité simple et directe'. Also see
    André Bazin, 'Le langage de notre temps', in *Regards neufs sur le cinéma* (Paris: Peuple
    et Culture, 1954).

18 André Bazin, 'L'auteur de *La Grande Illusion* n'a pas perdu confiance dans la liberté de
    création', *Écran Français* 230 (28 November 1949): n.p. YABA. On the Middle Ages and
    the cinema, see also André Bazin, 'Peut-on s'intéresser au cinéma?' in *Misc B: Bulletin
    Intérieur: Maison des Lettres*: '. . . *la diffusion du cinéma est le plus grand fait esthético-
    social qui se soit produit depuis le moyen-age*' (the widespread distribution of cinema is
    the greatest aesthetic-social event since the Middle Ages.)

19 André Bazin, 'Amédée Ayfre, Dieu au cinéma', *Cahiers du Cinéma* 25 (July 1953): n.p.
    YABA. Also see Mélisande Leventopoulos, 'D'André Bazin à Amédée Ayfre: les
    circulations du personnalisme dans la cinéphilie chrétienne', in *Contextes, L'engagement
    créateur, Écritures et langages du personnalisme chrétien au XXe siècle* 12 (September
    2012): http://contextes.revues.org/5513; Mélisande Leventopoulus, 'Une église
    moderne en images: la cause cinématographique du père Raymond Pichard (1947–54)',
    1895 63 (Spring 2011): 70–89. Père Raymond Pichard was the priest who financed
    Georges Rouquier's *Lourdes et ses miracles* (1955).

20 André Bazin, 'Theater and Cinema, Part II', in *What is Cinema? Vol. 1*, 107.

21 Lucien Goldmann, *The Hidden God: A Study of Tragic Vision in the Pensées of Pascal
    and the Tragedies of Racine* [1964], trans. Philip Thody (London and New York: Verso,
    2016).

22 Bazin, 'Les églises romanes de Saintonge', 61.

23 Bazin, 'Les églises romanes de Saintonge', 55.

24 Saint Augustine of Hippo, *On Christian Doctrine*, trans. D.W. Robertson, Jr. (New York:
    Liberal Arts Press, 1958), xiii.

25 Tom Levin, 'Iconology at the Movies: Panofsky's Film Theory', in Angela Dalle Vacche
    (ed.), *The Visual Turn: Classical Film Theory and Art History* (New Brunswick, NJ:
    Rutgers University Press, 2003), 85–114.

26 Christophe Gauthier, 'Une branche nouvelle sur l'arbre des formes? Focillon, Élie Faure
    et le cinéma', in Irène Bessier and Jean Gili (eds), *Histoire du cinéma, problématique des
    sources* (Paris: INHA-Universite de Paris1-Maison des sciences de l'homme-AFRHC,
    2004), 295–310.

27 Tom Conley, 'Evolution and Event in *Qu'est-ce que le cinéma?*' in Dudley Andrew (ed.)
    with Hervé Joubert-Laurencin, *Opening Bazin* (New York: Oxford University Press,
    2011), 32–41.

28 Andre Bazin, 'Farrebique ou le paradoxe du realism', *Esprit* (1 April 1947): n.p. YABA.

29 André Bazin, 'André Gide', *France Observateur* 96 (13 March 1952): n.p. YABA.

30 André Bazin, 'Les enfants de l'amour', *France Observateur* 185 (26 November 1953): n.p. YABA.

31 Bazin, 'Les églises romanes de Saintonge', 58.

32 André Bazin, 'La Cybernétique d'André Cayatte', *Cahiers du Cinéma* 36 (1 June 1954): n.p. YABA. Bazin's breathing metaphor is important. See André Bazin, 'Le Toit', *Parisien Libéré* 3800 (29 November 1956): n.p. YABA: 'le souffle humain du néorealism'.

33 Régis Debray, *Dieu, un itinéraire* (Paris: Odile Jacob, 2001).

34 André Bazin, '*Il Bidone* après *La Strada*', *Parisien Libéré* 3572 (5 March 1956): n.p. YABA.

6

Projecting cultural diplomacy: Cold War politics, films on art, and Willard Van Dyke's The Photographer

NATASHA RITSMA

In 1948, *The Photographer*, a 26-minute film on art focusing on Edward Weston's artistic practice, lifestyle and inspiration, was screened to audiences around the world. One of the first films on art to solely focus on the work and life of a photographer, this film was directed by Willard van Dyke, one of America's leading documentarians. As the first and only film on art funded, produced and internationally distributed by the US State Department, it functions as a unique case study of how a narrative focused on a single American artist was strategically used to win the hearts and minds of the global public through soft power. This biographical film positions Weston as the quintessential American artist, emphasizing the merits of hard work and rugged individualism, as well as celebrating America's natural beauty. As the International Motion Picture Service screened this film to international audiences, Weston was transformed into an iconic cultural figure of the Cold War while simultaneously symbolizing

American patriotism and modernist sophistication. This chapter looks at the cultural, diplomatic, political and personal factors that shaped the production and circulation of *The Photographer*. This film had a dual function, to position Edward Weston as a great American artist while strategically challenging the ideological and cultural propaganda of the Soviets during the Cold War period for a global audience.

After the conclusion of the Second World War and the emergence of the United States as the leading global military power, the United States government became increasingly concerned with America's image overseas. The onset of the Cold War brought on an onslaught of disparaging propaganda from Moscow attacking every aspect of American life and character. Due to the fact that the Office of War Information (OWI) was dissolved in 1945, the State Department needed an agency to assume OWI's overseas cultural and informational propaganda activities. Accordingly, the State Department established the International Motion Picture Service (IMPS) to assume the overseas administration of promotional information and cultural programmes.[1] In contrast to the non-intervention stance that the United States government attempted to publicly convey during the Cold War, its agencies were greatly invested in conveying a positive image of America and its people by promoting and indirectly funding cultural and public diplomacy programmes including films, art exhibitions and performances as a means of combating the negative image of Americans.

Films on art and post-war American culture

Films on art were part of a larger movement that brought together high art, mass culture and national identity following the Second World War when art became an increasingly significant aspect of American culture. Not only was the United States asserting itself as the new cultural leader of the world, it drastically transformed the trajectory of what constitutes modern art. The decade following the end of the Second World War was marked by economic growth, increased leisure time, and technological advancements that prompted an expansive interest in the visual arts across America and influenced aspects of everyday life such as home improvement, interior design and the amateur crafts movement not usually associated with the rarefied halls of art museums. A 1952 *Reader's Digest* article described the extent of this change by stating, 'Once in a great while a society explodes in a flood of new ideas, new tastes, new standards. A fresh and exciting age emerges, alive with expanding opportunities.'[2] Museums, cultural and educational institutions and the government collaborated to encourage an unprecedented enthusiasm for the visual arts. More new art museums were founded in the United States during the 1950s than any other time in history.[3]

Interest in and promotion of the arts was evident in the popular press like *Life* and *Reader's Digest* as well as in mainstream media outlets like radio and network television that regularly reported on developments related to American art. In 1951, the Henry Francis Dupont Winterthur Museum established the first American art and culture-training centre. Critics and theorists who wrote for art publications focused on American art, while organizations such as the College Art Association (CAA) highlighted previously ignored American art.[4] Additionally, in 1952, the editors of the *Partisan Review* organized a highly publicized symposium, 'Our Country and Our Culture', which explicitly concerned itself with American art.[5] Furthermore, art appreciation groups were formed, and art education and appreciation was incorporated into the public school and university curricula. By the mid-1950s, when New York had 'officially' replaced Paris as the capital of modern art, doctoral graduates whose research focused on American art found themselves in high demand filling academic and museum positions throughout the nation.[6]

This multifaceted movement that included the American popular press, educational and professional institutions, as well as international high culture publications ensured the continuation of the importance of the American art scene for decades to come. Government, corporate, philanthropic, cultural and educational institutions were exceedingly optimistic about the potential of films on art to advance art education and appreciation, and promoted the use of these films, which numbered more than 1,500 by 1956.[7] Their endeavours are exemplified by four catalogues titled *Films on Art*, that were published by the American Federation of Arts, UNESCO, the International Art Film

Federation and Indiana University, all of which attempted to facilitate the use of these films by listing and indexing them.[8] In the March 1952 issue of *Educational Screen,* art educator Nathan Resnick affirmed that films on art 'could truly batter down the barriers which confine our art treasures to sepulcher and bring them out where everyone can see them'.[9] In another *Educational Screen* article published in January 1954, Barbara Chapin, chairwoman of the New York Division of the American Association of University Women (AAUW), echoed a similar sentiment and referred to these films as presenting new ways of seeing 'treasures and travels and special visions of rare persons available to people everywhere. If we use them, what riches can develop in our cultural life!'[10]

Numerous scholars, such as Eva Cockcroft, Max Kozloff and Serge Guilbaut, have skillfully demonstrated how art was used to further America's political agenda immediately following the war. American art was positioned to symbolize the strength of American ideology and to represent the merits of American democracy as progressive, innovative and cutting edge in stark contrast to the highly regulated and controlled Soviet socialist realist art. However, these new innovations in American modern art were often difficult to comprehend for the untrained eye, and films on art were regarded as effective tools to help the American public appreciate modern art. While films on art were discussed in popular discourse and in trade journals as the great pedagogical equalizer, they also served as a form of indoctrination that encouraged citizens to appreciate a specific brand of American art.[11] Films on art sit between high and lowbrow culture, between commercial and non-profit enterprises, and between art as entertainment and art as edification. They were promoted and used by very diverse constituencies including museums, institutions of formal education, philanthropic organizations like the Carnegie, Rockefeller and Ford Foundations, non-profit organizations like the American Federation of Art, and membership-funded film societies like Cinema 16 as well as international cultural organizations like UNESCO.[12] After the end of the Second World War and the beginning of the Cold War, the films on art genre was vitalized by aesthetic, social, economic, technological, intellectual and political motivations and was backed by educational institutions, cultural organizations, media outlets and government organizations.

The Cold War and the art of cultural diplomacy

In the immediate aftermath of the Second World War, the American government received accounts from its agents around the world revealing that disparaging representations of Americans were being strategically disseminated to international audiences. Reports indicated that Americans were regarded as: uncultured and unappreciative of other cultures, materialistic, intolerant of others' views, unpredictable and unreliable, impractically idealistic, and blind to injustices in their own society.[13] Initially the US refrained from responding to these attacks. However, James F. Byrnes, a powerful political figure who was gravely concerned about the United States' delay in enacting vigorous public diplomacy initiatives, wrote a letter to President Harry S. Truman cautioning that America was 'the last of the great nations of the earth to engage in informing other peoples about its policies and institutions'.[14] In addition, after visits to Europe in 1946 and 1947, several members of Congress gave first-hand accounts of Communist propaganda designed to depict Americans in a negative light.[15] In response to these concerns, David Wilson, a staffer at the State Department who worked with the United States Mission to the United Nations, stated the need to expand cultural diplomacy as 'a means of making other people favourably disposed toward us, of diffusing among them an atmosphere of liking and respect for us which will aid in the implementation of our national policies'.[16]

Subsequently, strengthening the positive perception of the United States overseas was identified as the most important goal for American cultural diplomacy.[17] In January 1948, President Truman signed the United States Information and Educational Exchange Act, also known as the Smith-Mundt Act, to advance the understanding of the United States by other countries.[18] Moreover, only four months later, in April 1948, Truman signed the European Recovery Program (ERP) also known as the Marshall Plan that appropriated almost thirteen billion dollars to be dispersed over four years to help rebuild the European economies after the devastation of the Second World War. The impact of such post-war initiatives in shaping American perception overseas cannot be overstated. Substantial funds were directed toward 'soft power' initiatives; the fact that the United States was the only country whose economy benefited from the war allowed them to generously fund cultural diplomacy.[19] Richard MacCann maintained that:

> budgets for films [...] and other expensive representations of the U.S. image would never have been granted in such large amounts by the U.S. Congress without the overshadowing threat of Soviet infiltration [...] in every case, the Russian budget for propaganda was part of the plea for the American budget.[20]

Strategies for indirectly supporting cultural diplomacy were crucial for fighting the ideological and cultural propaganda of the Soviets during the Cold War period without appearing heavy-handed or overly didactic. Providing funding to showcase a range of American artistic achievements in the form of modern dance performances, jazz concerts and art exhibitions was paramount in demonstrating American cultural leadership. In her essay on the global impact of Louis Armstrong's music during the Cold War, the cultural historian Penny M. Von Eschen states,

> Indeed, cultural exchange was the commodity that closely pursued the quintessential Cold War commodities, oil and uranium, along with many others critical to America's seductive abundance. Tracing the steps of the artists offers a window into the sheer enormity and originality [...] of the U.S. global project of domination by way of modernization and development.[21]

Von Eschen highlights the fact that the State Department's cultural programmes functioned to showcase 'a distinctly American alternative to Soviet and European dominance in the arts, and that the programme committees became venues for debating what was considered "modern" and "uniquely American" in dance, art, and music'.[22]

Concerts, film screenings, performances and art exhibitions worked in tandem to promote a curated vision of American culture abroad; however, not all efforts went without challenges. One such example occurred in 1946 and greatly impacted the content and production of future cultural initiatives. In an effort to reach people around the world and convey a positive image of

America and its people, the State Department charged Joseph LeRoy Davidson, visual-arts specialist at the State Department, to curate an art exhibit to signal America's advancement in the fine arts 'for the government to use as a political tool abroad'.[23] Davidson curated the exhibition 'Advancing American Art' that featured paintings by many of the most celebrated twentieth-century American artists including Edward Hopper, Georgia O'Keeffe, Stuart Davis, Ben Shahn and Jacob Lawrence. William Benton, Assistant Secretary of State for Public Affairs and publisher of Encyclopedia Britannica (1943–73), celebrated this exhibition as a mechanism to challenge 'those abroad who thought of the United States as a nation of materialists', and to demonstrate 'that the same country which produces brilliant scientists and engineers also produces creative artists'.[24] The exhibition was to tour Europe, South America and Asia, and to demonstrate to the world America's new stature as a cultural leader, and to underscore the freedom of expression the United States government grants its artists in contrast to the Soviets.

Although the exhibition received positive reviews when it was shown at the Metropolitan Museum of Art as well as in Paris and Prague, in early 1947 it was withdrawn and brought back to the United States after conservative politicians and newspaper editors deemed it dangerous to America's image and accused its creators of furthering the Communist agenda. This conservative campaign to discredit the exhibition also resulted in reporting the artists who participated in the exhibition to the House Un-American Activities Committee for further investigation, the auctioning off of all the paintings, and the dismissal of Joseph LeRoy Davidson.[25]

Celluloid as soft power diplomacy

After the 'Advancing American Art' fiasco, effectively implementing soft power in the post-war political climate involved the intricate process of navigating numerous international and domestic cultural and political influences. Although State Department agencies sought to dissociate themselves from directly funding the arts, they needed to find a way to ideologically and culturally fight the Cold War without stirring controversy in the United States.

Hence, they strategized to use their financial resources to indirectly fund the arts through a variety of cultural tools. Films on art were recognized as such tools.

The dissolution of the OWI in 1945 threatened the financial survival of filmmaker and documentarian William Van Dyke and his production company Affiliated Films that had worked closely with the State Department during the war and produced propaganda films funded by OWI that promoted and idealized American cultural values, including *Oswego* (1943), *Steeltown* (1944), *Pacific Northwest* (1944) and *San Francisco* (1945). According to the art scholar and photographer James Enyeart, the producer Irving Jacoby, who worked with Van Dyke and who had contacts with the State Department, approached IMPS and proposed that Van Dyke's production company make a series of films featuring American artists to demonstrate America's cultural, intellectual and artistic wealth to international audiences.[26] Jacoby's proposal corresponded with the agency's desire to use films on art as a means for political and cultural propaganda. As Van Dyke's productions were of known quality to them, Jacoby's proposal was accepted and funds were assigned to Affiliated Films.

In producing this film, Van Dyke balanced numerous challenges in order to create a work that would honour Weston's oeuvre without provoking unwanted attention in Washington. Van Dyke selected the subject of his film, chose the locations where the film was shot, and oversaw the cinematography.[27] *The Photographer* strategically presented Edward Weston as the quintessential, rugged American artist, endowed with an extraordinary artistic vision, an observant eye and an exceptional set of skills. To nullify Soviet representations of Americans as materialistic, shallow and frivolous, the film strategically revealed Weston's modest lifestyle by having the camera enter Weston's humble home while commenting, 'He [Weston] feels rich though he owns nothing but his tools, his personal effects and his cats.' In another scene documenting Weston and his assistant in a car wash in Los Angeles, the commentator states,

> In Europe people say that this is America, Weston likes it and thinks it's fun, but he doesn't think it's America. Machines and gadgets are convenient, but they can't do our living for us. He won't let himself be used by them, he

tends to weigh their value against what he has to give for them in terms of freedom and self respect.

To counterpoint Cold War perceptions of Hollywood as representative of the entire nation, the voiceover explains 'LA is only a small part of America' as the film showcases California's diverse natural riches, from the Pacific Coast to the desert. The film follows Weston and his assistant as they travel throughout California exploring potential sites for his photographs. During these trips the camera reveals the grandeur and splendour of California's distinct landscapes where Weston, with the help of his assistant, sets up his camera for a shoot. Van Dyke documents Weston working at the same locations that his photographs made famous, such as Yosemite, Point Lobos and Death Valley. These sequences effectively document Weston's process in creating some of the most iconic photographs focusing on America's vast landscapes and striking natural beauty.

In post-production, Van Dyke's stunning cinematography was paired with Ben Maddow and Irving Jacoby's didactic commentary read by Mel Brandt. The voice-over and editing strategically protrayed Weston as an American artist that above all else values freedom. Positioning Weston as a free thinker and aesthetic pioneer successfully produced the highly calibrated message the State Department aimed to portray. This constructed representation of an American artist navigated a variety of choices regarding content and form. It's worth noting that although the film is an intimate portrait of Weston and his art, Van Dyke judiciously avoided using any of the nudes or other suggestive abstract photographs that are featured in many of Weston's works. Having already made films for the State Department, Van Dyke understood the parameters within which he was expected to operate and directed the film in a manner that satisfied the post-war conservative political environment, and met the State Department's goal of presenting an idealized image of America and American life while simultaneously portraying his friend in a positive light.

The Photographer marks a milestone in the history of the film on art genre as it was the first film to feature an American photographer, and was 'one of the very first films from any country to regard photography seriously as an art form'.[28] Throughout the film, Van Dyke strategically emphasizes the artistry Weston demonstrates as he composes, shoots and develops his photographs. Van Dyke's camera followed Weston into the darkroom documenting the artist developing a photograph 'with infinite skill' and demonstrating the interconnection between art and science. Referencing Weston's predecessors such as Nadar, Matthew Brady, Eugène Atget and Alfred Steigiltz, Van Dyke decisively inserts him in this prestigious lineage.

Beginning in 1948, *The Photographer* was distributed by the IMPS through UNESCO's international non-theatrical film circuit that was developed by the Allied Forces during the Second World War. This international non-theatrical film circuit facilitated the exhibition of *The Photographer* in locations around the world that would have been otherwise inaccessible during the Cold War period.[29] This extensive exposure transformed Weston into an iconic cultural figure while simultaneously conveying an idealized version of American values and America's modernist sophistication. In a letter to Van Dyke, Weston wrote, '... every now and then I meet someone who has seen it [*The Photographer*] in Siam or Alaska!'[30]

According to Richard Barsam, the early post-war films on art that were commissioned by IMPS including *The Photographer* (1948) were not intended for American viewers but for audiences in foreign countries.[31] However, there is evidence, through letters written by Van Dyke to Weston, that in 1950 a silent version of the film was screened in at least one theatre in Los Angeles with Weston narrating in real time, much like the travelogue programmes popular in the first half of the century.[32] A final version of the film was formally released in the United States in 1951, and was exhibited at film societies, museums and academic settings. It was declared an overall success and described as offering 'insight into the environment, the sources of inspiration and the creative processes of an artist',[33] and characterized as 'technically first rate in every department'.[34] *Educational Screen* published the following glowing review of the film:

> This truly remarkable motion picture through skillful editing, excellent camera work, penetrating interpretation of photography as an art, a sensitive presentation of Weston and his art does capture for its audience intimate and revealing incidents and experiences in the life of Edward Weston. For

both critical and lay audiences it offers much documentary evidence to establish photography as one of the important creative arts in America.[35]

Furthermore, the *Educational Screen's* review applauded Van Dyke's stunning cinematography depicting the California coast.[36]

The Photographer was at the forefront of the post-war American film on art movement and became a prominent example of early Cold War era cultural propaganda. Van Dyke sidestepped congressional criticism, censorship and other attempts of interference by making a quality film that represented America in a way that met with the State Department's approval and portrayed Weston as a serious, hardworking and stoic artist 'that shows American beauty in a language all can understand'.[37] By prudently producing a patriotic portrait of his friend that embodied the values the government wished to communicate, Van Dyke was capable of conferring upon his friend an international and domestic standing as one of the foremost artists of the time. In a letter to Weston, Van Dyke writes, 'I guess we did alright, no? It was wonderful to be able to do it for you, Edward, and I'm happy that I could express my love and appreciation in my own way.'[38]

In conclusion, mid-century films on art played an important role on the international front as soft power weapons of cultural diplomacy posed to counteract the ideological and cultural propaganda of the Soviets during the Cold War period without appearing heavy-handed or overly didactic. As filmmaker and artist Paul Haesaerts remarked, 'the art film has an exceptional power to penetrate deeply into the psyche, an imagination – to photograph, in a way, the very inside of certain minds or certain collective mentalities'.[39] Turner Shelton who became the head of IMPS in 1953, expounded on the important role films on art play in cultural diplomacy and proclaimed, 'Motion pictures [...] create an atmosphere of receptivity. They create an aura that makes people receptive to what we specifically have to say to them [...] I think motion pictures can make America understood.'[40] While *The Photographer* functioned as a strategic vehicle of cultural diplomacy that conveyed a positive, friendly and sophisticated image of America to international audiences and promoted photography as a fine art to domestic audiences, it also became one of the most viewed films on art in the mid-century.

Notes

1 Richard M. Barsam, *Nonfiction Film: A Critical History* (Bloomington: Indiana University Press, 1992), 278.

2 *Reader's Digest* as quoted in Douglas Miller and Marion Nowar, *The Fifties: The Way We Really Were* (New York: Doubleday and Company, 1977), 9.

3 Between the years 1950 and 1977, $561,700,000 was committed to the construction of 123 American art museums and visual arts centres across the country. Michael Kammen reports that in the mid-1950s museum attendance became a popular form of entertainment, almost matching the number of annual moviegoers of 1954 in *American Culture, American Tastes: Social Change and the 20th Century* (New York: Knopf, 1999), 117. Also see Francis Frascina (ed.), *Pollock and After: The Critical Debate* (New York: Harper and Row, 1985) for a series of essays addressing the rise of Abstract Expressionism and the politics of the Cold War.

4 Erika Doss, 'The Visual Arts in Post-1945 America', in Jean-Christophe Agnew (ed.), *A Companion to Post-1945 America* (Oxford: Blackwell Publishing, 2002).

5 Frances Stonor Saunders, *The Cultural Cold War: The CIA and the World of Arts and Letters* (New York: The New York Press, 1999), 159.

6 See Doss, 'The Visual Arts', and Serge Guilbaut, *How New York Stole the Idea of Modern Art: Abstract Expressionism, Freedom and the Cold War* (Chicago, IL: University of Chicago Press, 1983).

7 Theodore Bowie, *Films on Art: A Critical Guide* (Bloomington: Indiana University Audio-Visual Center, 1956), 6. In his Introduction, Bowie elaborates on the vast number of films on art created in the decade following the conclusion of the war.

8 Margaret I. Rufsvold and Carolyn Guss, *Guides to Newer Educational Media* (Chicago, IL: American Library Association, 1961), 67.

9 Nathan Resnick, 'A Modest Proposal on Art Films', *Educational Screen* (March 1952): 99.

10 Barbara Chapin, 'New Ways of Seeing', *Educational Screen* (January 1954): 13. AAUW was invested in exhibiting art films, because the organization regarded these films as a means of educating the public as well as pertinent tools for cultivating understanding of other societies and cultures and for fostering international relations.

11 Eva Cockcroft, 'Abstract Expressionism, Weapon of the Cold War', in Frascina (ed.), *Pollock and After*. Also see Guilbaut, *How New York Stole the Idea of Modern Art*.

12 For a detailed account of the relationship between philanthropic and government organizations in relation to the mobilization of non-theatrical film in the post-war era, see Charles Acland, 'Screen Technology, Mobilization, and Adult Education in the 1950s', in William J. Buxton (ed.), *Patronizing the Public: American Philanthropy's Transformation of Culture, Communication, and the Humanities* (New York: Lexington Books, 2009), 261–79.

13 Theodore A. Wilson, 'Selling America Via the Silver Screen? Efforts to Manage the Projection of American Culture Abroad, 1942–1947', in Reinhold Wagnleitner and Elaine Tyler May (eds), *Here, There, and Everywhere: The Foreign Politics of American Popular Culture* (Hanover: University Press of New England, 2000), 85.

14 Richard MacCann, *The People's Film: A Political History of U.S. Government Motion Pictures* (New York: Hastings House, 1973), 176.

15 MacCann, *The People's Film*, 176.

16 Wilson, 'Selling America', 84.

17 Guilbaut, *How New York Stole the Idea*, 193. For a comprehensive history of US cultural diplomacy see Michael L. Krenn, *The History of United States Cultural Diplomacy: 1770 to the Present Day* (London: Bloomsbury, 2017).

18 Guilbaut, *How New York Stole the Idea,* 190.

19 Reinhold Wagnleitner, 'The Irony of American Culture Abroad: Austria and the Cold War', in Lary May (ed.), *Recasting America: Culture and Politics in the Age of the Cold War* (Chicago, IL: University of Chicago Press, 1989), 286.

20 MacCann, *The People's Film*, 194.

21 Penny M. Von Eschen, 'Satchmo Blows Up the World: Jazz, Race, and Empire during the Cold War', in Wagnleitner and Tyler May (eds), *Here, There, and Everywhere*, 164.

22 Von Eschen, 'Satchmo Blows Up the World', 166.

23 Dennis Harper, 'Advancing American Art: Leroy Davidson's "Blind Date with Destiny"', in Scott Bishop et al., *Art Interrupted: Advancing American Art and the Politics of Cultural Diplomacy* (Athens: Georgia Museum of Art, 2012), 8.

24 William Benton, 'Vernissage: Advancing American Art', *Art News* (October 1946): 19.

25 This action effectively ended the careers of many of these artists.

26 James Enyeart, *Willard Van Dyke: Changing the World Through Photography* (Albuquerque: University of New Mexico Press, 2008), 245.

27 For a more detailed account, see L.S. Calmes, *The Letters Between Edward Weston and Willard Van Dyke* (Tucson: The University of Arizona Press, 2005) and Enyeart's *Willard Van Dyke*.

28 Barsam, *Nonfiction Film*, 296.

29 Zoe Druick, 'Reaching the Multimillions: Liberal Internationalism and the Establishment of Documentary Film', in Lee Grieveson and Haidee Wasson (eds), *Inventing Film Studies* (Durham, NC: Duke University Press, 2008), 81–102.

30 Calmes, *The Letters,* 49.

31 Barsam, *Nonfiction Film*, 279.

32 Calmes, *The Letters,* 44–5. Letters 58 and 59.

33 William McK. Chapman (ed.), 'The Films', in *Films on Art* (New York: American Federation of Arts, 1952), 126.

34 Theodore Bowie, *Films on Art: A Critical Guide* (Indiana University Audio-Visual Center, Bloomington, IN, 1956), 23.

35 L.C. Larson, Carolyn Guss, Betty Stoops, 'Evaluation of New Films', *Educational Screen* (January 1952): 27.

36 Larson, Guss, Stoops, 'Evaluation of New Films', *Educational Screen*, 27.

37 Quote from *The Photographer* (1948). Produced by Willard Van Dyke for USIS (United States Information Service) distributed by United World Films.

38 Calmes, *The Letters,* 45.

39 Paul Haesaerts, as quoted in George Amberg, 'Art, Films, and Art Films', *Magazine of Art,* (March 1952): 132.

40 MacCann, *The People's Film,* 178.

7

Henry Moore *and* A Sculptor's Landscape: *modernity, the land and the bomb in two television films by John Read*

JOHN WYVER

At a conference in Ghent in December 2013, I introduced a screening of a 35mm print of *A Sculptor's Landscape*, a half-hour BBC Television documentary about Henry Moore.[1] Observing Moore at work in his studios and the grounds of his home in Hertfordshire, and showcasing both sculptures and drawings, the 1958 film was written and directed by John Read (1923–2011).[2] As the audience watched the pin-sharp monochrome images of Moore's art set in a rural Britain from more than fifty years before, the accompanying soundtrack was simply Humphrey Searle's modernist score mixed with a range of audio effects. The original television narration spoken by the distinguished classical actor Ralph Richardson was missing; nor was this the only puzzling aspect of the fine print generously made available by the Cinematek Brussels. Stranger still was why this archive should possess a pristine copy of this particular British arts documentary. Its presence can only be a consequence of Expo '58, the world's fair held in the Belgian capital in the summer of the year in which Read's film was completed. Henry Moore was one of the participating artists in the event's 'Fifty Years of Modern Art' exhibition, and although to date it has proved impossible to confirm any screenings, the film print that we viewed must surely have been shown, with a now-lost Flemish or French narration track, in conjunction with this presentation of the artist.

The British pavilion at Expo '58 was an angular modernist structure created by architects Howard V. Lobb and Partners working with John Ratcliff.[3] The self-conscious alignment of national identity with modernity was qualified by the pavilion's interior commissioned from designer James Gardner. Here a future-facing 'Hall of Technology' was flanked by a 'Hall of Tradition' lit by stained-glass windows, hung with heraldic banners and showcasing Pietro Annigoni's celebrated portrait of Elizabeth II. Moreover, as Elizabeth Darling has written, 'In a souvenir brochure published by the *Daily Mail* – then as now a deeply traditional and conservative paper – the pavilion was described as representing "the country in which tradition is stubbornly and gracefully preserved," but it also "shows clearly the United Kingdom is still foremost amongst the pioneers in this nuclear age." [...] Britain's modernity was proclaimed and projected through the exterior of the pavilion but conveyed more ambiguously within.'[4]

This ambivalent conjunction of past and present is also a defining characteristic of *A Sculptor's Landscape* (first broadcast 28 June 1958), just as it is of John Read's earlier BBC profile *Henry Moore* (1951).[5] In both films, Moore's modernism, and the modernist visual style of the cinematography and editing, are contrasted with and contained by a supposed timelessness of the land and of the human figure. The films negotiate other tensions too, including those between the construction of Moore as an individual genius and his practice as a public, socially engaged figure, and between Moore the Englishman born and bred in Yorkshire, and Moore the internationalist. The key difference between the films, however, is that the later *A Sculptor's Landscape* was made in the shadow of the atomic bomb and the threat of nuclear annihilation. Despite the second film nowhere explicitly addressing these concerns, in its treatment of landscape, of the human figure and of Moore's developing work, the film betrays the nuclear anxieties that since the early 1950s had changed the world.

Exploring the tensions and highlighting the determining forces, this chapter outlines the production frameworks of *Henry Moore* and *A Sculptor's Landscape*, locating them within the emerging tradition of the visual arts on British television in the 1950s. It details the shared approaches and concerns of the two films and foregrounds the contrast between them determined by this new factor of nuclear fear.

A unique collaboration

A Sculptor's Landscape, broadcast seven years after *Henry Moore*, was the second of six films that John Read made with the artist for BBC Television between 1951 and 1979. Steven Jacobs has related the earlier films in this sequence to a post-war flourishing of arts documentaries concerned with the representation of sculpture including *Jacques Lipchitz* (1951), directed by Frank Stauffacher, and Alain Resnais and Chris Marker's *Les Statues meurent aussi* (1953).[6] Demonstrating both a consistent approach and a sense of development, Read's films are distinguished by their clarity and confidence, and represent a unique collaboration between a major creative figure, a distinctive filmmaker and a broadcaster.[7] Throughout a career at the BBC that lasted until 1978, Read wrote and directed numerous films about visual artists, including other documentaries during the 1950s about prominent painters, several of whom were identified after the Second World War as 'neo-Romantic' artists:[8] *Graham Sutherland* (1953), *John Piper* (1953), and two 1956 films on Stanley Spencer, *Cookham Village* and *War and Peace*. Each of these films is a significant document of British modernism and yet, like so many documentaries engaged with the visual arts, they remain largely unknown, including amongst cultural historians with an interest in this period. Such neglect has been in part because archival access has until recently been limited. Yet despite the centrality of these artists to British post-war culture, there has also been a resistance amongst scholars working with traditional hierarchies of the value of historical sources who have consistently privileged printed materials over the moving image.

Born in 1923, John Read was the son of the noted art critic Herbert Read and his first wife, Evelyn. He spent much of his childhood living in Edinburgh with his mother after she and Herbert separated. Fascinated by the cinema from early on, he made his first film when he studied after the war in Oxford and in 1948 he published the article 'Is There a Documentary Art?' in the film journal *Sight & Sound*. In this, he laid out principles that would underpin all of his work for the BBC across three decades, and at the same time he detailed both a personal and a social understanding of post-war reconstruction and regeneration that would run throughout his work:

> Documentary is the natural expression of the modern democratic community in terms of creative leadership. As such, it is a form of public service in the new and ever-widening field of adult education. [...] Much of our learning and knowledge of life is apprehended through our senses moved by poets, actors and painters, arousing in us the sense of pleasure that is also understanding. The highest purposes of Documentary can be achieved in a like manner, where the educational is implicit in the artistic.[9]

The article helped secure Read a lowly position with the documentary producer John Grierson, who was former head of the GPO Film Unit and at this point the controller of the Central Office of Information's film operations, and then, with his father's assistance, a position with the fledgling BBC television service. Working in the Alexandra Palace studios, he began to produce live presentations illustrated with photographs about subjects such as English pub signs and the Elgin Marbles. He also worked on a weekend magazine series with host Joan Gilbert and, on being instructed to appeal to a more up-market audience, he introduced art spots, including one with artist John Minton discussing his painting *The Death of Nelson*. As had been the case between 1936 and 1939 and since the single channel's resumption after the war in 1946, almost all BBC television broadcasts at the time were made with multiple electronic cameras and transmitted live from a small studio or as an outside broadcast. Filmed productions were rare in the schedules, although after 1947 the Corporation began to make short films, having reassured suspicious feature film producers and the film technicians' union that it had no interest in competing in the theatrical marketplace. As John Read later recalled, there was widespread resistance to film throughout the television service: 'The attitude then was: it was the great new electronic medium, the wonder of seeing it as it happens –

or, often, seeing it go wrong as it went wrong. I suppose they had to make claims for the new medium. But I saw [television] as a marvellous method of film distribution.'[10]

In the run-up to the May 1951 opening of the Festival of Britain, Read was offered the chance to make a feature about Henry Moore, almost certainly because of the personal and professional connections between his father and the artist. As Ben Cranfield has written,

Herbert Read and Henry Moore were not just connected by their ubiquity within the canonical formation of mid-twentieth century modernism and their over-exposure as doyens of British art: the development of their respective work as critic and artist was enmeshed for nearly forty years, from the first time Read visited Moore's studio in 1931 to Read's death in 1968 [...] Moore remained more solidly in Read's favour than any other artist, contemporary or historic [...] Read described Moore's work and process in the manner of Vasari, the Renaissance father of biographically dominated art history, tellingly the story of genius as an unfolding and indisputable fact.[11]

In 1950, both in Britain and abroad, and in part thanks to Herbert Read's promotional efforts, Moore was increasingly recognized as a singular genius. In the United States in 1946, the artist had been honoured with an exhibition at New York's Museum of Modern Art, the first solo show there by a British artist, and at the Venice Biennale in 1948 he had won the prestigious sculpture prize. After concentrating in the early years of the war on his Tube shelter drawings, and then working as an official war artist making drawings of miners, he had returned to carving in 1943. A number of high-profile public commissions followed including a *Family Group* for a Stevenage school. Geoffrey Grigson's 1944 book *Henry Moore*, published in the 'Penguin Modern Painters' series, sold 48,000 copies in its first four years. And as Andrew Stephenson has argued, this was a period in Moore's life 'when he was eager to comment publicly on the civic responsibilities of the artist and patron in post-war reconstruction and become energetically involved with the advisory committees directing public arts organisations, museums and galleries'.[12]

Planning a feature about Moore in 1950, John Read argued on pragmatic grounds that it was essential that he should be able to use film. The artist's sculptures were too bulky to bring in any quantity to the studio and Moore himself stressed how they should be seen in natural light against the landscape. The artist had a keen interest in how his works were photographed, and as Elizabeth Brown has written, 'Henry Moore photographed his own sculptures frequently, often beginning with a specific function in mind.'[13] In her perceptive essay, Brown analysed the ways in which throughout his career Moore used photography to highlight specific details and finishes and to create for his works particular moods and visual effects. In a later interview John Read acknowledged Moore's influence on the cinematography in his films: 'I remember learning everything from Moore about photographing sculpture, and especially about the use of natural light for "modelling"; he taught me, and I think the cameraman too.'[14] All of the sculptures were newly filmed from the original artworks by Alan Lawson, chief cameraman at BBC's Television Newsreel. He employed innovative cinematographic techniques, a number of which were reprised in the making of *A Sculptor's Landscape*. Light and shadow moving across the sculptures contributes to the sense of their plastic form and jump cuts are used to animate qualities in materials. In her detailed and rigorous consideration of the film, Katerina Loukopoulou suggested the jump cuts 'make common materials appear strange through their sudden appearance. They also make the viewer aware of the film's editing, pointing reflexively to film's capacity to construct a visual rhetoric. Just as modernist sculpture frequently departed from wholly representational forms, so these jump cuts depart from the realism of conventional editing.'[15] The attempt at de-familiarization is continued with works filmed against the sky, and so abstracted from any sense of scale. Read and Lawson, almost certainly with Moore's approval, frequently set the camera in motion, most strikingly in the closing sequence, for which the sculpture was placed on a large turntable in the open air and spun around in front of the camera. The camera then joined the sculpture on the spinning platform, and the images, including the backgrounds glimpsed through the artwork, create a rapidly changing pattern in which the previously clear relationships between figure and ground shift, change and collapse.

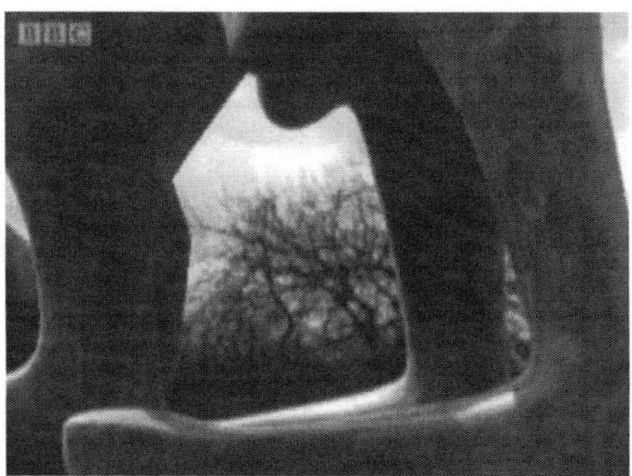

Figure 7.1 *Spinning on a turntable with the sculpture, Alan Lawson's camera films through the limbs of* Reclining Figure *(1951) in* Henry Moore *(John Read, 1951). Digital still. BBC Television.*

Yet if the film's form is at times giddily modernist and challenging, the tone of its narration is defensively conservative, and this combination is repeated in *A Sculptor's Landscape*. The format of the 1951 film is essentially that of an illustrated radio talk, with Read's elegant commentary read by actor Bernard Miles constantly stressing historical precedents for Moore's work. There is a single sequence in which Moore speaks with synchronous sound and addresses the camera directly. Filmed at his home in Hoglands, this was a far from trivial technical achievement at the time. Speaking in what appears to be a carefully rehearsed manner, the artist locates his practice in a response to natural forms. 'The central tradition of sculpture,' he explains to the viewer, 'is rooted in a respect for the materials of sculpture. One can learn from all sorts of natural forms, such as these. Take for instance this stone. It has a hole right through it. It has a strong, slow, structural rhythm which perhaps shows nature's way of working stone.'

Near the start of *Henry Moore* there is a focus on the artist's hands, working with tools, carving stone and modelling clay. The impulse to capture creation on celluloid is strong throughout the film. A cut from a blank sketchbook page to a close-up of Moore's eyes, underlined as so much of the film is by William Alwyn's music, is intended to suggest 'inspiration'. The second half of the film follows the creation of *Reclining Figure* (1951, now in the Scottish National Gallery of Modern Art) that the artist began in October 1950 for the following year's Festival of Britain. There is a fascination in witnessing those aspects of Moore's working processes, especially the casting of bronze, that he was prepared to reveal to the camera. But this is clearly incomplete – Moore's studio assistants, for example, are only glimpsed in the background (although they are explicitly acknowledged in *A Sculptor's Landscape*), and, as Philip Hayward has discussed as a general feature (and failure) of documentaries about visual artists, the *actual moment* of creation inevitably eludes both the filmmaker and the viewer.[16]

The film was broadcast on the evening of 30 April 1951.[17] The following day, a retrospective exhibition of the artist's works organized by the Arts Council of Great Britain, 'Sculpture and Drawings by Henry Moore', was shown to the press at London's Tate Gallery. That same evening, on London's South Bank, King George VI opened the Festival of Britain. Adjacent to the 'Origin of the Land' exhibit, and around the corner from a display devoted to the still comparatively new medium of television, was a plinth on which was mounted Moore's *Reclining Figure*. Television, exhibition and festival reinforced Moore's status as *the* emblematic visual artist of the moment. Moreover, *Henry Moore* was just one of more than 2,000 broadcasts, mostly on radio, made by the BBC about every aspect of the Festival of Britain. The Festival and broadcasting forged a productive partnership which together constructed an image of the nation that both looked back to the triumphs of the first Elizabethan age and anticipated the second that would begin when Princess Elizabeth ascended to the throne.[18] *Henry Moore* was promoted as one finely balanced expression of this conjunction of tradition and modernity.

Return to Hoglands

Five years after his first film profile, having made documentaries with Graham Sutherland, John Piper and Stanley Spencer as well as programmes about the landscapes of the Lake District and English parish churches, John Read returned to Moore as a potential subject. He was planning a series titled *The Artist Speaks* that would put into practice ideas that the director had expressed in a 1957 article:

I do not myself believe that the art film is a legitimate instrument of criticism. The opportunities for contrived argument are too many and the impact of the screen too authoritarian. I prefer to think that sympathetic interpretation and the identification of the audience with the artist are more legitimate objectives. When possible the artist should be in the film to speak for himself and I prefer building up commentary and explanation from the artist's own opinions and statements, leaving the spectator to form his own judgement.[19]

The respect for the artists with whom he filmed that Read expresses here, together with his sense that his documentaries were created essentially in their service, remained firmly consistent throughout his long career. Read understood his practice as that of a facilitator and educator, developing a broader and better-informed audience for modern art within a framework of public service broadcasting derived from John Reith and of the understanding of culture from the Victorian critic Matthew Arnold and his influential study *Culture and Anarchy*. Unlike other makers of films about sculpture in these years, such as Carl Theodor Dreyer or Henri Alekan, Read resisted the idea that he was a creative artist who imposed his own sensibilities and concerns on his depiction of his subjects and their artworks.[20] Such reticence and modesty were common attributes of programme makers working for BBC Television in the post-war years.

Read's sense of his subservient role in working with Moore is caught in an October 1956 internal memo preserved in the BBC Written Archives at Caversham in which he recounted a recent visit to Moore's home and studios at Hoglands. Read had invited the artist to contribute to his new series, but 'This he firmly declined to do for reasons I fully understand and respect [...] He did offer to give full co-operation and assistance in making with me a further film study of his more recent sculpture.'[21] Read did not detail Moore's reasons for his reluctance but it is likely that the artist had no interest in being featured in a series with other contemporary artists. Throughout the documentaries with John Read, and indeed in almost all of the films made during his lifetime, the artist is always presented as individual, distinct, separate from the other artists of his time, and where there are comparative references to other artists it is invariably to the giants of the past, to Michelangelo mostly, Leonardo, Cezanne and Rodin, or to anonymous makers of Chacmool figures or African masks.[22]

The correspondence between Read and Moore during the preparations for the second film reveal the ways that Read welcomed the artist as a collaborator, and how the director saw himself as a conduit for the artist's self-expression. Moore sent Read a copy of a talk written by him for the British Council called 'Sculpture in the Open Air', and parts of this were incorporated into the script. After Moore declined being part of *The Artist Speaks*, John Read reassured the artist that, 'I have reported back that the thing to do is to follow your own wishes and to make a film about your sculpture in its setting.'[23] The following July, Read wrote again to Moore that he 'would be most grateful if you could find time to look through the enclosed script [...] I would like to discuss with you more exactly which drawings and sketches we might use in the film, and also the selection of sculpture to be shown.'[24] Reflecting on the process once the film was finished, Read wrote, 'All through the making of the film I tried to keep the artist as close to the actual filming as possible [...] This collaboration rarely became a difficulty and it created freedom of action rather than inhibited it.'[25] Both *Henry Moore* and *A Sculptor's Landscape* should therefore be seen as in many ways Moore's expression of ideas and concerns that the artist wished to emphasize. Yet inevitably the collaborative process of filmmaking entailed mediation by the director, cinematographer and others, and the final result is inflected both by the intentions of the production team and by broader social and cultural currents as well as by the interests and concerns of the viewer's active engagement with the film. I wish to argue that in the case of *A Sculptor's Landscape*, for example, concerns about nuclear war in the late 1950s saturate the film although neither the narration nor Moore himself makes any reference to the topic.

A Sculptor's Landscape opens where *Henry Moore* closes, with a sequence of sculptures abstracted against the sky. Filmed so that they appear similarly sized, they dissolve into each other as they turn, blending together almost as if they are a metamorphosing organism. As is the case throughout both films, the works are not identified by either title or date, even though they come from more than twenty years of Moore's career. As a consequence, they are cut free

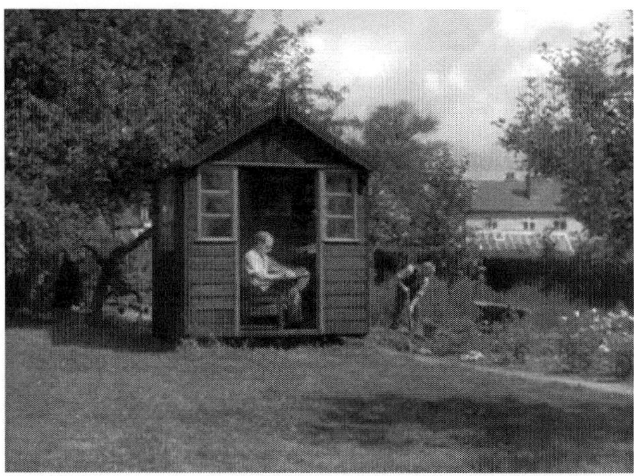

Figure 7.2 *Henry Moore sketches in the doorway of a shed in the grounds of Hoglands in* Henry Moore *(John Read, 1951). Digital still. BBC Television.*

from history, at the same time as their singular origin is reinforced; as the script says of Moore, aligning his creativity with that of a writer, 'his handwriting is on everything he creates'. The first location, to which the film frequently returns, is Hoglands, with its studios located in the extensive grounds. Moore is immediately distanced from urban society and rooted in the English landscape; we are told that he 'has lived in the country for many years. His home is in a Hertfordshire village, among country lanes, leafy hedgerows and green fields'. Scenes shot around the working studios of Hoglands emphasize the rural location and its remoteness from the city. A visit to the Battersea open-air sculpture exhibition places *Warrior with Shield* (1953–4) alongside the work of other artists including Reg Butler and Elizabeth Frink who remain unidentified.

On the return to Hoglands, Moore is discovered seated in the doorway of a potting shed, enclosed in a leafy bower and with a gardener tending a vegetable patch to the side. He is exploring visual ideas through doodles and drawings, and it is almost as if these thoughts are growing from the same soil as the cabbages. Sculptures are seen elsewhere in the extensive grounds of Hoglands and the film briefly visits Brimham Rocks in North Yorkshire. Moore is portrayed by John Read as inspired by rocks and roots, the shapes of the land

and of the female body. One shot, for example, tracks left to right along a drawing of a reclining female figure and then dissolves to a landscape of hills in the distance, echoing the shapes of the drawn body and especially its raised knees, a placid lake in the middle-ground, and close to the camera a dry stone wall also suggestive of the contours of the body. A cut to another wild landscape motivates a right to left pan, once more linking the land and Moore's abstracted bodies. A move in on a round hole in another drawing of a body cuts to a similar hole in a cliff at Brimham and then to a similar opening in a sculpture through which a treeline can be glimpsed. The accompanying narration, written by Read, speaks of the 'timeless, epic quality' of Moore's work, with its 'ancient and primitive associations'; associations between the human figure and landscape are stressed at several points in the commentary, including the reflection that, 'One of the most characteristic aspects of Moore's work is the way the suggestion of the human figure merges into the forms of the landscape, without either of these losing their separate identity.' A tight equivalence is established between the female body, the nation's landscape untouched by tourism, agriculture or other agents of historical change, and Moore's art.

In the most striking sequence, we are shown the then recently installed group of works close to the Glenkiln Reservoir in Scotland: *Standing Figure* (1950), *King and Queen* (1952–3) and *Upright Motive No.1: Glenkiln Cross* (1955–6). Filming these, with background sheep but no humans or other signs of the modern world in shot, involved a four-day trip driving to Scotland and back, undertaken by a crew under cinematographer Walter Lassally. Moore's works are shown as if they have been part of the landscape for centuries, a quality reinforced by the high contrast monochrome images that remove the works from a historical moment in a way in which colour cinematography would not. The visual language of sculptural modernism that had been developed by Moore (and others) since the 1930s is subjected to a process that the critics Jane Beckett and Fiona Russell have described as being 'intertwined with, held safe, and contained, by a mythology of pastoral England'.[26] Ideas of antiquity and timelessness are central to this operation, as is the focus on Moore's *musée imaginaire* of found objects, flints and bones, arrayed throughout the artist's studios. In 1944, Herbert Read contributed the introduction to the monograph *Henry Moore: Sculpture and Drawings*, the most comprehensive study of the artist to date. This text revised the modernist and moderately politicized discourse about Moore of the 1930s, and according to Beckett and Russell,

> initiated a rereading of Moore as a post-war humanist and introduced a number of new elements into the discussion of his work, notably an emphasis on the public commissions, a notion of Moore's 'Englishness', and a description of Moore's reworking of sculptural form, now positioned as having a fundamentally human content. This was by no means a fixed view of Moore's new sculpture in the 1940s and 1950s, which [...] could still be read as disturbing, but it gradually became the dominant account.[27]

John Read's films work to establish this vision of Moore, grounding the sculptures in the land and the body at the same time as they construct a persona for the artist as intuitive rather than intellectual, heroic yet determinedly down-to-earth, modern and forward-looking, yet at heart profoundly traditional. Moreover, his modernized classicism and his explicit humanism are set forth in the documentaries in the context of a post-war return to order and societal reconstruction. Yet there are glimpses in *A Sculptor's Landscape* of alternative constructions of Moore, including the

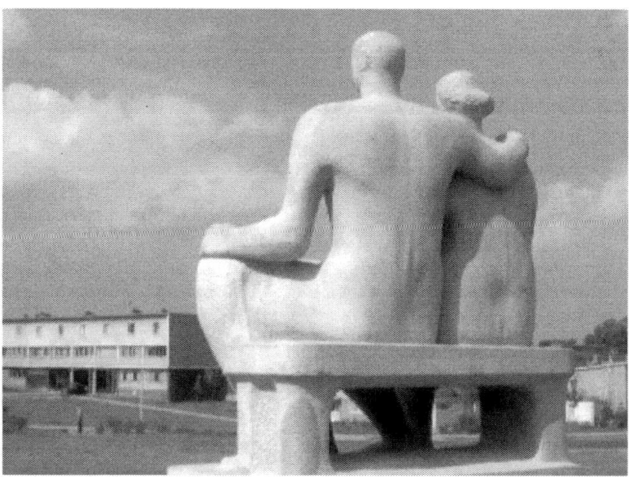

Figure 7.3 *New social housing in Harlow New Town is juxtaposed with* Harlow Family Group *(1954–5) in* A Sculptor's Landscape *(John Read, 1958). Digital still. BBC Television.*

understanding of the artist as an increasingly international figure, exemplified by the half-size model *UNESCO Reclining Figure* (1957–8) being loaded for transport to the Italian quarry where its marble will be cut. To underline his 'English-ness', however, the commentary for *A Sculptor's Landscape* twice mentions that Moore is the son of a Yorkshire miner. Equally notable is a sequence that features *Harlow Family Group* (1954–5) in its original parkland setting with the houses of Harlow New Town in the distance. In one shot, the gaze of the carved child appears captivated by the distant homes, and in the next the male's arm draped over the female figure's shoulder seems almost to embrace the dwellings as well. Here is the film's only explicit presentation of the social milieu in shots of urban Britain populated by the children of a generation looking forward to a reconstructed future.

Despite the fact that in the fifteen years after the end of the war most of Moore's large-scale work was made for urban spaces, the brief Harlow sequence is the only one of its kind in *A Sculptor's Landscape*. Instead, the film's presentation of major works in the landscape fulfils the two modes that Penelope Curtis and Fiona Russell have identified in the post-war still photography of Moore's work. One of these, they suggested, 'is a sculpture of comfort and renewal, figured upon a harmony with the historical landscape. The emptied out body of a reclining female figure is filled by the landscape which it frames or holds.'[28] This is a sculpture of apparent continuity, draining the landscape of 'its historical uneasiness and particularity'.[29] One reclining female form is filmed in a lush meadow with a gentle treeline beyond. 'His reclining figures,' the film's commentary relates, 'which spread like a range of hills, seem as massive and as sure as the earth herself.' In the other mode, employed especially in the Glenkiln sequence, sculptures are iconized as 'ageless, rather than aged, overtly prehistoric rather than historical'. *Standing Figure, King and Queen* and *Glenkiln Cross*, as filmed by Read and his team, exemplify Curtis and Russell's analysis: 'This is a sculpture which is singular, anomalous, set apart from the continuum of everyday life and history. It and the landscape it inhabits offer little hope of renewal, other than to gather up our fears within its frame.'[30] The fears that might be seen as gathered up within the frames of Moore's sculptures as filmed by Read in these depopulated landscapes were, in the Britain of 1958, overwhelmingly those of nuclear annihilation.

Henry Moore and the bomb

Awareness of the nuclear threat had developed rapidly over the previous decade, and had been focused by the country's 'Operation Grapple' nuclear tests in the Pacific Ocean between May 1957 and September 1958, as well as by the potentially catastrophic fire at the Windscale nuclear reactor facility in October 1957.[31] The National Council for the Abolition of Nuclear Weapons Tests (NCANWT) was set up in February 1957, and this was a precursor to the Campaign for Nuclear Disarmament (CND) established in November that year. Henry Moore, along with the artist Barbara Hepworth, was a sponsor of both organizations, reflecting a commitment to this cause that had also seen him as early as 1950 sign a letter to *The Times* opposing the use of nuclear weapons in Korea. Moore himself chose not to make explicit connections between his politics and sculptures, leaving them free to be co-opted by liberal humanists in his home country, across Europe and in the United States. But as Robert Barstow has argued,

> Henry Moore produced sculpture in the 1950s and 1960s that was widely seen as a direct response to the prevailing climate of nuclear anxiety. Even [the leftist critic John] Berger, an unlikely champion of Moore, proposed that his *Falling Warrior* (1956–57) become an emblem for the CND and the preliminary studies the subject of a CND-sponsored exhibition.[32]

Catherine Jolivette has observed that the male nude is rare in Moore's work, with the 'warrior' sculptures of the 1950s, including *Warrior with Shield* and *Maquette for Fallen Warrior* (1956) almost the only examples to put alongside *Falling Warrior*. 'In these works,' she has written, 'the heroic figure is rendered vulnerable, protected only by a shield, his ribs exposed, limbs tense with fear and hollowed features – round staring eyes, or a mouth agape with pain.'[33] Both *Warrior with Shield* and *Falling Warrior* are prominent in *A Sculptor's Landscape*, the former on display in the Battersea exhibition and the latter being unceremoniously transported by and then lifted out of a wheelbarrow. For all that the film notes the classical precedents for such a work, the images suggest that it might be an abject corpse being carted to a grave pit, the detritus of a nuclear attack.

Other sculptures by Moore featured in the film can also be seen, at least in retrospect, to speak of the Cold War politics of the moment. Towards the end of the 1950s, Britain was still involved in societal reconstruction, a process in which, as Gregory Salter has detailed, 'the nuclear family had become central'.[34] The family was also important to Moore's work during the decade, and this is acknowledged in *A Sculptor's Landscape* with numerous images of *maquettes* for family groups, with the inclusion of 'Harlow Family Group' and a line in the commentary confiding that 'sometimes [Moore] just draws to amuse his young daughter'. In a richly detailed analysis of the Cold War at home focused on John Bratby's paintings but equally applicable to Moore's work, Salter has explored the significance of the family in the art of the decade:

> The family serves as a site for Cold War ideals (democracy and consensus) as well as anxieties (breakdown of society, destruction of the self, annihilation through nuclear war). In many ways the domestic arena is a refuge from the battles of the Cold War. But it is also the locus of the internalisation of the many anxieties from which Britons hoped to escape.[35]

The nuclear anxieties are perhaps also signalled by the harsh, modernist score by Humphrey Searle that plays a disturbing and determining role in *A Sculptor's Landscape*, especially so when – as during the 2013 Ghent screening – the narration is stripped away. The music is strikingly different from the romantic, pastoral accompaniment that William Alwyn contributed to *Henry Moore*. There are other elements on the soundtrack that also suggest a gathering storm: the wind whistling around the Glenkiln sculptures and an unexplained noise that sounds like thunder at the close of an earlier sequence highlighting the terrace outside one of Moore's studios.

Nor is it only the insistent wind that suggests that the Glenkiln landscape is constructed somewhat differently from those shown previously in the film. These earlier landscapes might be seen as similar to those celebrated in the 1950s by the historian W.G. Hoskins, who David Matless in his foundational study *Landscape and Englishness* identified as 'a key figure in the emergence of an anti-modern, anti-state, anti-progress culture of landscape from the late 1940s'.[36] Matless has suggested that Hoskins typified a powerful post-war response to change, for which 'turning away is the only possible sensible gesture, away from an England of roads, bombs and planners and towards a humbler ground of deserted village and obscure country church, of ridge and furrow and bench ends'.[37] But the eruption of Moore's assertive, challenging figures into the landscape, their insistent verticality disrupting the equivalence of the reclining body and gently rolling hillsides, and the manner in which the film presents them dominating the surrounding vistas suggests that here 'turning away' from modernity is not an option. Nor is the avoidance of modern conflict, or at least preparations for such, since the commentary speaks of *Standing Figure* as 'stand[ing] like a sentinel' and *King and Queen* seated on rising ground 'in a position of command'. And the consequences of the conflict are then suggested by a hard cut to *Fallen Warrior* being wheeled towards the camera on a barrow that has become a bier.

Catherine Jolivette has written that in the art of the 1950s 'representations of landscape [...] [were revealed] to be sites of anxiety, rather than security'.[38] She argues that images of Britain's geography and geology were mobilized by artists and by the wider culture both in support of a backward-looking pastoral ruralism and to suggest how precarious was both the land and the nation in an age in which nuclear war appeared increasingly likely. In *A Sculptor's Landscape* Henry Moore's art and the fields, hills, lakes and moorlands of Britain are

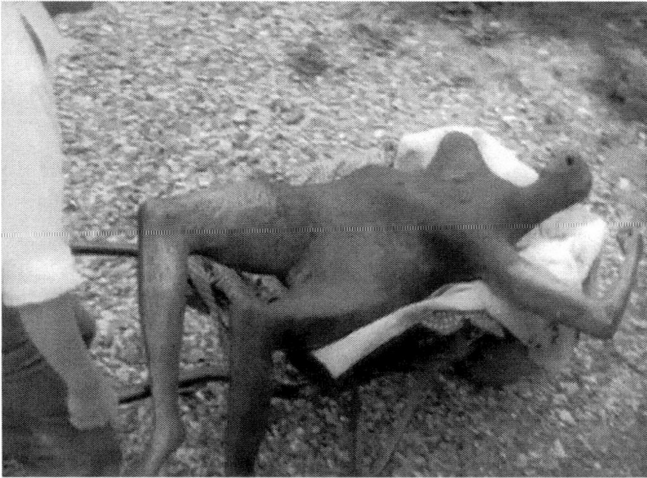

Figure 7.4 *A cast of* Falling Warrior *(1956–7) is unceremoniously transported in a wheelbarrow in* A Sculptor's Landscape *(John Read, 1951). Digital still. BBC Television.*

presented within both of these frameworks, resulting in a film that is both complex and contradictory.

Conclusion

John Read's two films, *Henry Moore* and *A Sculptor's Landscape*, together with his other artist profiles made for BBC Television in the 1950s and with the television arts magazine *Monitor* that began in February 1958, contributed along with many other cultural manifestations, many of which were supported by the Arts Council of Great Britain, to changing conceptions of the arts and to developing audiences for exhibitions, concerts, theatre and dance. As Katerina Loukopoulou has argued, 'these films were part of the wartime and post-war momentum of a neo-romantic belief in the transformative power of the arts, endorsed by a wide political spectrum of artists, filmmakers and critics'.[39] As he made clear in a 1983 interview, John Read saw his work as celebrating the central role of art and artists to develop and extend the progressive, anti-materialist ideals that had been given form during the war and the years of the progressive Labour administration immediately afterwards:

> The basic reason for doing it [making arts films] is simply that you've got to stand up for the imaginative world, the imaginative element in the human personality, because I think that's constantly threatened. It's a very materialistic society; it's an increasingly technological society, or economic society; and there are other values – people do have imagination and sensibilities, and I think that does need constant exposition.[40]

Henry Moore and *A Sculptor's Landscape* can be seen as exemplary expositions of this approach, and ones that were viewed by significant audiences both in their initial broadcasts and also in the extensive non-theatrical distribution that they received courtesy of the Arts Council of Great Britain. At the same time, they can be understood as revealing much about the politics of the decade in which they were created and about contemporary conceptions of the land, of the nation, of the family, of ideas of the past and the future, and of the fear of nuclear annihilation that, thankfully, at least to date, have proved to be unfounded.

Notes

1　'Art & Cinema: On the Aesthetics, History, and Theory of the Art Documentary' was held at the KASKcinema, Ghent, 7 December 2013. This paper is developed from my introduction, and I am grateful to organizer Steven Jacobs for the invitation to participate in both the event and this collection. The conference also featured contributions by Jacobs himself and Angela della Vache, who also contribute to the current volume.

2　On Read, see John Wyver, 'John Read', in *Oxford Dictionary of National Biography*, https://doi.org/10.1093/ref:odnb/104066, accessed 6 June 2018.

3　See Jonathan Woodham, 'Entre Plusieurs Mondes: Le Site Britannique', in Rika Devos and Mil de Kooning (eds), *L'Architecture Moderne À L'Expo 58: 'Pour Un Monde Plus Humain'* (Essen: Mercator Foundation, 2006), 246–61.

4　Elizabeth Darling, '"Britain Today" at Expo 67', in Rhona Richman Kenneally, Johanne Sloan, *Expo 67: Not Just a Souvenir* (Toronto: University of Toronto Press, 2010); *Daily Mail, The British Pavilion from Brussels* (London: Associated Newspapers, 1959), n.p.

5　*Henry Moore* can be viewed online in the United Kingdom in the 'BBC British Art and Artists' archive collection, http://www.bbc.co.uk/archive/henrymoore/8801.shtml; *A Sculptor's Landscape* is also available, http://www.bbc.co.uk/archive/henrymoore/8802.shtml; both accessed 10 April 2018.

6　See Steven Jacobs, 'Carving cameras on Thorvaldsen and Rodin: mid-twentieth century documentaries on sculpture' in Steven Jacobs, Susan Fellman, Vito Adriaensens, Lisa Colpaert, *Screening Statues: Sculpture and Cinema* (Edinburgh: Edinburgh University Press, 2017), 67.

7　The later films are *Henry Moore: One Yorkshire Man Looks at his World* (1967), which reprises sections of the first two films as well as taking Moore to his home town of Castleford; the 1974 pair *The Language of Sculpture* (which was partly shot in Florence) and *Henry Moore at Home*; and the elegiac *Henry Moore at Eighty* (1978), which pays particular attention to the artist's works on paper. For discussion of these films and of British television's presentation of Henry Moore more generally, see John Wyver, 'Myriad mediations: Henry Moore and his works on screen 1937–83', in *Henry Moore: Sculptural Process and Public Identity* (London: Tate Research Publication, 2015), http://www.tate.org.uk/art/research-publications/henry-moore/john-wyver-myriad-mediations-henry-moore-and-his-works-on-screen-1937-83-r1151304; accessed 2 April 2018.

8　On British 'neo-Romanticism', see David A. Mellor (ed.), *A Paradise Lost: The Neo-Romantic Imagination in Britain 1935–55* (London: Lund Humphries/Barbican Art Gallery, 1987).

9　John Read, 'Is There a Documentary Art?' in *Sight & Sound*, 17, 68 (1948–9): 157.

10　Quoted in 'P.L.' [Peter Lennon], 'Portrait maker', in *The Listener* (15 January 1983): 27.

11 Ben Cranfield, '"A stimulation to greater effort of living": The importance of Henry Moore's "credible compromise" to Herbert Read's aesthetics and politics', in *Henry Moore: Sculptural Process and Public Identity* (London: Tate Research Publication, 2015), http://www.tate.org.uk/art/research-publications/henry-moore/ben-cranfield-a-stimulation-to-greater-effort-of-living-the-importance-of-henry-moores-r1151301; accessed 2 April 2018.

12 Andrew Stephenson, 'Fashioning a post-war reputation: Henry Moore as a civic sculptor *c.* 1943–58', in *Henry Moore*, http://www.tate.org.uk/art/research-publications/henry-moore/andrew-stephenson-fashioning-a-post-war-reputation-henry-moore-as-a-civic-sculptor-c1943-r1151305; accessed 2 April 2018.

13 Elizabeth Brown, 'Moore looking: photography and the presentation of sculpture', in Dorothy Kosinski, *Henry Moore: Sculpting the 20th Century* (New Haven, CT, and London: Yale University Press, 2001), 288.

14 Author's interview with John Read, 12 May 1995.

15 Katerina Loukopoulou, 'The mobile framing of Henry Moore's sculpture in post-war Britain', in *Visual Culture in Britain*, 13, 1 (Fall 2012): 73.

16 See Philip Hayward 'Introduction – representing representations', in Hayward (ed.), *Picture This: Media Representations of Visual Art and Artists*, 2nd edition (Luton: University of Luton Press, 1998), 7.

17 *Radio Times*, 27 April 1951, 44; the listing was accompanied in the listings magazine by a feature article written by the art critic Eric Newton, 'The evolution of a genius', 42.

18 On the Festival of Britain, see Harriet Atkinson, *The Festival of Britain: A Land and its People* (London: I.B. Tauris, 2012).

19 John Read, 'The art film and television', *Athene*, 7, 4 (June 1956): 18.

20 On Dreyer's *Thorvaldsen* (1949) and Alekan's *L'Enfer de Rodin* (1957), see Jacobs, 'Carving cameras'.

21 John Read, 'letter to Assistant Head Talks, Television, 18 October 1956' Folder: BBC Written Archives Centre (WAC), Caversham, TEL1/C/1494/1313A.

22 See Wyver, 'Myriad mediations'.

23 John Read, 'letter to Henry Moore, 23 October 1956', WAC TEL1/C/1494/1313A.

24 John Read, 'letter to Henry Moore, 16 July 1957', WAC TEL1/C/1494/1313A.

25 John Read, 'Filming *A Sculptor's Landscape*', *Painter and Sculptor*, Summer 1958, 4.

26 Jane Beckett and Fiona Russell, 'Introduction', in Beckett and Russell (eds), *Henry Moore: Critical Essays* (Aldershot: Ashgate, 2003), 12.

27 Beckett and Russell, *Henry Moore*, 6.

28 Penelope Curtis and Fiona Russell, 'Henry Moore and the post-war British landscape: monuments and modern', in Beckett and Russell (eds), *Henry Moore*, 140.

29 Beckett and Russell, *Henry Moore*, 140.

30 Beckett and Russell, *Henry Moore*, 140.

31 On Operation Grapple, see the detailed Wikipedia entry, https://en.wikipedia.org/wiki/Operation_Grapple, accessed 10 June 2018; on the Windscale fire, see Lorna Arnold, *Windscale, 1957: Anatomy of a Nuclear Accident* (New York: St Martin's Press, 1992).

32 Robert Barstow, 'Geometries of hope and fear: the iconography of atomic science and nuclear anxiety in the modern sculpture of world war and nuclear Britain', in Catherine Jolivette (ed.), *British Art in the Nuclear Age* (Farnham: Ashgate, 2014), 63.

33 Catherine Jolivette, *Landscape, Art and Identity in 1950s Britain* (Abingdon: Ashgate, 2009), 59.

34 Gregory Salter, 'Cold War at home: John Bratby, the self and the nuclear threat', in Jolivette (ed.), *British Art in the Nuclear Age*, 153.

35 Salter, *British Art in the Nuclear Age*, 155.

36 David Matless, *Landscape and Englishness* (London: Reaktion Books, 1998), 274.

37 Matless, *Landscape and Englishness*, 276.

38 Jolivette, *Landscape, Art and Identity*, 2.

39 Katerina Loukopoulou, *A Cultural History of Films on Art*, Unpublished PhD. thesis, School of Art, Film and Visual Media (Birkbeck College, University of London, 2010), 22.

40 Quoted in 'P.L.' [Peter Lennon], 'Portrait maker', 27.

8

Creative process, material inscription and Dudley Shaw Ashton's Figures in a Landscape *(1953)*

LUCY REYNOLDS

Two circular forms of curved white marble sit in the sand under the rocky arches of a cliff. Framed in close up, the angle of the camera exaggerates the scale of these small sculptures so that they appear to dominate the view of the Cornish coastline behind them. The solidity and stillness of the marble forms counterpoint the agitated surf running beneath them, which, glimpsed through small apertures carved into them, sets in motion a play of rhythmic relations between contrasting and complementary surfaces and spaces. The spell of this intense interplay of the organic and man-made is broken by the interposition of one hand – then another – which lifts the smaller sculpture of the two, and slots it into the hole within the larger. The hands pause, resting on the co-joined sculptures, anonymous except for the punctuating rhythm of a further stone, flat, dark and round, set into their owner's ring.

It is a fleeting, if indelible, sequence in the 1953 film *Figures in a Landscape*, and contains many of the distinctive features that the filmmaker Dudley Shaw Ashton (1909–85) brings to his portrait of the sculptor Barbara Hepworth.

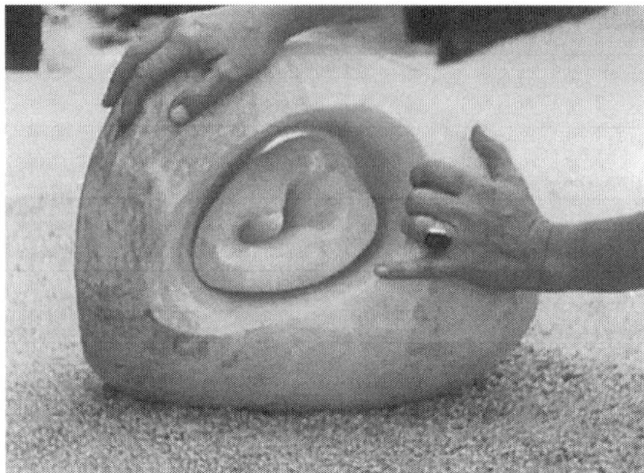

Figure 8.1 Figures in a Landscape *(Dudley Shaw Ashton, 1953). Digital still. Courtesy of the British Film Institute.*

It is striking that the artist's hands upon the sculptures in the surf marks Hepworth's first appearance in the film, which begins with arresting images of the Zennor peninsula in Cornwall in which a number of her sculptures – in small groupings and in isolation – appear against its atmospheric cliffs, standing stones and quarries. These unpeopled images of the landscape are accompanied by the archaeologist Jacquetta Hawkes' meditation on human presence in the Cornish landscape, voiced by poet Cecil Day-Lewis, and to the accompaniment of an original sound score by modernist composer Priaulx Rainier. By situating Hepworth's sculptures directly within the contours and against the landmarks of Cornwall's southern-most tip, where she had famously established her St Ives studio, Shaw Ashton audaciously literalizes his argument for the profound relationship between the artist's work and its Cornish context. Yet the artist and her sculptures embody not only the influence of land on individual creative endeavour, but also reflect how the film's images of these figures in the landscape sought to project more widely a cohesive vision of nationhood at a transitional time. Made on the cusp of the country's post-war regeneration, and the brink of a new modernity, Shaw Ashton's film is illuminating for how it encapsulates this uncertain moment.

As Dudley Shaw Ashton's most well-known film, *Figures in a Landscape* has found most frequent reference within the framework of Hepworth scholarship, rather than documentary film history. His studied framing of the worker could be seen as out of step with the more free-wheeling expressions of everyday experience portrayed by Lindsay Anderson, Lorenza Moretti and the new generation of filmmakers associated to documentary forms in Britain's immediate post-war culture. Priaulx Rainier's atonal score, the patrician voice-over of Cecil Day-Lewis and the artful, Surrealist infused, juxtapositions of *Figures in a Landscape* contrast starkly to the representations of working-class culture in Anderson's contemporaneous *O Dreamland* (1953), for example; whose portrait of a seaside funfair was described by the critic Gavin Lambert as 'like a blow in the face', which 'assaults eye and ear with a rough-edged but sharp-centred impression'.[1] Rather, *Figures in a Landscape* could be seen to ascribe to all the class bound, generational conventions which Anderson's 'Free Cinema' screenings, and the burgeoning new strain of realism in British arts culture, from theatre and poetry to pop art, sought to eschew.

Yet, whilst the solemn didacticism of *Figures in a Landscape* might not chime with the desire to document authentic experience sought by Andersen or playwrights such as John Osbourne, it alludes to a more complex moment in British film history than mere generational opposition. *Figures in a Landscape* could be read as a potent reflection of how the cultural hiatus created by the Second World War was to have repercussions on the art produced in the decade that followed. Rendered dormant by five years of fighting, the Blitz and war-time privations, it could be argued that the cultural canons of modernist form which had dominated British cultural life and its institutions in the 1920s and 1930s, still remained the primary co-ordinates for a cultural landscape utterly changed in the war's aftermath. Shaw Ashton's focus on Hepworth reflects not only his own investment in these pre-war touchstones, but also points to the role assigned to artists such as Hepworth, who had a high profile before the war, to act as agents of cultural regeneration in the decade that followed.

Ashton and Cornwall: landscape at stake

Despite a successful premiere at the Venice Film Festival in 1954, *Figures in a Landscape* was seen as a curiosity with which Hepworth herself remained dissatisfied, in comparison to more prominent portrayals of her practice in film and television, in particular John Read's 1961 documentary for the BBC, *Barbara Hepworth*. Inga Fraser notes that the artist felt her 'keen sense of scale and sensitivity to movement' was 'distorted' in Shaw Ashton's film,[2] and was displeased with how Shaw Ashton's interest in the representation of the creative process overshadowed her artistic autonomy:

> The portrayal of her sculpture was mediated via a combination of Shaw Ashton's visual focus on the uncanny, Rainier's esoteric score, Hawkes's poetic narrative and Day-Lewis's theatrical delivery [...] it is conceivable that with these additional artistic contributions Hepworth felt her own narrative and conception of sculpture too much compromised.[3]

Fraser's observation certainly supports the privileging of process characteristic of Shaw Aston, including the foregrounding of the film's other elements such as sound and commentary. Furthermore, as she argues, *Figures in a Landscape* has 'set the tone for future portrayals, especially in the emphasis on the connection between her art and the Cornish landscape' and as a result obscured other potential readings of Hepworth's work, particularly relating to the earlier influences of international modernism.[4]

However, rather than seeing *Figures in a Landscape* as a summation of Hepworth's work to date, the film might be more fruitfully considered as a reflection of the artist's concerns at a particular, and potent, time in both her practice as well as wider societal and national shifts. Both artist and filmmaker experienced how landscape came to be at stake and was nationally asserted in a different way from the previous era of international modernism in which both were protagonists. And whilst Shaw Ashton's focus on artist and landscape might indeed be considered narrow, it is important to stress that this was a period when Hepworth identified herself strongly with her Cornish environment. In 1952 she clearly articulates this idea in an auto biographical insert to the catalogue she developed on her work with Herbert Read. Setting her observations chronologically between 1939 and 1946, which charted her arrival and settlement in Cornwall, she describes herself as part of the landscape, rather than an observer of it, writing eloquently of how: 'From the sculptor's point of view one can either be the spectator of the object or the object itself. I was the figure in the landscape.'[5]

Hepworth's declaration suggests not only her own agency in positioning her practice, but also why Shaw Ashton was drawn to her work in order to explore a wider argument. Rather than standing apart from her environment as an artistically autonomous presence, the camera inscribes Hepworth within the landscape alongside her sculptures. Appearing first through her disembodied hands, Shaw Ashton asserts Hepworth's creative process as a sculptor and stone carver, in order to position her as a point of artistic continuity within Hawkes' narrative of a landscape overwritten with centuries of human – habitation and labour. Shaw Ashton's images and Hawkes' narrative reflect the stabilizing role deployed for the British landscape in officially endorsed culture at this transitional period in the early 1950s. The film brings to mind Robert Burden's observation on how images of landscape are used to allay and stabilize times of national anxiety: '[at] moments in history when landscape needed to represent something essentialist about the national culture – as nostalgia for an imagined organic past or idyllic childhood (a symbolic regression); as counterweight to an industrializing economy; as consolation for the horrors of war'.[6] In this way, Shaw Ashton's film might thus be considered compelling, not only for its unusual portrait of an artist at work in her environment but also for its assertion of landscape as deeply and enduringly connected to creative endeavour, in a reflection of the anxieties and sensitivities of a country for whom notions of land, both domestic and international, were in crisis.

Other subjects of Shaw Ashton's films from the 1950s, such as Henry Moore's sculpture *Reclining Figure*, situated outside the new UNESCO building in Paris, which he made for the British Film Institute (BFI) in 1958, for example, or 1959's *Coventry Cathedral*, which documents the bombed cathedral's reconstruction, reflect the tentative construction of a post-war culture then at work across Europe, where official endorsements of culture by established artists such as these might be harnessed as hopeful messages for future transnational unities. Yet again, in his desire to explore more profound questions about creative labour, Shaw Ashton goes beyond official narratives of regeneration. In *Coventry Cathedral*, with its pans across Basil Spence's architectural drawings and the artist Graham Sutherland at work on preliminary drawings for its tapestry, the camera becomes a tool for his more profound and enduring enquiry into the material processes of the maker.

Like many of the films about artists and art works which Shaw Ashton would go on to make for cultural institutions such as the BFI and the Arts Council in the decades that followed, *Figures in a Landscape* shows an unusual sensitivity to creative process rather than artistic persona. His emphasis on the former is borne out in the first sentence of the 'Preliminary Rough Outline' for the film, which Shaw Ashton proposed in 1952 to the British Film Institute's newly established Experimental Film Fund, when he writes that 'the film should be experimental in its approach to the modern movement in art. Initially it should be so in its method of showing the influences which have been at work on the creative mind of the artist.'[7] Poetically epitomized as the sculptor's hand reaches into the surf to rest on her sculptures in *Figures in a Landscape* and apparent across a body of films on artists as various as Francis Bacon (*Francis Bacon: Paintings 1944–1962*, 1963) and Nicolas Poussin (*Poussin – The Seven Sacraments,* 1968), Shaw Ashton used a number of experimental strategies, such as visual and musical counterpoint and unconventional framing, in his attempt to understand what motivated and determined the creative methods in question. In his first letter to Jacquetta Hawkes in 1952, concerning her engagement to conceive the script for *Figures in a Landscape*, Shaw Ashton puts this point clearly, writing that: 'The film is not intended to be in any way didactic but is rather a form of film form on landscape and its reference to the work of one particular artist.'[8] With this in mind, *Figures in a Landscape* and the art documentaries which followed it until his final 1976 film, *Sam Smith: Genuine England,*[9] might be considered discursive rather than didactic, asserting the process of art making as a complex dialogic, and active, enquiry between the artist and their environment. Echoing documentary forebears such as Alberto Cavalcanti or John Grierson, Shaw Ashton frequently commissioned original sound scores and scripts to heighten his cinematographic experimentation, seeing the collaborative consultations with Hawkes and from experimental composers such as Rainier as bringing further creative dimension to his portraits.

Like Shaw Ashton, and despite the prominence afforded them through official channels such as the 1951 Festival of Britain or the Venice Biennale, Hepworth and her contemporaries Henry Moore and Sutherland, could also be understood as increasingly out of step with a new post-war mood at odds with the officially sanctioned optimism that the Festival attempted to assert. At the same time that the sculptures of Moore or Hepworth were being reframed as post-war embodiments of a universal symbolism by state-endorsed institutions, another generation of artists were perceiving them as elitist and establishment. For the artists Eduardo Paolozzi and Richard Hamilton, and the critics Lawrence Alloway and Reyner Banham, meeting as the Independent Group at the Institute of Contemporary Art (ICA) in 1952, the popular forms of burgeoning commercial culture, from comic books to advertisements, were far more relevant to the art of post-war experience than the mute formalism of Hepworth or Moore's sculpture.

Ashton's films on art and the development of *Figures*

Whilst *Figures in a Landscape* may have contributed, even negatively, to Hepworth scholarship, Shaw Ashton's wider film corpus has gained little recognition within film historical discourse. A reason for his marginality could be partly attributed to his lack of visibility, as a filmmaker operating outside both the professional canon of the British film industry and its London apex. His filmmaking experience was honed not in film school but through his engagement in Britain's wide-spread and established amateur film culture in the years leading up to the Second World War. Documentary was an increasingly popular form at Film Society screenings throughout the 1930s, which Jamie Sexton relates to the 'growing (if never total) disillusion with commercial cinema'.[10]

In 1938, Shaw Ashton won an award from *Amateur Cine World* for the short film *Land Fall*, which recorded the construction of the modernist house he commissioned from the architect Oliver Hill in 1938 at Poole in Dorset. *Amateur Cine World* was one of the key publications to reflect the growing regional spread of the film club movement, aided by the establishment of the Institute of Amateur Cinematographers in 1932 and the Independent Film-makers Association in 1933. That the latter's stated aim was to 'bring together and assist those who are interested in the production of Documentary,

Experimental, and Educational films'[11] underlines the documentary and fact-based focus of many amateur filmmakers such as Shaw Ashton, and also reflects the influence of Soviet and British documentary films by Basil Wright, John Grierson, Dziga Vertov and Sergei Eisenstein, which they were encountering in the pages of amateur film publications and at film society screenings. Based in Dorset rather than London, Shaw Ashton's exposure to this culture came through the Bournemouth Film Society, particularly during and in the years following the war.

Whilst he was not involved in the London milieu of Ivor Montagu's Film Society and other well-known screening spaces for alternative cinema form, Shaw Ashton did, however, benefit from the regional networks of amateur film enthusiasts, which had spread since the 1930s, and from the connections he made through them socially. For example, Thorold Dickinson, an influential figure in post-war British cinema for his work with Ealing Studios as an editor and director, and later as the pioneer of film studies at the Slade School of Art, became a close friend, having taken a cottage not far from *Land Fall*. Thorold's later position as Chief of Film Services for UNESCO from 1956–60, for example, undoubtedly had a bearing on Shaw Ashton's 1959 commission to depict Henry Moore's *Reclining Figure* outside the UNESCO building.

At the same time, *Land Fall*, the subject of Shaw Ashton's winning film, indicates his strong affiliations to the wider currents of modernism in arts and design, which allowed him, as a young man of means with a family trust fund, to commission Hill to build his house, having first considered and consulted Wells Coates – later responsible for the Royal Festival Hall – and Berthold Lubetkin. According to the Pevsner guide to *The Buildings of England*, Shaw Ashton's film of his house – in 'the International Modern Style [...] made the career of the owner'.[12] In *Land Fall*'s carefully composed frames of workers shifting bricks and rendering plaster, and pans across the completed house's sinuous modernist planes, it is possible to trace the twin co-ordinates of modernism in the visual arts and design and the politically infused experimentalism of the pre-war era documentary, which would later inform Shaw Ashton's documentary films on art and, in the case of Hepworth and her sculpture, the depiction of modernist forms situated within the British landscape.

Pevsner's allusion to Shaw Ashton's future direction reflects the career in art documentary which he went on to establish, often but not exclusively through his production company Samaritan films, the credits of which first appear on his 1961 visual improvisation on Claude Debussy's composition, *La Cathedrale Engloutie,* made for the Marlborough Gallery with sponsorship from the Arts Council. It was the devaluations of his trust fund stock following the war, which catapulted Shaw Ashton from amateur to professional, driven by the need to turn creative interest into commercial gain, beginning with public safety information films for children, such as *Trouble in Toy Town* (1946). However, rather than moving into the more commercial realms of advertising or the film industry, he built a career close to his amateur interest and knowledge in the visual arts, taking advantage of the buoyant post-war film funding becoming available through public bodies and institutions such as the British Film Institute and the Arts Council of Great Britain, for whom he documented the lives and work of artists and architects as various as Poussin, Claude Lorrain and Francis Bacon. However, the early promise of the BFI's Experimental Film Fund as a regular source of funding did not materialize. As the decade progressed the fund moved away from its originally stated intention to document films about artists, and to reflect the educational aims of amateur film production, towards more varied short film forms such as experimental fiction.[13] Working in a freelance capacity and predominately in the small field of educational arts documentary for a cinema context, rather than the burgeoning televisual arts programming strands then becoming more established, with the arts magazine series *Monitor* (BBC 1958–65) and high profile television arts commentators such as the art historian Kenneth Clark, Shaw Ashton's career was based on pitching ideas to arts commissioners such as the Arts Council and the educational independents which had emerged from the government-sponsored Crown Film Unit, such as the Blackheath Film Unit. These attempts would, as his son Peter Shaw Ashton recalls, occasionally 'hit a bullseye'.[14] The precariousness of finding funding to pursue his film projects accounts for Shaw Ashton's relatively small output compared to other filmmakers, such as John Read, who was also producing documentaries on artists in the post-war period.

Ashton and Hepworth: geometry and abstraction

Shaw Ashton was clearly attracted to Hepworth's method of working marble, wood or granite, seeing her approach as a profound enquiry into how to represent objects in space, at the same time that he identified it with pre-war modes of modernism. Hepworth was committed to overturning previous conventions of sculptural practice that employed maquettes and models, choosing instead to adhere to the modernist maxim of 'truth to materials' and to carve directly into stone. Her slow and incremental chiselling away at the stone or wood's surfaces, manifested the desire to understand the material's intrinsic nature, and the spatial dynamics it occupied. Through his representations of Hepworth in the act of carving, Shaw Ashton's intent was to offer an insight into the often mystified processes of creative labour, which are frequently divorced from the completed art object. His imperative, as I have argued, finds its roots in earlier representations of labour encountered through film society culture, seen not only in the films of the Soviet avant-garde, such as Vertov, but the portrayal of the British working class by the indigenous documentary movement of the GPO film unit: Alberto Cavalcanti's *Coal Face* (1935), for example, or Humphrey Jennings' 1939 *Spare Time,* which presented a portrait of Britain at work and leisure. *Figures in a Landscape* makes the case that processes of creative practice such as Hepworth's operate under the same dynamic and are worthy of equal attention to their working-class counterparts. First represented through the agency of her hands, as signifiers of her creative instrumentalization, Hepworth is framed throughout the film in haptic attachment to her sculptures; proximately positioned either in the act of chiselling or touching, and represented in an ongoing engagement with them through Shaw Ashton's use of textural close-ups and assertive fixed frames.

Hepworth's focus on direct carving into her material drew on skills that she had learnt during time spent in Italy on a travelling scholarship in the late 1920s, and her interest in this way of working was encouraged by close friendships with European artists from Constantin Brancusi and Piet Mondrian to Sophie Taeuber-Arp and Hans Arp, who had briefly made London – and significantly in the case of her close friendship with Nam Gaubo, Cornwall, their home in the decade to come. Reinforced by her connection to influential figures in the British modernist firmament like Herbert Read, as well as her second husband Ben Nicolson, her affinities, like those of Shaw Ashton, were to the international modernist movement that had its ascendancy during the 1930s. Furthermore, she was highly instrumental in the discourses circulating around abstraction and the Constructivism movement, seen in her involvement as the designer of the 1937 publication *Circle: International Survey of Constructivist Art,* which featured the work of artists, architects and designers including Le Corbusier, Brancusi and László Moholy-Nagy. Whilst Hepworth had long considered the landscape around her as key to the forms and formulations of her sculptures, her enquiry into her relationship to landscape intensified following her move, on the eve of war, from London to St Ives in the Penwith peninsula of Cornwall in 1939. It was here that she began to look more closely at the corporeal and spatial dynamics of human relationships to landscape and to identify herself as the 'figure in the landscape', writing in 1946 of how: 'first and last there is the human figure which in the country becomes a free and moving part of a greater whole'.[15] The need that she writes of in 1952 to 'discover some absolute essence in sculptural terms giving the quality of human relationships' (36) can be glimpsed in the relational interplay of tension and harmony between grouped spheres, forms and taut strings, presented in the film in works such as *Wave* (1943), *Conoid, Sphere and Hollow II* (1937) or *Group 1* (1952).

Certainly, as Catherine Jolivette has argued very cogently, the figure in the landscape, particularly through the sculptures of her close contemporary Henry Moore, to whom she was compared throughout her career – often disparagingly – was figured as female, and linked to a spurious relationship between the land and an essentialised female body as signifier of nature. As Jolivette contends:

> Her work, though far more concerned with geometry and abstraction than Moore's, was frequently discussed in terms of the sculptor's gendered body, and in relation to her maternity, which in turn, was construed to grant her a closer connection to nature and to the land.[16]

Rather, Jolivette suggests an affinity to the landscape that was for Hepworth 'emotional and intellectual, not corporeal',[17] and I would argue that Shaw

Ashton's film is consciously engaged in making the argument for a tangible connection between sculpted matter and geological matter facilitated by, rather than situated in, her body. His use of comparative proximity between artist and landscape is less concerned with the artist's gendered body, than in an attempt to investigate and convey through the medium of the camera how external, contingent and localized features of the Cornish landscape have a significant role in the development of her work. In his outline to the BFI, he writes how its first section should be devoted to: 'the influences of landscape, natural form and the continuous Cornish feeling for shape, light and texture and how these influences have been heightened and turned into a form of visual poetry by the artist"[18]

Indeed, the cut that follows Shaw Ashton's images of her marble sculptures in the sand brings the viewer into abrupt confrontation with the eye of the sculptor, gazing back at them through an aperture of her own making, carved out of the wooden centre of the 1949 sculpture *Lyric Form*. Carrying the viewer from the open spaces inside Hepworth's sculpture to the eye of the artist herself, Shaw Ashton's self-reflexive choreography of images possesses a Vertovian resonance. But, looking beyond its Kino Eye allusions, Shaw Ashton's film also makes the argument that sculpture too can be an instrument for seeing more closely, throwing into relief the environment around it through its equivalent, or contrasting, surfaces and shapes. Resting on sand rather than a plinth, Hepworth's sculptures in the surf also assert a Surrealist incongruity. Indeed, Shaw Ashton refers directly in his preliminary outline to 'the deliberate placing of her figures in the natural landscape giving something of the surprise of a Surrealist painting'.[19] It is telling that he uses the word 'surprise' rather than shock; for the challenge to the viewer is not imparted by the slitting of an eye, but by the confident authorial gaze of the artist, asserting her creative presence as she looks back into the camera.

Figures in a Landscape's use of striking juxtapositions references a Surrealism more akin to British contemporaries such as filmmaker and artist Humphrey Jennings and painter Paul Nash than European counterparts such as Breton or Buñuel. Nash's nationally distinct version of Surrealism during the 1930s and 1940s strongly engaged with the incongruities of forms in the landscape, a motif which was to be continued in a more emotive strain by artists of the so called neo-romantic school during and in the aftermath of the war, such as Graham Sutherland or John Minton. In one of the few contemporaneous articles on the film in a 1954 issue of *Architectural Review*, Reyner Banham makes reference to Nash's famous 1935 assertion of 'a statue in a ditch or the middle of a ploughed field', to argue for the Surrealist shock tactic of incongruous juxtaposition in the film, as a means through which the viewer may see both landscape and sculpture anew. He writes that 'the object itself becomes far more provocative than it would be in a man-made setting while the relative values of all the other objects in the landscape are resolved and altered'.[20] Yet, in *Figures in a Landscape*, I would argue that the altered spatial relations between form and landscape, which Banham refers to as 'a kind of field of aesthetic force',[21] are opened up to a more complex set of reciprocities than that offered by Surrealist counterpoint; one in which the artist and cinematographer (Shaw Ashton himself) act as dynamic agents of interaction between sculpture and its setting. Developing further on her notion of being a figure in a landscape, Hepworth herself spoke of how 'every sculpture contained to a greater or lesser degree the ever-changing forms and contours embodying my own response to a given position'.[22] In wooden works such as *Pelagos* (1946) and *Wave* (1944) – both depicted in the film – we can, according to Chris Stephens, see this reflected as 'a sense of tension, of energy held in equilibrium',[23] which expresses this phenomenological exchange. Positioned

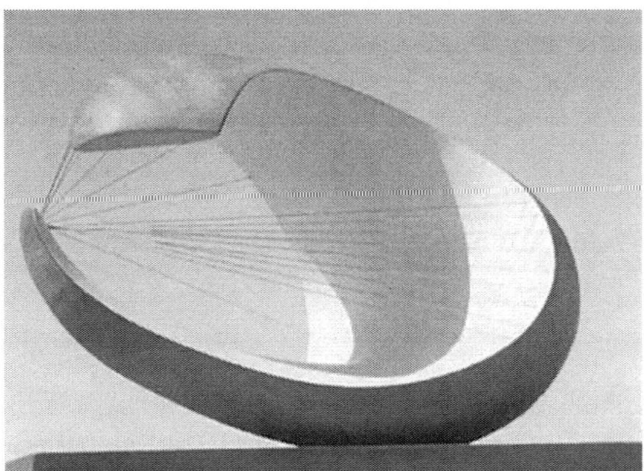

Figure 8.2 *Barbara Hepworth's sculpture* Wave, *as featured in* Figures in a Landscape *(Dudley Shaw Ashton, 1953). Digital still. Courtesy of the British Film Institute.*

against Cornwall's tin mines, shorelines and megalithic stones through the camera's shifting alignments of scale, light, distance, view and contour, Shaw Ashton is able to make a more nuanced argument for the potency of the sculptural form, beyond mere comparative contrast.

For, to return to Hepworth's point about the human figure 'as a free and moving part of the whole', the case that Shaw Ashton makes, along with Hepworth and the other contributors to the film's conception and realization, is for the human being not as separated out from the contours of the landscape but greatly implicated in it, historically, socially and politically. Shaw Ashton's focus on land and landscape, and his choice of Hawkes and Hepworth as its interlocutors, reflects how it was a subject very much at stake in the cultural discourse of the period. The representation of Britain through its landscape, which had helped to promote the notion of a cohesive national identity during the war, and which was asserted at regenerative projects such as the 1951 Festival of Britain, was itself being eroded by geographical factors both domestic and international. Britain's territorial dominance abroad was increasingly in question as more parts of the empire asserted their independence or marked new immigrations into the country. At the same time, the recent ravages and ruination of bomb damage was still markedly visible across the country as the slow process of rebuilding began. Territorial metaphors, always conflicted in British history and culture, thus took on new significance for a country still uncertainly held in post-war recovery, and finding, as Jolivette notes, that, due to unfolding events abroad and conditions at home: 'the very significations of nationhood and a collective British identity were subject to examination and revision'.[24] Furthermore, the catastrophic effects of atomic power wielded at Nagasaki and Hiroshima brought a new dimension of anxiety to the image of landscape as a space of desolation and destruction beyond Britain's domestic bomb damage, imbuing it with a fragility and vulnerability in the face of more widespread forms of atomic annihilation. The anguished sculptures by artists such as Reg Butler could be seen as responses to this global precarity, heralded by Herbert Read on the advent of the show of sculptures in which they were included at the 1952 Venice Biennale as representative of the 'geometry of fear'. As Robert Burstow observes:

Coming at a moment when the ideological conflict of the Cold War had been transformed into military confrontation in Korea and increased risk of nuclear warfare, Read's memorable phrase slipped into the discourse of post-war British sculpture, shifting the associations of 'geometry' away from the Constructive art of Utopian Socialism (familiar to regular Biennale visitors from Hepworth's 1950 exhibit) towards an Expressionist art of dystopian anxiety.[25]

National narratives: the film's reception

Rather than endorse these reflections of nuclear anxiety, official culture countered the 'geometry of fear' with alternative narratives connecting British identity to its geography. Contemporaneous to the production and conception of the film, the timing of Elizabeth II's coronation in 1953, for example, signalled the stability of sovereignty over Britain's increasingly fragmented international territories. The 1951 Festival of Britain also asserted the image of land as a national signifier of continuity, endurance and solidity against the backdrop of nuclear crisis. In displays such as 'Britain at Land' and 'the Living World', geological and archaeological exhibits and information helped to reinforce territorial identifications between the British people and their land, fabricated through a narrative of its geography as an ancient and enduring habitation.

Made between 1952 and 1953 when these concerns at home and abroad were at their apex, *Figures in a Landscape* also offers a compelling reflection of how images of land and art might be used to allay such fears of annihilation. The timeless stability, which official culture had associated to Hepworth's sculptures, was further determined by their placement in corresponding patterns and contours of landscape also designated as symbols of stability, through their archaic reference to Cornish myth and history. Shaw Ashton's choice of the archaeologist Jacquetta Hawkes as 'ideal' to write the commentary also reinforced this narrative of Cornish land, particularly since she was responsible for the Land exhibitions at the Festival of Britain and thus had a role in profoundly influencing the post-war narrative of social cohesion based on notions of national terrain. Hawkes was a well-known public intellectual in British culture at the time, she had popularized archaeology through her television appearances, such as the quiz series *Animal, Vegetable, Mineral*. Most significantly, her best-selling book *A Land* (1951), a lyrical chronicle of Britain's geographical development and the human role in its formation, had caught the public imagination with its timely argument for the continuities across time between the British people and their environment.

It was her poetic, yet accessible, language that Shaw Ashton wished to engage. But importantly, her argument for the peopled histories of the land, as much inscribed with myth and culture, as by geographic sedimentation, echoed back to the resonant figure in the landscape shared by Hepworth and himself. In the suggestive and alliterate embellishments of her script, she alludes to earlier figures of 'ancient pagans' in the landscape: 'the granite knew the feel of its crystalline surface from the touch of their fingers. There were figures in the landscape'.[26] Hawkes started to develop her script at the end of 1952, guided by the footage that Shaw Ashton had already shot; and a close bond developed between them.

The South African composer Priaulx Rainier, known for her spare, experimental scores and also with a residence in St Ives, was not Shaw Ashton's first choice for the film, as Hawkes had been.[27] She became involved through her close friendship with Hepworth, for whom she had composed in the past. As correspondence shows, Rainier became a significant point of communication between Shaw Ashton, Hawkes and an increasingly disengaged Hepworth. Hepworth had not only displayed concerns about the wording of Hawkes' script in the final months of production, but was also suffering a series of personal tragedies: this included the break-up of her marriage to Nicolson, but more significantly, the death of her eldest son in a plane crash while serving in the Korean War in early 1953. Rainier worked closely with Hawkes and Ashton to develop the score in dialogue with Hawkes' script and in response to Shaw Ashton's images. Her attention to the balance and rhythm between image, voice and music is apparent in a letter to Hawkes of March 1953, when she writes of how:

> Yesterday I saw the film twice with Dudley reading the script as far as he
> was able. The shortened phrases in the new version are much better leaving

space to absorb visually [...] This showed one how fragmentary sound should be except in long unbroken sequences. I am hard at it now.[28]

Following the addition of the poet Cecil Day-Lewis' voice-over commentary, the film was finished in time to launch as the British short film entry for the fourteenth Venice Film Festival (20 August to 4 September 1953), at the same time inaugurating the BFI's Experimental Film Fund, as its first production. Despite this early visibility, and the endorsement of key figures in British film and art culture such as Edgar Anstey and Roland Penrose on the accompanying BFI publicity, beyond Reyner Baynam's sustained consideration in *Architectural Review*, the film garnered few further reviews outside the amateur film press.[29] Information surviving in the BFI archives suggests that, beyond its screening at the Venezuela Film Festival the following year, *Figures in a Landscape* relied on regional educational circuits for its distribution and received little further attention until more recent curatorial and scholarly attention in a new millennium.[30]

The reasons for the lack of visibility at the time of its making for either the film or its filmmaker in the intervening years return us to its author's lack of purchase and provincialism amongst film industrial networks, at the same time that the formal experimentations of both filmmaker and artist as appearing increasingly out of step with the concerns of a society and culture looking forward after the privations of war time and its aftermath. As I have observed, the film reflects thus the cultural hiatus in which it was conceived, where pre-war modernism was pressed into the service of bolstering regeneration efforts and Cold War fears. However, with hindsight, *Figures in a Landscape* functions as a rich repository for the conflicting ideas around culture and national identity playing out across Cornwall's idealized landscape. Already dated at its release, Hawkes' grandiose narrative of the land's temporal inscriptions and its historic continuities now finally reveal an archival potency on retrospective viewing. Read beyond a staged formalism out of step with new freedoms, the audacious materialism of Hepworth's situated sculptures also takes on new weight.

But even as *Figures in a Landscape* may seem out of time, it is also prescient of how Shaw Ashton, Hepworth and Hawkes' engagement with questions of the landscape might shift from a celebration of historical potency to one of environmental urgency. For Hepworth, the 'war ended a certain idealism' and, like Hawkes, she was 'a passionate advocate' for post-war social reconstruction. Revelations of the Holocaust and Hiroshima caused 'the relationship of the individual to their social and natural environment', to become as Christopher Stephens notes 'an overriding concern',[31] for Hepworth. All of the film's protagonists were later to become involved with the anti-nuclear activism precipitated by the Campaign for Nuclear Disarmament later founded by Hawkes and her husband J.P. Priestly. Despite not being an active participant in the fighting,[32] Shaw Ashton, as his son remembers, was also profoundly politicized by revelations of war-time atrocity, and its atomic aftermath. Whether in *Figures . . .* or his later films on Bacon, Mantegna or Sam Smith, Shaw Ashton's politics were implicit within the experimental rationale of his filmmaking, and his enduring interest in creative instrumentalization. However, there is no doubt that, in tandem with Hawkes and Hepworth, he identified himself as the figure in the landscape, finding in this position a resonant space from which to respond and reflect the political conditions of a Britain in transition.

Notes

1　Mark Cousins and Kevin Macdonald, *Imagining Reality* (London: Faber and Faber, 1996), 212.

2　Inga Fraser, 'Media and Movement: Barbara Hepworth beyond the Lens', in Penelope Curtis and Chris Stephens (eds), *Barbara Hepworth: Sculpture for the Modern World* (London: Tate Publishing, 2015), 78.

3　Fraser, 'Media and Movement', 78.

4　Inga Fraser, 'Hepworth on Film', in *Tate Etc*, 34 (Summer 2015), http://www.tate.org.uk/context-comment/articles/hepworth-on-film (accessed 4 January 2018).

5　Barbara Hepworth, 'The War, Cornwall, and Artist in Landscape', in Herbert Read, *Barbara Hepworth Carvings and Drawings* (London: Lund Humphries, 1952), 60.

6　Robert Burden, 'Introduction: Englishness and Spatial Practices', in Robert Burden and Stephan Kohl, *Landscape and Englishness* (Amsterdam/New York: Rodopi, 2006), 24.

7　Dudley Shaw Ashton, 'Preliminary Rough Outline Treatment for Proposed Film on the Work of Barbara Hepworth', Jacquetta Hawkes Archive, Bradford University, 1.

8   Letter from Dudley Shaw Ashton to Jacquetta Hawkes (4 September 1952), Jacquetta Hawkes Archive, Bradford University.

9   *Sam Smith: Genuine England* was commissioned by the Arts Council and the Crafts Advisory Committee for BBC2's *Arena* arts series, on the occasion of an exhibition of the wood sculptor Sam Smith.

10   Jamie Sexton, *Alternative Film Culture in Interwar Britain* (Exeter: University of Exeter Press, 2008), 104.

11   'Notice of Formation of Independent Film-Makers Association', *Cinema Quarterly*, 2, 1 (Autumn 1933): 70, quoted and footnoted in Sexton, 106.

12   John Newman and Nikolaus Pevsner, *The Buildings of England: Dorset* (London: Penguin Books, 1972), 337.

13   For an in-depth study of the BFI Experimental Film Fund, see Michele Pierson, 'Amateurism and Experiment: The BFI's Experimental Film Fund (1952–1966)', in *The Moving Image*, 5, 1 (2005): 68–94 and Christophe Dupin, 'The BFI and Film Production: Half a Century of Innovative Independent Film-Making', in Geoffrey Nowell-Smith and Christophe Dupin (eds), *The British Film Institute, the Government and Film Culture, 1933–2000* (Manchester/New York: Manchester University Press, 2012).

14   Interview between Peter Shaw Ashton and the author, 30 November 2017.

15   Hepworth, *Barbara Hepworth Carvings and Drawings*, 280.

16   Catherine Jolivette, *Landscape, Art and Identity in 1950s Britain* (Abingdon: Ashgate Publishing, 2009), 64.

17   Jolivette, *Landscape, Art and Identity in 1950s Britain*, 53.

18   Dudley Shaw Ashton, 'Preliminary Rough Outline Treatment for Proposed Film on the Work of Barbara Hepworth', Jacquetta Hawkes Archive, Bradford University, 1952, 2.

19   Shaw Ashton, 'Preliminary Rough Outline Treatment for Proposed Film on the Work of Barbara Hepworth.

20   Banham, Reyner, 'Object Lesson', *Architectural Review* CXV, 689 (May 1954): 404.

21   Reyner, 'Object Lesson', 406.

22   Hepworth, *Barbara Hepworth Carvings and Drawings*, 60.

23   Chris Stephens, 'Landscape Sculpture', in Chris Stephens (ed.), *Barbara Hepworth: Centenary* (London: Tate, 2003), 65.

24   Jolivette, *Landscape, Art and Identity in 1950s Britain*, 16.

25   Robert Burstow, 'Geometries of Hope and Fear: The Iconography of Atomic Science and Nuclear Anxiety in the Modern Sculpture of World War and Cold War Britain', in Catherine Jolivette (ed.), *British Art in the Nuclear Age* (Routledge: London, 2014), 53.

26 Jacquetta Hawkes, working copy of script for *Figures in a Landscape*, Jacquetta Hawkes Archive, Bradford, 1953, 3.

27 According to Shaw Ashton's Preliminary Rough Outline for the BFI, he was considering James Butt for the composer, as recommended by the composer Imogen Holst: 'I suggest that the music should be written by James Butt, who had been very highly recommended to me by Imogen Holst after I had made enquiries through the Arts Council in connection with the Battersea film last year. I was also in touch with a small chamber orchestra.' Shaw Ashton, 'Preliminary Rough Outline Treatment for Proposed Film on the Work of Barbara Hepworth, 3.

28 Letter to Jacquetta Hawkes from Priaulx Rainier dated 17 February 1953, Jacquetta Hawkes archive, Bradford University.

29 See Register of Releases in *The Film User*, March 1954.

30 It found new visibility as part of the Arts Council funded LUX touring film programme, curated by Lucy Reynolds, entitled *Describing Form*, which toured nationally to the Henry Moore Institute, Tate Britain, Mead Gallery, Kettles Yard, Spacex, New Art Centre, Roche Court, Hull Film Festival, Chapter Arts Centre, Cardiff, Outpost Gallery, Norwich between 2005–2006.

31 Chris Stephens, 'The Quality of Human Relationships', in Chris Stephens (ed.), *Barbara Hepworth: Centenary* (London: Tate, 2003), 35.

32 Due to his severe asthmatic condition, Shaw Ashton was not able to fight in the Second World War and served as a home guard in the Dorset area.

9

Neoplasticism and cinema: Ilya Bolotowsky's experimental films on art

HENNING ENGELKE

In the late 1950s, the artist Ilya Bolotowsky shot a film at Leo Castelli's gallery on East 77th Street in New York. The scene was the elegant, and in its time quite famous, spiral staircase leading up to the exhibition space. A dancer in tights, captured from various angles, performs on the stairs, adapting her movements to the curved shape of the architectural structure. Castelli's face, in close up, comes into view. More people appear, climbing up and down the stairs, others sit on the chequered tiles at the bottom. At some point, a prismatic lens splits up the image. The spiral curve of a Nautilus shell, turning around its own axis, is superimposed over images of the staircase. Rotating ever more rapidly, the view from the top of the stairs is eventually converted into an abstract spiral-shape. It is as if the gallery space – at that time an important venue for a rapidly changing artworld – were transformed in the image of Marcel Duchamp's painting *Nu descendant un escalier no. 2* (1912) and his film *Anémic cinéma* (1926). Some shots, on the other hand, seem to undermine the aura of high-art in a kind of obscure irony: spliced in at the beginning of the film, we see home movie-style footage of a college graduation ceremony.[1]

Poised between historical document, artistic *hommage*, home movie and cinematic experiment, this short and probably unfinished film, titled *The Nautilus Shell*, condenses central elements of Ilya Bolotowsky's filmmaking: the combination of aesthetic exploration with an insider's record of the 1950s art world, happening-like improvization oscillating between sincerity and irony. The odd footage at the beginning may well have ended up on the reel by accident, but its ironic effect still matches the playful approach of other works. Bolotowsky's films surprised many of his contemporaries, familiar with the strict geometric order of his paintings. Following the example of Piet Mondrian, but vastly extending the latter's primary colour scheme, he sought to evoke in his paintings 'a feeling of timeless harmony and dynamic equilibrium', emerging from the tensions between strictly non-figurative, rectangular colour blocks.[2] The free-wheeling aesthetic exploration, wealth of art historical allusion, loose narrative structures and representational imagery of his films seemed irreconcilable with the controlled minimalism of the paintings. Commenting on this contradiction, the experimental filmmaker Stan Vanderbeek described

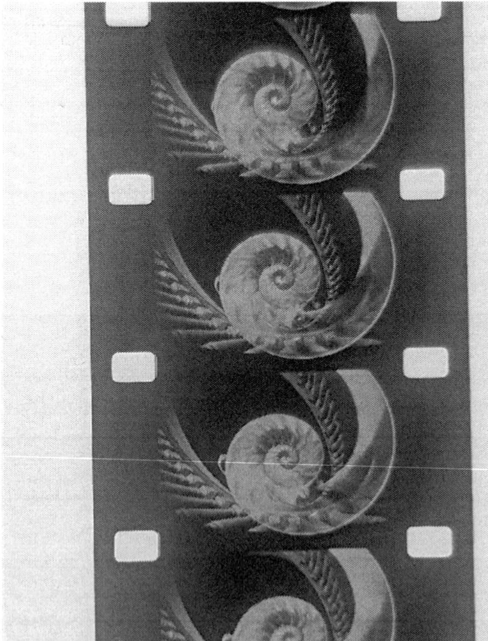

Figure 9.1 *Ilya Bolotowsky,* The Nautilus Shell *(c. 1957–58). Courtesy of Andrew Bolotowsky.*

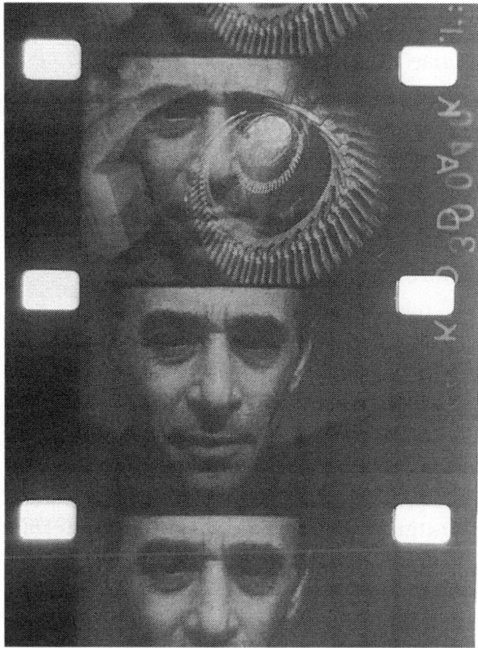

Figure 9.2 *Leo Castelli appearing in Ilya Bolotowsky's* The Nautilus Shell *(c. 1957–58). Courtesy of Andrew Bolotowsky.*

Bolotowsky as 'a marvelous example of an extremely rigid geometric painter who makes the most romantic nineteenth-century movies'.[3] Bolotowsky himself suggested that filmmaking helped him to keep 'all irrelevant literary, representational, romantic, and surrealist elements' out of his paintings.[4]

This remark does not necessarily mean that Bolotowsky considered filmmaking a mere auxiliary to painting or an outlet for improper artistic urges. He may equally have regarded painting and filmmaking as complementary activities. The sheer quantity of films and the amount of work invested in them supports this view. From 1953 to 1970, Bolotwsky made more than forty films, ranging from very brief, almost unedited records of encounters with artist colleagues and friends, exhibition openings, drawing classes and museum visits to more elaborate films. He described his cinematic work as consisting of 'creative, experimental black-and-white films and documentaries of artists'.[5] Open to aesthetic conceptions other than his own, he filmed painters like George L.K. Morris, Jean Xceron, Balcomb Greene, Wolf Kahn, Alice

Baber, and Milton and Sally Avery, but also, continuing through the 1950s and 1960s, sculptors Louise Nevelson, David Smith, Jose de Rivera or Ruth Asawa, dancer and choreographer Midi Garth, the art dealer Sam Kootz and, twice, Marcel Duchamp. Often the artists and their artworks are shown in the private spaces of their homes and studios, occasionally Bolotowsky focuses on a specific artwork and, in a few isolated instances, on the process of artistic production. The more finished experimental films similarly rely on the participation and collaboration of other artists, the dancer Yvonne Rainer performs in *Subways* (1958), the painters Leon Polk Smith and Knut Stiles appear in a number of films.

Viewed from today's perspective, Bolotowsky's films provide fascinating glimpses into the mid-twentieth-century New York art world. They are not straight 'records', though. Even Bolotowsky's most simple 'documentaries of artists' deploy cinematic devices such as multiple exposures, prismatic images, deliberate out-of-focus shots and unusual camera angles. Sometimes he seems to have used film as a kind of sketchpad to note down creative ideas resulting from his encounters with artists.[6] The longer works use similar techniques, often to evoke mythological themes, as in *Narcissus in a Gothic Mood* (1960/64), *The Last Orpheus* (1962) or the somewhat more enigmatic *Metanoia* (1961). Rarely depicting artworks, except by allusion or quotation, they are nevertheless 'about' art in the sense that they engage, through cinematic myths, with artistic concepts. These films, in particular, seem to reflect back on Bolotowsky's own work as a painter and his position within a changing artworld. After all, he continued to paint in a non-objective mode that had been deemed 'obsolete' since he adopted it in the mid 1940s. His paintings, while appreciated by collectors and included in important museum collections, never received the public attention given to his Abstract Expressionist colleagues, some of whom he had known and worked with since the 1930s. It may be for this reason that his films resist the idea of a linear chronology of styles that dominated modernist discourse on art. But his cinematic work goes beyond the personal. Through film, Bolotowsky was able to situate his painting – dedicated to 'timeless' formal tensions and harmonies – in the context of a changing art world and changing media. This becomes evident in *The Nautilus Shell*, where Duchamp's already canonized works – notably a 'last' painting evoking Eadweard Muybridge's proto-filmic chronophotographies and the film *Anémic cinéma* – quite literally interfere with the current artistic business of Leo Castelli's gallery.

What I wish to discuss in what follows is how film not only contrasts with Bolotowsky's painting – as he may seem to indicate in the above quote – but also complements it, and is in some way important for his work as a painter. Reflecting on painting and film not in abstract terms, but through concrete aesthetic procedures, his films can, moreover, shed a light on the complex interrelations between media, histories and artistic myths that have been repressed in modernist discourse on art with its focus on medium specificity, autonomy and, as Michael Fried claims, 'presentness'.[7] Although Bolotowsky's paintings aspired to a kind of absolute formal purity, his films show that even at this extreme pole, painting was part of a larger system of image production or, as David Joselit has termed it, an 'interrelated image ecology'.[8] It is in this respect that his films, as I will argue in concluding, intersect and contrast with the policies and histories of American art documentaries of the 1950s, shaped by modernist conceptions of art and liberal subjectivity as well as integration into programmes of democratic education and cultural diplomacy.

Encounters in the art world

Bolotowsky was already an established painter when he started to make films in 1953. An emigrant from Russia, he had arrived in New York as an adolescent with his parents in 1923 and subsequently studied at the National Academy of Design. In the 1930s he became intensely involved, alongside artists such as Mark Rothko and Adolph Gottlieb, with the American abstract painting movement.[9] For several years he worked for the Works Progress Administration (WPA) Federal Arts Project, creating a number of abstract murals for public buildings in New York such as the Williamsburg Housing Project (1936), the Hall of Medical Sciences at the 1939 New York World's Fair, and the Chronic Diseases Hospital (1941). His murals, like most of his easel paintings of this time, drew on a somewhat eclectic but aesthetically efficient combination of biomorphic shapes and diagonal lines (inspired, according to Bolotowsky, by Russian Suprematism).[10]

It was only after his military service in Alaska, and after Mondrian's death in 1944, that he took up the Neoplasticist style that would shape the rest of his career.[11] Through his many contacts in the New York art scene he would have been aware of the upcoming surge, manifesting itself in the work of Gottlieb, Rothko, Arshile Gorky or Hans Hofmann, in more spontaneous forms of abstraction. But he nevertheless staunchly adhered to geometric abstraction, deepening the non-objective approach he had pursued since the 1930s. Some of his colleagues from this time, like Harry Holtzman, Burgoyne Diller, Fritz Glarner, Charmion von Wiegand and Leon Polk Smith, continued along similar lines, which increasingly fell out of favour with the official art world. From 1946 to 1948, Bolotowsky temporarily replaced Josef Albers, who was on a leave of absence, as Head of the Art Department at the influential Black Mountain College.[12] This was certainly a prestigious position, but Bolotowsky's turn towards teaching, which became a constant preoccupation throughout his career, also indicates the need to supplement his income from the sale of paintings. Despite his renown as a painter, he never achieved the prominence of his Abstract Expressionist colleagues and his art increasingly came to occupy a place that fell outside the scope of standard accounts of art history on the 'rise of American painting'.[13] From 1948 to 1957, he taught art at the University of Wyoming in Laramie, but he stayed in contact with his colleagues in New York, where he regularly exhibited at Grace Borgenicht Gallery and where he returned from 1954 to 1956 for a stint as adjunct professor at Brooklyn College.

Both the increasing predominance of Abstract Expressionism and his teaching experiences formed a background for Bolotowsky's filmmaking. A grant for 'experimental film work' from the University of Wyoming Graduate School in 1953 allowed him to make his first films.[14] He started modestly on 8mm, filming a drawing class and a model, a visit to the Denver Art Museum and his experiments with Duchamp-inspired spiral discs, rotating on a potter's wheel. His productivity and ambitions as a filmmaker increased during his time at Brooklyn College when he was able to reconnect with his New York colleagues. A substantial number of films from this period were made on the occasion of his visits with artists friends, as if he wanted to capture on film his encounters with people and artworks. Bolotwsky's 1956 colour film on the

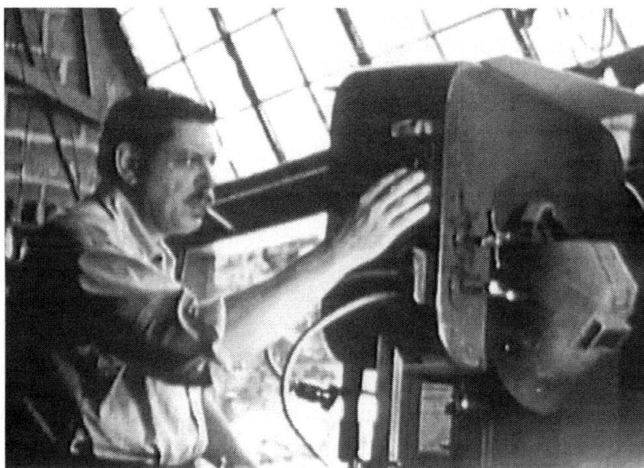

Figure 9.3 *Ilya Bolotowsky* David Smith *(1956). Digital still. Courtesy of Andrew Bolotowsky.*

sculptor David Smith shows the famous steel sculptures outside Smith's studio in Bolton Landing alongside the artist at work, his home and his family.

The Dancer Midi Garth (1956) similarly combines shots – both in colour and black-and-white – of quotidian actions inside Garth's studio, with indoor and outdoor dance scenes, sometimes by a lake, and views of the porch of a house.

Rather than implying a connection between artistic creation and surroundings, Bolotowsky's loosely arranged shots with their intimacy and spontaneity suggest an open, exploratory approach. A more conventional art documentary like Herbert Matter's *Works of Calder* (1950) seeks, for instance, to explain Calder's mobiles through comparison with natural objects near his studio, waves rippling on a beach or leaves moving in the wind. Bolotowsky, instead, appears to use film to record his perceptions and ideas, resulting from the encounter with artists and their artworks. Representation merges with reflections on art and film. Frequently, the sense of film as a means of aesthetic exploration and heightened perception is supplemented by art historical allusions that oscillate between seriousness, irony and obscure personal humour. Setting the lens on infinity and only bringing into focus a rotating metal sculpture at the very end of the single-shot *Jose de Rivera* (1958) creates a cinematic pun on the sculptor's preoccupation with 'infinite' bands of polished metal. In the black-and-white (and rather underexposed) *Louise Nevelson* (1956) the sculptor 'sits' for her cinematic portrait in a way reminiscent of James McNeill Whistler's painting of his mother – *Arrangement in Gray and Black No. 1* (1871) – whose foregrounding of colour and tonalities played an important role for American abstract painting. Superimposed images of Nevelson's studio and her sculptures do not so much cohere into some general art historical comment or explanation, but rather explore multiple possibilities of cinematic engagement with aesthetic perception. The intricate structures of Nevelson's sculptures are brought into dynamic interaction with each other, forming an 'arrangement in gray and black' with an art historical reference of the artist's portrait. The colour film showing Duchamp in his studio on West 14th Street (1956) with his back mostly turned toward the camera, on the other hand, hints at a shared sense of artistic irony.

Reflections on painting

Bolotowsky continued to make similar films on other artists until the mid-1960s, but early on, he also began making longer and more ambitious films. Drawing on some of the same techniques used in the shorter films, and casting many artist friends, these films are mainly distinguished by their suggestion of loose, but nevertheless evident fictional narratives and by people assuming certain 'roles'. The interplay of formal exploration and art historical allusion, however, continues the approach of the shorter films. *The Nautilus Shell* with its combination of staged performance and documentary footage underlines this continuity. It is also noticeable in the 17-minute *Fire Escapes* (1956) with its rich structure of references, aesthetic exploration and cinematic reflection which merit closer scrutiny.

While in his short films Bolotowsky documented visits with artists, shooting *Fire Escapes*, possibly his first 16mm film, provided him with the occasion for assembling a group of artist friends along with family members. The cast includes the fellow Neoplasticist painter Leon Polk Smith, the philosopher Lucian Krukowski, the sculptor Michael Lekakis and the painter Knut Stiles, a former student of Bolotowsky at Black Mountain College and a collaborator on several of his films. The photographer and filmmaker Vladimir Telberg is credited along with Bolotowsky as the creator of the 'camera angles'. Telberg is best known for his surrealist inspired photomontages, he was closely associated with Anaïs Nin's literary and artistic circle and he was also a member of the short-lived but influential Independent Filmmakers Association whose members included, among others, Maya Deren, Willard Maas, Marie Menken and Nin's husband Ian Hugo. Telberg's expertise in creating multi-layered images is evident in *Fire Escapes*, but his surrealist approach is transformed through Bolotowsky's specific engagement with art and art history.

Although the connection between scenes is loose, *Fire Escapes* hints, through association and allusion, at a kind of narrative development. A recurring female figure played by two different actresses, may even be regarded as something like a protagonist. The film begins with a brief tilted view from a window onto flat roofs and a fire escape landing, followed by prismatically distorted images, reminiscent of Mondrian's painting *Composition With Lines* (1917). The female 'protagonist', dressed in tights, climbs down the fire escape, with multiple exposures of her body underlining the reference, again, to Duchamp's *Nu descendant un escalier*. For the next several minutes we see people walking up and down flights of stairs, moving back and forth, passing each other, and climbing over the handrails, all in a kind of choreographed pattern.

Human figures stand out against and merge with the intricate grid of the architecture and its play of light and shadow. In-camera superimpositions, tilted views and prismatic distortions enhance this effect, flattening the image and creating a sense of spatial disorientation. Such abstraction then gives way to more conventional images. As in early film comedies, multiple actions are condensed within the space of a single shot – a man running around with an umbrella, the 'protagonist' sunbathing, a boy carrying a bucket, a newspaper drifting in the wind. Briefly, the film returns to the people on the fire escapes. Towards the end, the female protagonist knocks on a door and miraculously vanishes. In another reference to early cinema, this is achieved through a substitution splice. Instead of the protagonist, we then see, in the very last shots, another woman with a baby in her arms climbing up yet another flight of stairs into the glaring sunshine. The end title ambiguously reads 'Fire Escape' rather than, as at the beginning, 'Fire Escapes'.

One might regard *Fire Escapes* as a treatise on the intertwined histories of art and film: a passage leading through the geometric spaces of the modern city, the semi-abstraction of city symphonies and cubism, surrealist collage and the spaces of early movies, towards the sacred tranquillity of pure light – what Bolotowsky called his striving 'for the timelessness of Platonic ideas'.[15] An exclusive focus on such symbolic aspects, however, would neglect the film's irony and play, its happening-like openness, and its engagement with the relationship of painting and film on an aesthetic level. The film's ironic approach is evident, for instance, in a shot, interrupting the opening stairs sequence, of three men intently and somewhat confusedly looking at something. This is revealed by a nearly abstract prismatic 'reverse-shot' to be the curiously distorted action of the film itself.

If this seems like a comment on the confusion that abstract art often evoked, the back-and-forth movement of the people within and across the actual grid-pattern of the fire escapes hints at the balanced tensions of Bolotowsky's paintings themselves, even if in temporal succession and in the three dimensional space of architectural diagonals. The virtual movement evoked in the dynamic equilibrium of his paintings, in such scenes, becomes actual movement. This transformation brings into focus problems associated with the relationship between film and painting but also contradictory claims inherent in Neoplasticism itself.[16]

When Bolotowsky evokes the grid patterns of his paintings in the structure of fire escapes, or when he cinematically emulates paintings by Mondrian and

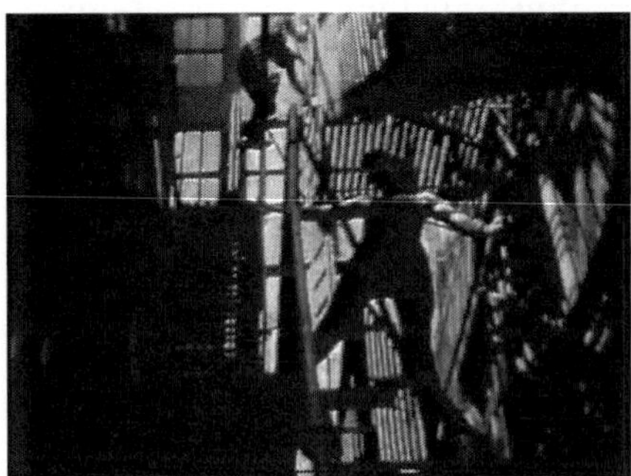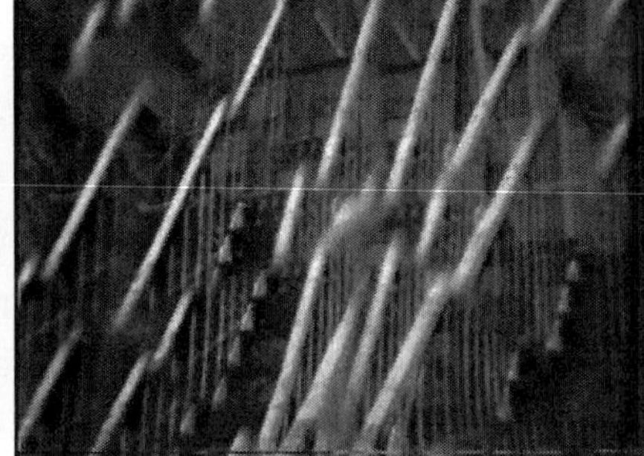

Figure 9.4 and 9.5. *Ilya Bolotowsky* Fire Escapes *(1956). Digital still. Courtesy of Andrew Bolotowsky.*

Duchamp (a constant point of reference in his films from the 1950s), he lends 'reality' to abstract art in a way reminiscent of André Bazin's observation that in art documentaries 'what is symbolic and abstract takes on the solid reality of a piece of ore'.[17] In one sense, he thereby affirms the distinction between film and painting (appropriating Wilhelm Worringer's art historical terms): the one 'an art of empathy' with an 'eye that sees from nature', the other an art of conceptual 'abstraction'.[18] In another sense, however, *Fire Escapes* also presents a 'reality' that is, at least in part, shaped by principles of abstract art that Rosalind Krauss associates with 'a paradigm or model for the antidevelopmental, the antinarrative, the antihistorical'.[19] One might think here of Mondrian's belief, emerging from his engagement with Theosophy and Kabbalah, that his paintings revealed truths about the actual world.[20] Apparently less mystically inclined than Mondrian, Bolotowsky was nevertheless convinced that the 'universal' quality he sought to achieve, was 'best expressed as a Platonic idea or archetype of an ideal, harmonious relationship'.[21]

I will discuss Bolotowsky's cinematic involvement with myth more extensively in the next section. *Fire Escapes*, however, also presents the idea of timelessness through narrative devices, the 'antidevelopmental' is inserted, one could say, into a developmental – historical – structure. For Bolotowsky this had a personal dimension. *Fire Escapes* creates a complex, but certainly not arbitrary, web of interconnections between inner and outer space, chance and order, film and painting, the sacred and the profane. It evokes not only multiply layered spaces but also – in contradistinction to the idea of a linear passage – heterogeneous temporalities. This, in turn, reflects back on Bolotwsky's criticism (at least in part biographically motivated) of the idea of art history as a 'one-goal development', emerging from 'the nineteenth-century idea of progress' that 'may be responsible for the "tradition of the new" and the resulting idea of "obsolescence in art"'.[22]

Myths of cinema and painting

When Bolotowsky wrote or spoke about his paintings, he usually described them in matter-of-fact terms as solutions to aesthetic problems. References to spiritual dimensions, prominent in the writings of Mondrian, are sparse. In his films, however, Bolotowsky sometimes went further. In an interview in 1974, Bolotowsky remarked that, in these films, 'the plot develops out of the visual elements and generally there's some connection with some myth, either a Greek myth, or some myth I adapt to fit my own interpretation'.[23] Such an orientation towards mythological structures and motifs was a common feature of 1950s experimental film. The critic Parker Tyler, for instance, regarded experimental film as a conscious reflection of the unconscious myths of Hollywood cinema. Despite its capacity to represent 'reality', or rather because of it, film seemed, as he stated in a symposium on 'Symbolism, Myth and Film', particularly suited to depict symbolic worlds in which nothing 'is what it seems', transforming real space into 'abstract and imaginative space'.[24]

Although Bolotowsky kept a certain distance from the various groups and factions of the experimental film scene in New York, he sometimes collaborated, as mentioned above, with other filmmakers, and he was certainly familiar with contemporary experimental film. He also personally knew Parker Tyler, who, in his function as an art critic, had written appreciatively about his paintings.[25] But while experimental film provided a model or template, Bolotowsky's engagement with myth also extended to his paintings. It may seem, as if he coped with the split between spirituality and materialism – which Rosalind Krauss regards as the core of the 'schizophrenic' structure of the grid in modernist painting – by releasing in one medium what he needed to repress in the other (as he seems to indicate in the aforementioned quote). Shifting from one medium to another, however, simultaneously challenges the conceptions of autonomy and medium specificity presupposed in Krauss's modernist conception of the grid.

Through the creation of myth, *Metanoia*, one of Bolotowsky's most ambitious and aesthetically successful films, explores such interrelationships between film and painting, physical and spiritual reality. The film, shot in 1960 and completed in 1962, exists in two versions. The first one (also titled *Positive Negative*) consists of a negative and a positive reel, each showing the complete action. The second version, which was more widely shown, is entirely in the negative. Made strange by the reversal of tonal values, the film depicts arrangements of windows and doorways that appear as grey and black fields

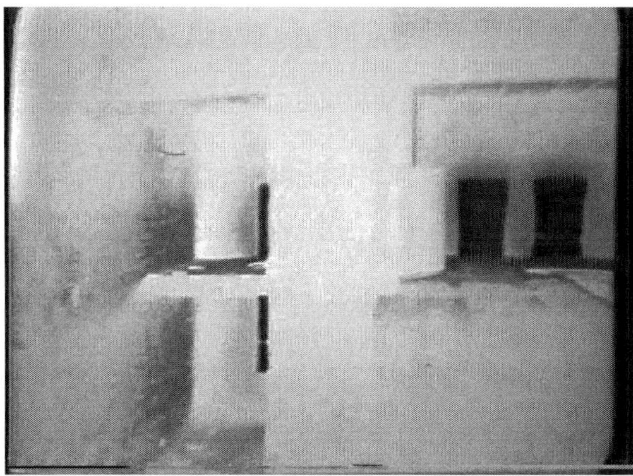

Figure 9.6 *Ilya Bolotowsky* Metanoia *(1961). Digital still. Courtesy of Andrew Bolotowsky.*

on a dirty white ground. These fields somewhat resemble the flat colour blocks of Bolotowsky's paintings, but they can also be recognized as parts of intricate spatial structures.

Shooting in the vast interior of an abandoned brewery with collapsed floors and precarious catwalks, Bolotowsky used semi-transparent mirrors to further complicate spatial relations. People move through this inscrutable arrangement of interlocking spaces – most prominently a male figure wearing an Eskimo mask surrounded by a halo-like ring of irregularly shaped attachments.[26]

A small hooded figure opens a door, and the protagonist with the Eskimo mask appears, his white silhouette standing out against the black doorway.

We then see him walking in measured steps, rising from the ground, climbing through the disturbing architecture, balancing over an abyss or suspending himself from a wall – his chest rising and falling with each breath. Other figures appear and disappear, often in multi-layered images with confusing dimensions and spatial relationships. Windows are opened and closed again in one scene, appearing as opaque surfaces flooded with black light. Sometimes the mask is held up in the air, then, towards the end, the protagonist takes it off and solemnly places it on the ground. The film concludes with an image of the protagonist approaching the camera, one arm raised over his head, the mask double exposed above him into a separate 'frame'.

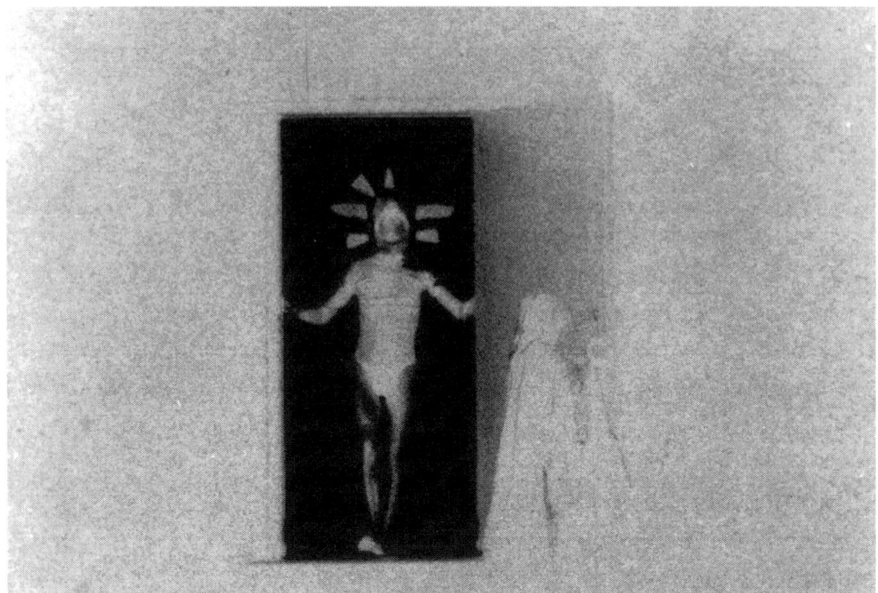

Figure 9.7 *Ilya Bolotowsky* Metanoia *(1961). Digital still. Courtesy of Andrew Bolotowsky.*

In its choreographed structure and use of cinematic effects *Metanoia* merges the exploration of filmic space with images that suggest both shamanistic ritual and modern dance. The sound track, a composition for the modern ballet, underlines this latter reference, while also contributing to the film's dramatic effect. The main conflict, as Bolotowsky describes it, is between two opposing ways of perceiving the protagonist, as 'a poor lost soul in a tremendous, frightening world' and as 'a triumphal [...] god-like figure'.[27] Recognizing the interrelation between these two aspects, between physicality and spirituality, may be part of the transformation suggested in the film's title, which literally means remorse or repentance. As a theological and psychological term, 'metanoia' refers to a fundamental spiritual or therapeutic conversion often associated with an existential crisis, a dramatic event or a mental breakdown. Such an idea of radical change, of turning around, is conveyed already, on a perceptual and metaphorical level, by the positive-negative reversal. The intricate multi-layered cinematic spaces and planes similarly challenge 'normal' perception.

One might object that this reading overburdens the film with meaning. In a contemporaneous programme note *Metanoia* is succinctly described as 'dark vision of classic simplicity by noted painter'.[28] On the other hand, to create complexity out of simple forms was precisely the aim of Neoplasticist painting. Moreover, a quote from Antonin Artaud's essay 'On the Balinese Theatre' that serves as the film's epigraph explicitly introduces the idea of a spiritual conversion: 'Eyes of dreams which seem to absorb our own, eyes before which we ourselves appear to be *fantome*'. According to Artaud, it is a higher reality that, in the ritual performance, gazes back at us, radically transforming our own self-image. Artaud's gnostic search may have resonated with Bolotowsky's own ideas on art. What Artaud saw in the Balinese theatre was an art that transformed dancers into 'living hieroglyphs' (*'hiéroglyphes animés'*). Gestures became cyphers for states of mind, linked, ultimately, to 'the absolute'.[29] The strangeness of spaces, the measured, almost hieratic movement of the protagonist and the ritualistic use of the mask in *Metanoia* evokes something similar.

In this film, Bolotowsky associates himself, through cinematic 'myth', with a broader avant-garde tradition that considered art as an expression of the ideal abstract forces permeating the phenomenal world. Art, in this tradition, is a form that can, like Balinese dances or shamanistic rituals, potentially render these forces accessible to perception and lead to a fundamental transformation of consciousness – to metanoia. But in connecting gesture to timelessness, Bolotowsky not only expressed, in the medium of film, his artistic convictions, and, at the same time, distanced himself from the individually expressive painterly gestures of Abstract Expressionism so influentially represented in Paul Falkenberg and Hans Namuth's film *Jackson Pollock 51* (1951). He also manifested his separation from a contemporary art world driven by the idea of historical progression.

Striving for 'the absolute' in both its aesthetic and esoteric meaning, Neoplasticism could be understood, as Jack Burnham observes, to not simply represent 'another "ism" within the progression of twentieth century abstract styles'.[30] Mondrian himself frequently suggested that Neoplasticism was but a step towards the 'realisation of pure art in our surroundings [...] a plastic expression of the equally balanced proportion of the polarity of life'.[31] Questions of redundancy and originality, from this perspective, became of secondary importance. Neoplasticism rather offered a scheme of formal/spiritual evolution in its own right, a higher order, detached from art history as we usually understand it. This conception provided a rationale for the continuation of Neoplasticist painting by Mondrian's American 'followers'. They nevertheless had to cope with the art world's demand – shared by the avant-garde and consumerist ideology – for originality and innovation. It is these contingent historical circumstances that Neoplasticist painting, in its avoidance of all figurative, symbolic and narrative 'content', was categorically incapable of expressing.

When Bolotowsky turned to film he found a way to relate his painting, through another visual medium, to ideas and discourses that were essential to but could not be part of painting. Robert Haller observes: 'For Bolotowsky the world contains other invisible [images], images awkward to paint realistically, let alone by his highly formal, geometric style, but possible on film.'[32] Considering a film like *Metanoia*, simultaneously presenting transcendental ideals and physical reality, two dimensional shapes and strange, ritualistic spaces, one gets the sense that such images were not wholly external to Bolotowsky's paintings, but rather emerged from them. Film, on the other hand, could also inspire painting, as in the mural he made for the lobby of Cinema I in Manhattan (1963), creating, in neoplasticist style, 'an effect somewhat like an abstract motion picture'.[33]

Painting and film, materialism and myth, autonomy and openness do not so much contradict or exclude as complement and permeate each other.

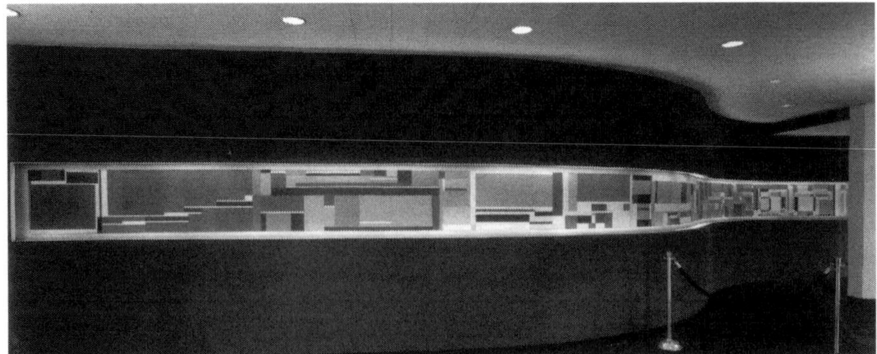

Figure 9.8 *Ilya Bolotowsky* Cinema I Mural *(1963). Courtesy of Andrew Bolotowsky.*

Policies and histories of art and film

It is only from the perspective of modernist medium specificity and artistic autonomy that such heterogeneity must appear as 'schizophrenic' in the negative sense of 'a delusionary concept'. This heterogeneity also points to another history of abstraction in America, obscured by the rise of modernist ideologies of art and the construction of 'national' art histories – a history of interrelated media, where painterly 'purity' merges with social and cultural concerns and which unfolds outside the perceptual regime of the museum. If this other history has gained increasing attention in recent decades, it fell outside the dominant ideologies and institutional policies of the 1950s art world.

Bolotowsky's films were not widely distributed. He personally showed them at galleries, art schools and artist's venues such as the famous Club on New York's Lower East Side. *Metanoia* was screened at Cinema 16 in New York which was then one of the most prominent venues for independent and experimental film, in 1962, and was awarded first prize at the Midwestern Film Festival in Chicago in the following year. Such public recognition was an exception. The generally limited circulation can be attributed to financial and personal reasons as well as to changing distribution economies and the transformation of the experimental film scene in the early 1960s. The short 'artist documentaries', on the other hand, were incompatible with standard genres of educational films on art. Yet, Bolotowsky's cinematic work as a whole – simultaneously reflecting on art and film – raised issues that lay at the core of debates on the status of films on art, and, more generally, the question of film as an art form. In the US, these issues circumscribed (like the shared 16mm non-theatrical film sector) a multifaceted field of intersection and competition between experimental film cultures and art documentaries.[34] The critic Arthur Knight, for instance, claimed that it was only through 'the application of film art, the aesthetic of cinema' that films could create a 'visually exciting art experience'.[35] What defined 'film art/art films', however, in the eyes of powerful institutions such as the Museum of Modern Art or UNESCO was significantly shaped by the very ideologies of art and art history that Bolotowsky's films challenged.

When films on art became a major element in strategies of democratic education and cultural diplomacy after the Second World War (see Dimitrios Latsis' and Natasha Ritsma's chapters in this volume), it was under the premise of artistic autonomy. The relationship between film and art was certainly the subject of a highly productive debate – as the theories of André Bazin and Siegfried Kracauer attest to. But its stakes were set by modernist conceptions. Paul Falkenberg and Hans Namuth's *Jackson Pollock 51* (1951) could thus function 'in a dialogic relation with Pollock's paintings as objects', despite its innovative depiction of the process of painting.[36] Introducing a 'closed system of interpretation' the film reinforced art historical narratives that celebrated Abstract Expressionism as the 'first' American abstractionist movement and epitome of liberal consumerist subjectivity.

Unfashionable as Bolotowsky's ideas on art may have appeared, his paintings and films point beyond narrow modernist orthodoxy. Painting may have had priority for Bolotowsky, but his films also demonstrate that he was aware of them as part of larger systems of image production. Through cinematic myth he was able to acknowledge heterogeneity, complementarity and copresence – of painting in cinema and cinema in painting, but also of different temporalities and histories. In his films the modernist myth of 'the absolute' is disassociated from rigid conceptions of an artistic medium and historical teleologies – even at what might seem to be the culmination of the pursuit for aesthetic 'purity'. What his work also highlights is the need to consider the histories, policies and aesthetics of 'art' and 'films on art' not isolated from each other, but as elements of interrelated image ecologies and media histories.

Notes

1   With few exceptions, Bolotowsky's films, including *The Nautilus Shell*, only exist as 16mm camera originals. A release print of *Metanoia* was distributed by Cinema 16, this film was also transferred, along with *Fire Escapes* and *Narcissus in a Gothic Mood*, to Betamax video for an exhibition at SUNY Stony Brook in 1985. I wish to thank Andrew Bolotowsky for making his father's films available to me, for sharing his recollections and for providing images for this article. Thanks are also due to Andrew Lampert and Robert Haller for allowing me to view the films on an editing table at Anthology Film Archives.

2   Quoted in Lawrence Campbell, 'Squaring the circle and vice-versa', *Art News* 68, 1 (1970): 40.

3   Willard Van Dyke, 'Interview with Stan Vanderbeek', unpublished transcript (1 February 1966), 19, MoMA Film Study Center, file on Stan Vanderbeek.

4   Ilya Bolotowsky, 'On Neoplasticism and my own work', *Leonardo* 2, 3 (1969): 230.

5   Ilya Bolotowsky, 'Statment', *Film Comment* 2, 3 (1964): 12.

6   Bolotowsky's use of sketches in painting varied greatly. According to Andrew Bolotowsky, his father 'never followed a formula for developing a painting', sometimes sketching with a ball point pen, or creating a collage out of a cut up silkscreen print, or using no sketch at all (e-mail to the author, 25 May 2018). The use of film as a 'sketchpad' seems to fit in with such a practice.

7   Michael Fried, *Art and Objecthood* (Chicago, IL/London: University of Chicago Press, 1998), 167.

8   David Joselit, *Feedback: Television Against Democracy* (Cambridge, MA/London: MIT Press 2007), 45.

9   Bolotowsky, 'On Neoplasticism', 222–4; Ilya Bolotowsky/Henry Geldzahler, 'Adventures with Bolotowsky', *Archives of American Art Journal* 22, 1 (1982): 22–6; Susan C. Larsen, 'The American Abstract Artists: A Documentary History, 1936–1941', *Archives of American Art Journal* 14, 1 (1974): 2, 7.

10 Bolotowsky, 'On Neoplasticism', 224.

11 Bolotowsky, 'On Neoplasticism', 224.

12 For a general account see Vincent Katz and Martin Brody (eds), *Black Mountain College: Experiment in Art* (Cambridge, MA: MIT Press, 2003); Bolotowsky's teaching is referenced in: Helen Molesworth/Ruth Erickson (ed.), *Leap Before You Look: Black Mountain College, 1933–1957* (New Haven, CT: Yale University Press (2015), 182 and 354.

13 In the 1970s some exhibitions attempted to correct this view by including work by Bolotowsky. See Stephen Prokopoff (ed.), *Post Mondrian Abstraction in America* (Chicago Museum of Contemporary Art, 1973); Nancy J. Troy (ed.), *Mondrian and Neo-Plasticism in America.* (New Haven, CT: Yale University Art Gallery, 1979). Bolotowsky had a one-man retrospective at the Guggenheim, see Adelyn D. Breeskin (ed.), *Ilya Bolotowsky* (New York: The Solomon R. Guggenheim Foundation, 1974).

14 Breeskin (ed.), *Ilya Bolotowsky*, 121.

15 Bolotowsky, 'On Neoplasticism', 230.

16 Rosalind Krauss, 'Grids', *October* 9 (1979): 60.

17 André Bazin, *What is Cinema?* Vol. I (Berkeley/Los Angeles, CA: University of California Press, 1967), 168.

18 Louise Averill Svendsen, 'Interview with Ilya Bolotowsky', in Breeskin (ed.), *Ilya Bolotowsky*, 22.

19 Krauss, 'Grids', 64.

20 Jack Burnham, 'Mondrian's American Circle', *Arts Magazine* 48, 1 (1973): 38.

21 Bolotowsky, 'On Neoplasticism', 226.

22 Bolotowsky, 'On Neoplasticism', 221.

23 Svendsen, 'Interview with Ilya Bolotowsky', 22.

24 Parker Tyler, 'Symbolism, Myth and Film', sound recording, Anthology Film Archives, New York.

25 Parker Tyler, 'Ilya Bolotowsky', *Art News* 54, 9 (1956): 51.

26 Bolotowsky claims to have become interested in Eskimo art during his military service in Alaska (Breeskin (ed.), *Ilya Bolotowsky*, 121). The term 'Eskimo' is used here, as the mask is made by Alaskan people who, unlike the Inuit of Eastern Canada and Greenland, do not regard it as derogatory.

27 Svendsen, 'Interview with Ilya Bolotowsky', 22.

28 Cinema 16, programme note (5 December 1962), in Scott MacDonald (ed.), *Cinema 16: Documents Toward the History of the Film Society* (Philadelphia, PA: Temple University Press, 2002), 409.

29 Jane Goodall, 'Artaud and painting: the quest for a language of gnosis', *Paragraph* 12, 2 (1989): 110.

30 Burnham, 'Mondrian's American Circle', 39.

31 Mondrian, 'Neo-Plasticism', in Troy (ed.), *Mondrian and Neo-Plasticism*, 62.

32 Robert Haller, diary entry (24 March 2007), Anthology Film Archives, file on Ilya Bolotowsky.

33 Bolotowsky, 'On Neoplasticism', 226.

34 For a detailed discussion see Henning Engelke, *Metaphern einer anderen Filmgeschichte* (Marburg: Schüren, 2018), 127–35.

35 Arthur Knight, 'A Short History of Art films', in William McK. Chapman (ed.), *Films on Art* (New York: The American Federation of the Arts, 1952), 6.

36 Caterine M. Soussloff, 'Jackson Pollock's Post-Ritual Performance: Memories Arrested in Space', *TDR* 48, 1 (2004): 66.

Select bibliography: mid-twentieth-century art documentaries

Arnheim, Rudolf ([1934] 2004), 'Malerei und Film', in *Der Seele in der Silberschicht: Medientheoretische Texte: Photographie, Film, Rundfunk*, Frankfurt: Suhrkamp, 171–4.

Arnheim, Rudolf ([1939] 2004), 'Kunstwerke im Film', in *Der Seele in der Silberschicht: Medientheoretische Texte: Photographie, Film, Rundfunk*, Frankfurt: Suhrkamp, 262–5.

Aumont, Jacques (2007). *L'œil interminable. Cinéma et peinture* (Paris: Différence, 2007).

Bazin, André ([1950] 2007), 'Peinture et cinéma', in *Qu'est-ce que le cinéma?* Paris: Éditions du Cerf, 187–92.

Bazin, André ([1956] 2007), 'Un Film Bergsonien: *Le Mystère Picasso*', in *Qu'est-ce que le cinéma?* Paris: Éditions du Cerf, 193–202.

Bolen, Francis, ed. (1953), *Films on Art: Panorama 1953*, Paris: UNESCO.

Bowie, Theodore R. (1954), 'About Films on Art', *College Art Journal* 14, 1 (Autumn): 28–37.

Bowie, Theodore R. (1956), *Films on Art: A Critical Guide*, Bloomington, IN: Indiana University Audio-Visual Center.

Breteau, Gisèle (1985), *Abdécadaire des films sur l'art moderne et contemporain 1905–1984*, Paris: Centre Georges Pompidou/Centre national des arts plastiques, 1985.

Chapman, William Mck., ed. (1952), *Films on Art*, New York: American Federation of the Arts.

Covert, Nadine, ed. (1991), *Art on Screen: A Directory on Film and Videos about the Visual Arts* (New York/Los Angeles, CA: Metropolitan Museum of Art/J. Paul Getty Trust.

Dalle Vacche, Angela, ed. (2003), *The Visual Turn: Classical Film Theory and Art History* New Brunswick, NJ: Rutgers University Press.

Dalle Vacche, Angela, ed. (2012), *Film, Art, New Media: Museum without Walls?* New York: Palgrave Macmillan.

Del Monte, Marco (2009), *Il film sull'arte e la Mostra Internazionale del Cinema di Venezia*, PhD diss., Venice: Università Ca' Foscari.

Dix ans de films sur l'art (1952–1962): Peinture et sculpture (1966), Paris: UNESCO.

Druick, Zöe. (2011), 'UNESCO, Film and Education', in Charles Acland and Haidee Wasson (eds), *Useful Cinema*, Durham, NC: Duke University Press, 81–102.

Dufrêne, Thierry (2010), 'L'histoire de l'art à l'âge du cinéma', *Diogène* 3, 231: 137–49.

Duyck, Leon (2014), *FIFA: Fédération Internationale du Film d'Art: Onderzoek naar de samenstelling, doelstellingen, werking en activiteiten van de FIFA en de ondersteuning van de kunstdocumentaire na WOII tot en met de jaren '60*, Ghent University, MA diss.

Emmer, Luciano and Enrico Gras (1947), 'The Film Renaissance in Italy', *Hollywood Quarterly* 2, 4 (July): 353–58.

Esner, Rachel and Sandra Kisters, eds (2018), *The Mediatization of the Artist*, London: Palgrave Macmillan.

Etienne, Fanny (2002), *Films d'art, films sur l'art: Le regard d'un cineaste sur un artiste*, Paris: L'Harmattan.

Farwell, Beatrice (1963), 'Films on Art in Education', *Art Journal* 23, 1 (Autumn): 39–40.

Films on Art (1949), Paris: UNESCO.

Films on Art (1951), Paris: UNESCO/Brussels: Les Arts plastiques.

Films on Art: Panorama 1953 (1953), Paris: UNESCO.

Francastel, Pierre (1951), 'A Teacher's Point of View', in *Films on Art*, Paris: UNESCO/ Brussels: Les Arts plastiques, 13–16.

Frangne, Pierre-Henry, Gilles Mouëllic and Christophe Viart, eds (2009), *Filmer l'acte de création*, Rennes: Presses universitaires de Rennes.

Guermann, Francis, Frédéric Joyeux and Nicole Torres (1988), *Etats des lieux du film sur l'art*, Université de Nancy II, MA diss.

Hallas, Roger, ed. (2019), *Documenting the Visual Arts*, New York: Routledge.

Hayward, Philip, ed. (1988), *Picture This: Media Representations of Visual Art and Artists*, London: John Libbey.

Jacobs, Steven (2011), 'Camera and Canvas: Emmer, Storck, Resnais and the Post-war Art Film', in *Framing Pictures: Film and the Visual Arts*, Edinburgh: Edinburgh University Press, 1–37.

Jacobs, Steven (2013), *Art and Cinema: The Belgian Art Documentary*, Brussels: Cinematek.

Jacobs, Steven (2017), 'Carving Cameras on Thorvaldsen and Rodin: Mid-Twentieth-Century Documentaries on Sculpture', in Steven Jacobs, Susan Felleman, Vito Adriaensens, and Lisa Colpaert, *Screening Statues: Sculpture and Cinema*, Edinburgh: Edinburgh University Press, 65–84.

Jacobs, Steven and Birgit Cleppe (2019), 'A Museum of Moving Images: Mid-Twentieth-Century Art Documentaries on the Louvre,' *Oxford Art Journal* 42, 3: 373–93.

Knight, Arthur (1952), 'A Short History of Art Films', in William Mck. Chapman, ed., *Films on Art*, New York: The American Federation of Arts, 8–9.

Kracauer, Siegried (1960) 'The Film on Art', in *Theory of Film: The Redemption of Physical Reality*, Princeton, Princeton University Press, 195–201.

Lemaître, Henri (1956), *Beaux-arts et cinema*, Paris: Les Éditions du Cerf.

Loukopoulou, Katerina (2012), 'Museum at Large: Aesthetic Education through Film', in Devin Orgeron, Marsha Orgeron, and Dan Streible, eds, *Learning with the Lights Off: Educational film in the United States*, New York: Oxford University Press, 356–77.

Mirams, Gordon (1948), 'The Function of the Art Film/Le rôle du film d'art', *Museum*, 2, 3–4: 198–203.

Monotti, Francesco (1948), 'Art and the Camera Eye in Italy/L'art sous l'oeuil de la caméra en Italie', *Museum*, 2, 3–4: 204–5.

N.N. (1948), 'The Film and the Art Museum/Le film et les musées d'art', *Museum*, 2, 3–4: 196.

N.N. (1948), 'Use of the Motion Picture in Museums of the Present Day/L'utilisation du film dans les musées modernes', *Museum*, 2, 3–4: 208–9.

Raghianti, Carlo Ludovico (1951), *Répertoire général international des films sur l'art*, Rome: Edizone dell'Ateneo.

Ragghianti, Carlo Ludovico (1952), *Cinema arte figurativa*, Turin: Enaudi.

Regan, Suzanne (1981), *The Utilization of the Film Medium by American Art Museums*, PhD diss., University of Massachusetts, Amherst.

Ritsma, Natasha (2015), *The Postwar 'Arts Explosion' in an Age of Mechanical Reproduction: The Production, Circulation, and Exhibition of Nontheatrical Films on Art*, PhD diss., Indiana University.

Robert, Valentine, Laurent Le Forestier and François Albera, eds (2015), *Le Film sur l'art: Entre histoire de l'art et documentaire de création*, Rennes: Presses universitaires de Rennes.

Rocchetti, Pasquale and Cesare Molinari (1963), *Le Film sur l'art: Repertoire général international du film sur l'art 1953–1960*, Venezia: N. Pozza.

Saurisse, Pierre (2018), 'Creative Process and Magic: Artists on Screen in the 1940s', in Rachel Esner and Sandra Kisters (eds.), *The Mediatization of the Artist*, London: Palgrave Macmillan, 99–113.

Savoy, Bénédicte (2014), *Vom Faustkeil zur Handgranate: Filmpropaganda für die Berliner Museen 1934–1939*, Köln: Böhlau Verlag.

Scotini, Marco, ed. (2000), *Carlo Ludovico Ragghianti and the Cinematic Nature of Vision*, Milan: Charta.

Smith, Douglas (2004), 'Moving Pictures: The Art Documentaries of Alain Resnais and Henri-Georges Clouzot in Theoretical Context (Benjamin, Malraux and Bazin)', *Studies in European Cinema* 1, 3: 163–73.

Thiele, Jens (1976), *Das Kunstwerk im Film: Zur Problematik filmisher Präsentationsformen von Malerei und Grafik*, Bern: Herbert Lang/Frankfurt: Peter Lang.

Welscher, Judith (1985), 'The Filming of Art', *Daedalos: The Moving Image*, 114, 4 (Fall): 141–59.

Wyver, John (2007), *Vision On: Film, Television and the Arts in Britain*, London: Wallflower Press.

Ziegler, Rainer (2005), 'Kunst und Architektur im Kulturfilm', in Klaus Kreimeier, Antje Ehmann, Jeanpaul Goergen (eds), *Geschichte des dokumentarischen Films in Deutschland. Band 2: Weimarer Republik 1918–1933*, Stuttgart: Reclam, 219–27.

Index